I0810493

IMAGES
of America

SHARON

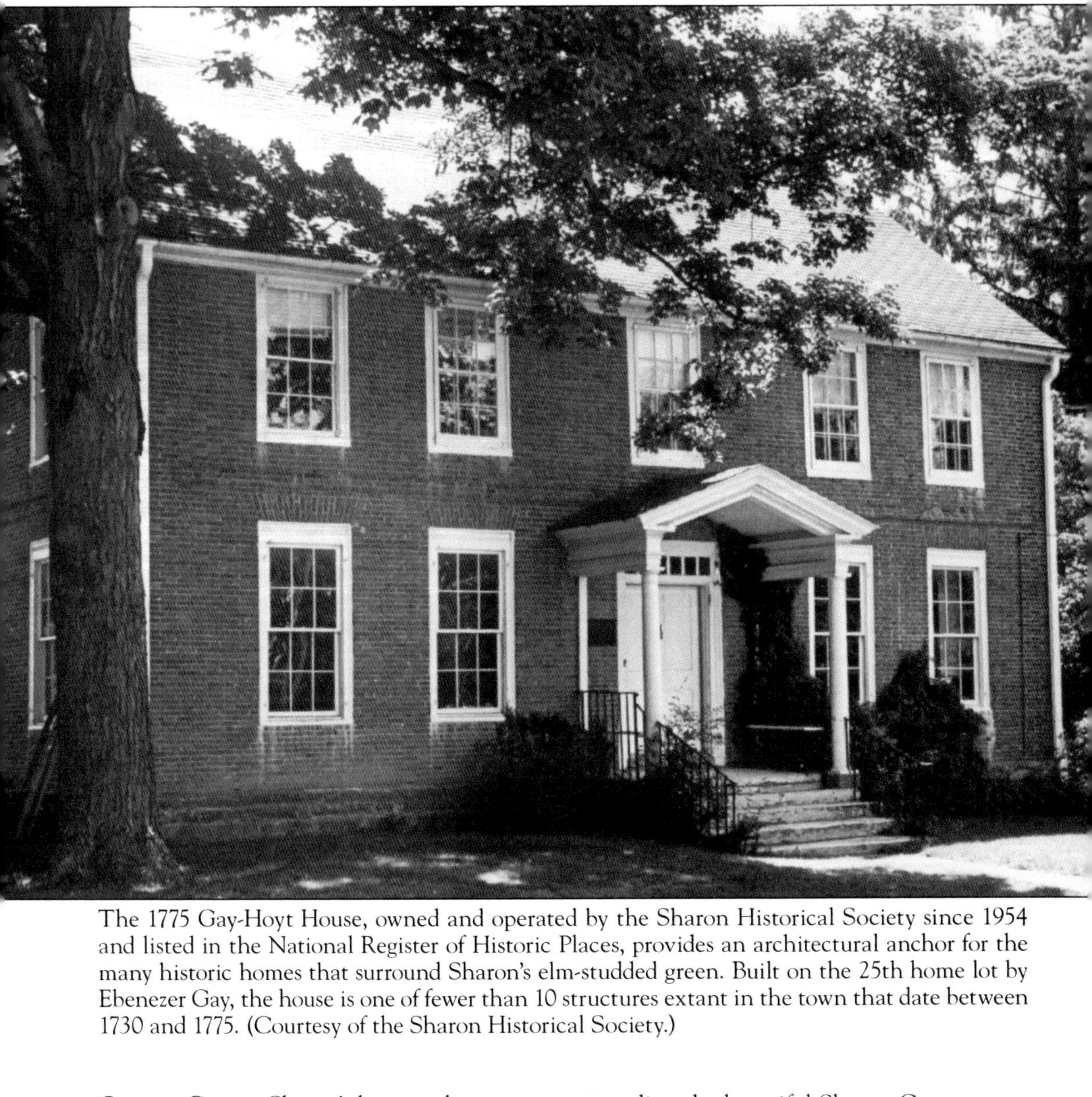

The 1775 Gay-Hoyt House, owned and operated by the Sharon Historical Society since 1954 and listed in the National Register of Historic Places, provides an architectural anchor for the many historic homes that surround Sharon's elm-studded green. Built on the 25th home lot by Ebenezer Gay, the house is one of fewer than 10 structures extant in the town that date between 1730 and 1775. (Courtesy of the Sharon Historical Society.)

On the Cover: Sharon's historic downtown, surrounding the beautiful Sharon Green, was a bustling business and trade center from the early 1800s through the mid-1970s. Located at the very northern end of the Sharon Green, what was first known as the Gillette Store was purchased by brothers Edward and Henry Gillette on September 1, 1860. Sales inventory included hardware and furnishings for the home, but the store also featured a room where men of the community could gather to discuss news of the day and to barter their skills. After Henry left Sharon in 1865 for a new business opportunity in Salisbury, Edward operated the store until 1893, when he took on his son E.F. Gillette Jr. as a partner, renaming the store E.F. Gillette & Son. The store sold everything from pickles to baby carriages, from patent medicine to nuts and bolts. When E.F. Jr. passed away in 1909, the store was inherited by his sister, Elizabeth Gillette Eggleston, who continued to operate the business as a general store and pharmacy. (Courtesy of the Sharon Historical Society.)

IMAGES
of America

SHARON

Sharon Historical Society

ARCADIA
PUBLISHING

ISBN 978-1-4671-2188-0

Published by Arcadia Publishing
Charleston, South Carolina

Printed in the United States of America

Library of Congress Control Number: 2013953621

For all general information, please contact Arcadia Publishing:
Telephone 843-853-2070
Fax 843-853-0044
E-mail sales@arcadiapublishing.com
For customer service and orders:
Toll-Free 1-888-313-2665

Visit us on the Internet at www.arcadiapublishing.com

The Sharon Historical Society was formed by a group of 21 Sharon residents on January 20, 1911. Organized under the name Poconnuck Historical Society (after the Poconnuck Native American tribe, which had resided in the area), the name was changed to the Sharon Historical Society in 1918. Its mission at the time was "to collect and preserve in some suitable place such articles as may tend to illustrate the life and history of the early settlers of this region, and to create and foster an interest in local history and tradition." Today, the Sharon Historical Society collects, preserves, and shares Sharon's stories, building bridges between the past, present, and future through its collections, exhibitions, and programs. Our goal is to maximize the power of personal and community stories and shared history to enrich and impact lives.

Contents

Acknowledgments		6
Introduction		7
1.	The Green and its Surrounds	9
2.	Doing Business	27
3.	Education, Arts, and Worship	43
4.	On the Farm	59
5.	Building a Strong Community	67
6.	Play Ball!	79
7.	They Came From New York	87
8.	Coming Together in Peace and in War	97
9.	Moments in Time, Friends, and Family	113
Bibliography		127

Acknowledgments

Since the Sharon Historical Society was founded in 1911, hundreds of volunteers have worked tirelessly to sort, accession, catalog, and research the thousands of archival documents in the museum's collection. Without the tens of thousands of hours that these people spent on their tasks, this book would not have been possible. Unless otherwise noted, all images appear courtesy of the Sharon Historical Society.

Few compilers of a small town's history can boast of the support of a citizen-patriot who is the caliber of Sharon's own James L. Buckley. He stands high in the hearts and admiration of his fellow townspeople, and we are most appreciative of his reflections. Sir, we are honored by your contribution to this book. Thank you.

The gathering of the photographs for this book was made easier because of the extensive collection of the Sharon Historical Society. We are also gratified at the number of Sharon residents, past and present, who were eager to share their personal photographs and memories. We are indebted to the following: Bonnie and Ray Aakjar, American Legion Post 126, Linda Amerighi, Barbara Bartram, Tom Bartram, Maureen Cahill, Doris Carberry, Tom Casey, David Chase Jr., Wally Chase, Marian Chatfield, Cynthia Conklin, Tom Euvrard, Kip Garovoy, Philip Grindrod, Jean Hansell, Harvey Hayden, Kathy Heacox, Helen and Lynn Humeston, Sally Jenkins, Barbara and Norm Johnson, Mary Lamb, Jayne Peterson Larsen, Barbara Carberry McEnroe, Emma "Dolly" Paley, Caroline Paton, Linda Kelsey Peterson, Everett "Bub" Pitcher, Esther Pollard, Barbara and Brent Prindle, Del Prindle, W. Peter Reyelt Jr., Tim Riley, Ted Roeske, the Sharon Woman's Club, Robert Thompson, Nancy Trowbridge, William Trowbridge, Bill Wilbur, Diane Wilbur, Ed Wilbur, and Catherine Wilcox.

Our thanks also go to Jamie Casey, who compiled, edited, and typed captions in their final form.

Thanks to Ed and Mary Kirby for reviewing the captions for historical accuracy.

Thanks also to Liz Shapiro, executive director of the Sharon Historical Society, who was indispensable with advice, encouragement, patience, and her vast knowledge of Sharon.

Lastly, this book could not have been completed without the technical skills, enthusiasm, and calming presence of Rosemary Davis, curator of collections for the Sharon Historical Society.

—Elizabeth M. Hall
David Chase Jr.
Kathryn M. Heacox

INTRODUCTION

In a lecture on conservatism, English-born professor Patrick Allitts, of Emory University, illustrated mankind's innate love of home by citing an encounter with a woman whom he met on a visit to his hometown of Daresbury, England. When she remarked that the world's best people lived there, Professor Allitts asked how she could tell, given the fact that she had never lived anywhere else. Her reply was, "I don't have to live anywhere else to *know* that Daresbury has the best people in the world." I suspect that that is what those of us who have grown up in Sharon might say about our own town, because in our case, it happens to be true. I can say this because I have lived in several other places, wonderful places, and I can confirm that ours is in fact the home of the best people on earth. It is also one of its loveliest towns.

There are so many things that set Sharon apart from the rest of the globe. First of all, there is the beauty of its natural setting. Its sparsely populated 59.6 square miles of open fields and woodlands are bordered on the east by an unspoiled Housatonic River; its hills (we called them mountains when I was a boy) provide wonderful views of the Taconic Range to the west and the Berkshires to the north; at its center lies one of the most beautiful villages in all New England. Almost 275 years have rolled by since Sharon's founding, but, over the course of at least the last 150 of them, the character of its green and of the houses that border it have remained essentially the same.

I suspect that the key to Sharon's enduring charm is the fact that it lies beyond commuting distance to anywhere. As a consequence, it has been spared the curse of being converted into a bedroom town and all that that implies in terms of the fragmentation of land, building developments, shopping malls, and traffic. And so it has remained what it has been since its earliest days—a self-contained community of diverse people with diverse interests and pursuits who nevertheless work together in close harmony in advancing the common good.

This has always been true. The men and women who settled Sharon were an energetic and resourceful lot. Most of them were drawn here by the region's iron resources, and they were soon at work constructing the blast furnaces and forges and limekilns and making the charcoal that together were required to produce the raw iron. Others cleared and cultivated the land or built the dams that powered the gristmills and sawmills that ground their grains and produced the lumber required to build their homes. Still other early residents followed a variety of occupations. There were the merchants and blacksmiths who met Sharon residents' needs, and the producers of shoes, hats, tanned leather, pottery, and even cigars who sold their goods within and beyond the town's borders. Together, they established a town government, planned the village's center and its subsidiary communities of Ellsworth and Amenia Union, built their churches, and then sprinkled the town with one-room schoolhouses that lay within walking distance of every child.

Thanks to their energy and ingenuity, within 20 years of its founding Sharon was a self-sufficient community of over 1,200 souls. By the end of the 18th century, its population exceeded 2,300, and among them were a significantly larger number of well-educated individuals than one would expect to find in a rural community at that time. Some have attributed this to the fact that Sharon was located midway on what in Colonial days was an important highway linking Hartford and Albany. Whatever the reason, Sharon produced one of Connecticut's first governors following the American Revolution and boasted enough doctors to organize the first medical society in the United States. One of those doctors would go on take advantage of that highway to import medicines from Europe for resale in Hartford, Albany, and as far away as New York City.

Sharon became affluent in the late 1700s and early 1800s as entrepreneurs attracted by the availability of iron began to manufacture a variety of goods in Sharon Valley and Amenia Union. These included plows, monkey wrenches (a Sharon invention), an early version of the machine gun (or rifled canon), explosive artillery shells used during the Civil War, and a locally invented mousetrap that earned Sharon Valley the title of "Mouse Trap Headquarters of the Western World." Fortunately, the world (western or otherwise) did not beat a path to the inventor's door. But whether it was mousetraps or some other magic ingredient, there has always been something about Sharon that has drawn a wonderful range of people and talents to the town. This was true even as the iron played out and the manufacturers moved away, causing Sharon's economy and population to experience significant declines.

It was during that period, in fact, that Sharon was discovered by what came to be known as the "summer people." They were a handful of New York families who were attracted by the quiet beauty of the village and the availability of a number of substantial homes that had been built during the 18th and early 19th centuries, and thus escaped the blight of Victorian architecture. In early June, after their children's schools had closed for the summer, they would move into their capacious Sharon homes with their nurses and maids and remain there until after Labor Day, when New York's schools reopened. Although they continued to make their livelihoods in the city, these families became integral parts of the Sharon community, and, in due course, they retired here.

The last century's summer people have now morphed into weekenders. As in the past, these once-upon-a-time outsiders quickly come to think of Sharon as home, and they and our town's full-time residents continue to work together in meeting our community's evolving needs with the energy and imagination that has characterized this remarkable place since its earliest days.

The photographs in this volume provide wonderful glimpses of Sharon over the past century and more. They record that the roads through town have now been paved and that new trees have been planted to replace the graceful elms that bordered the Green before they fell victim to Dutch elm disease. The photographs also confirm that, in most respects, the character of the town has remained essentially unchanged. These pictures are sure to bring waves of nostalgia to those who, like me, have long lived here and feel so blessed to call it home. They may even give those not so blessed some inkling of why it is plausible that Sharon, rather than Daresbury, should be the place where the best people on earth have chosen to live, as indeed they have.

You have my word for it.

—James L. Buckley
Sharon, Connecticut
December 2013

One

The Green and its Surrounds

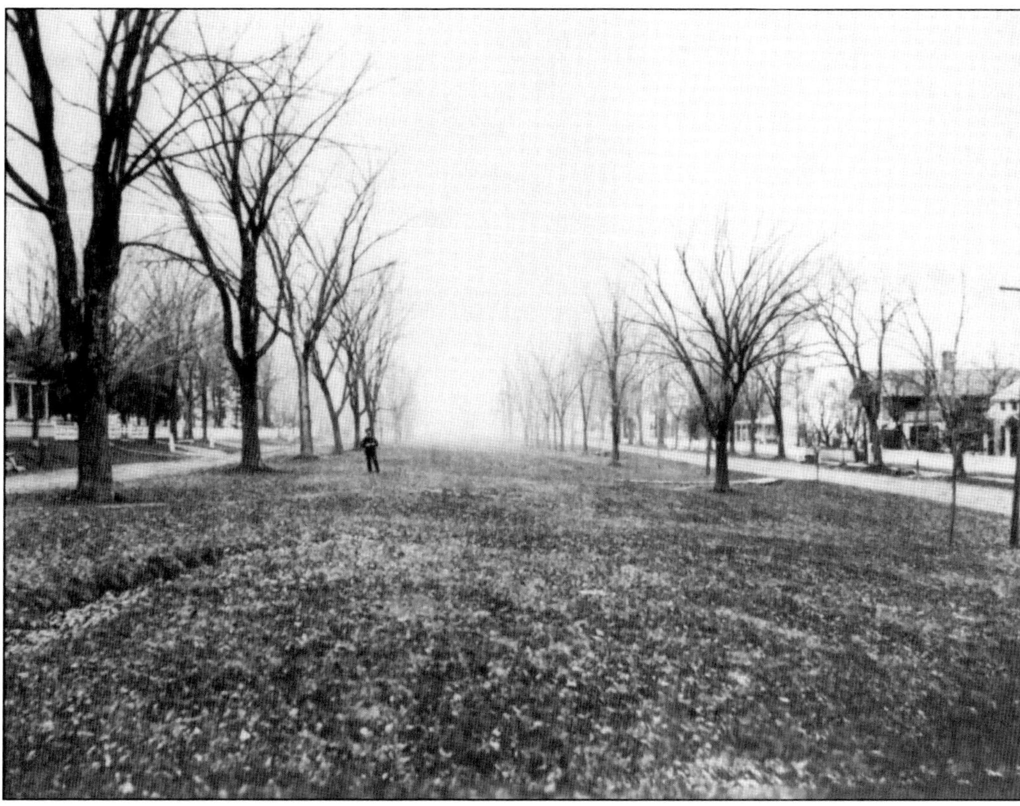

This is the earliest known photograph of the Sharon Green, believed to have been taken around 1889. Note the figure standing near the center of the frame, which offers a good perspective on the size of the elms planted in 1879. Although there are few fences enclosing homes on the Green today, note the proliferation of fences on both sides of the Green.

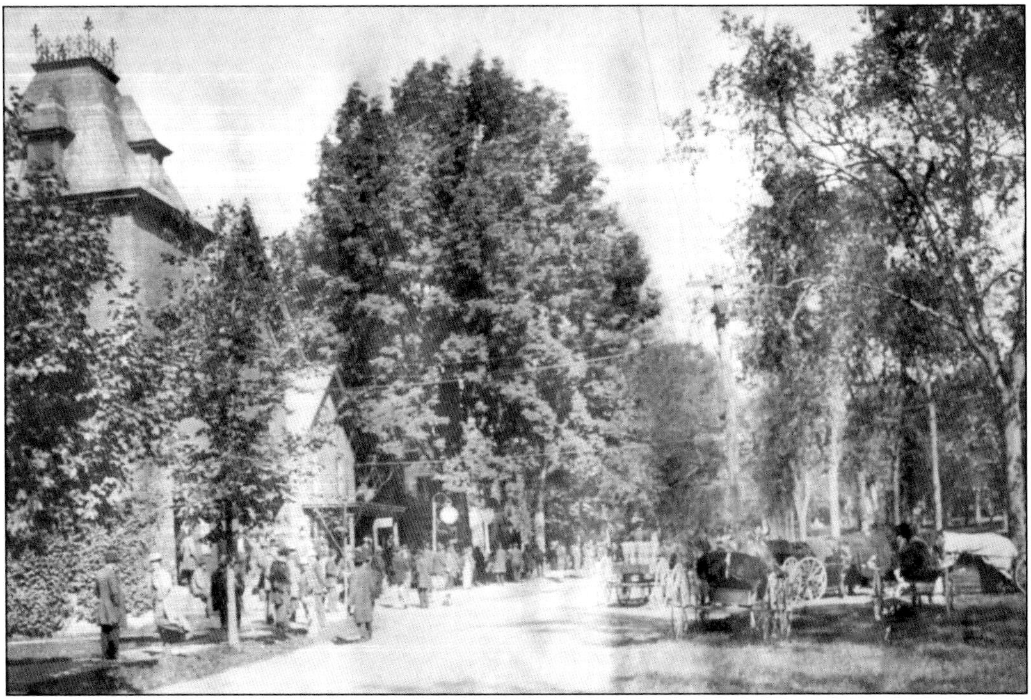

The town hall has occupied a prominent place on the Sharon Green since it was built in 1875, with Isaac Newton Bartram serving as contractor. Prior to that time, the "official" town hall was in an upstairs room at the Tavern House, an early name for the Sharon Inn. The recognizable tower was added in 1884, and a new facade of pediment, portico, and four columns was dedicated in 1924. This photograph was taken around 1900, possibly on the day of a town election or other notable occasion.

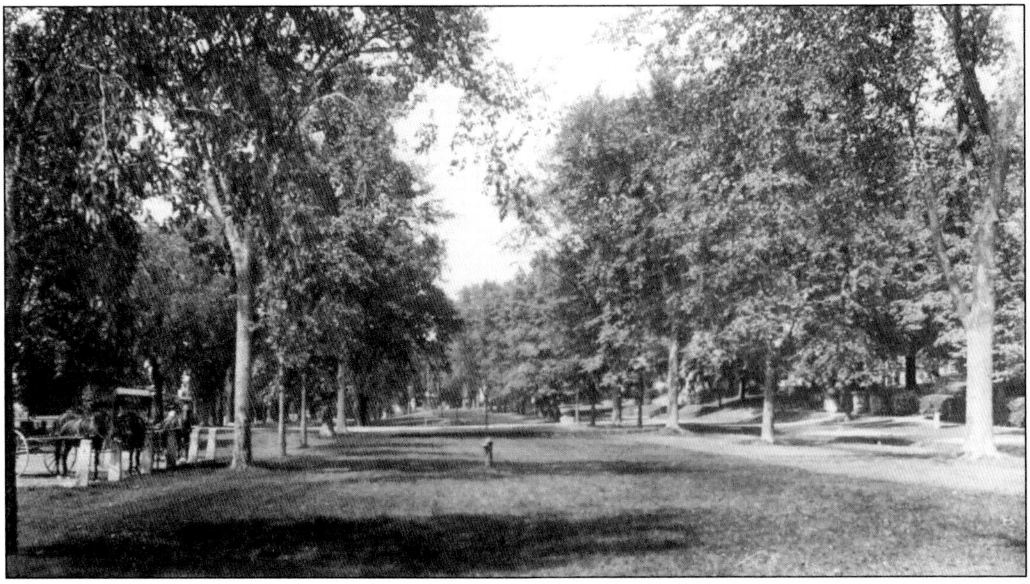

Shown here is a view of the Sharon Green looking north towards the King House. Horses and buggies are prominent features in many of Sharon's early photographs. These are hitched to the line of hitching posts made from Stockbridge marble across from town hall.

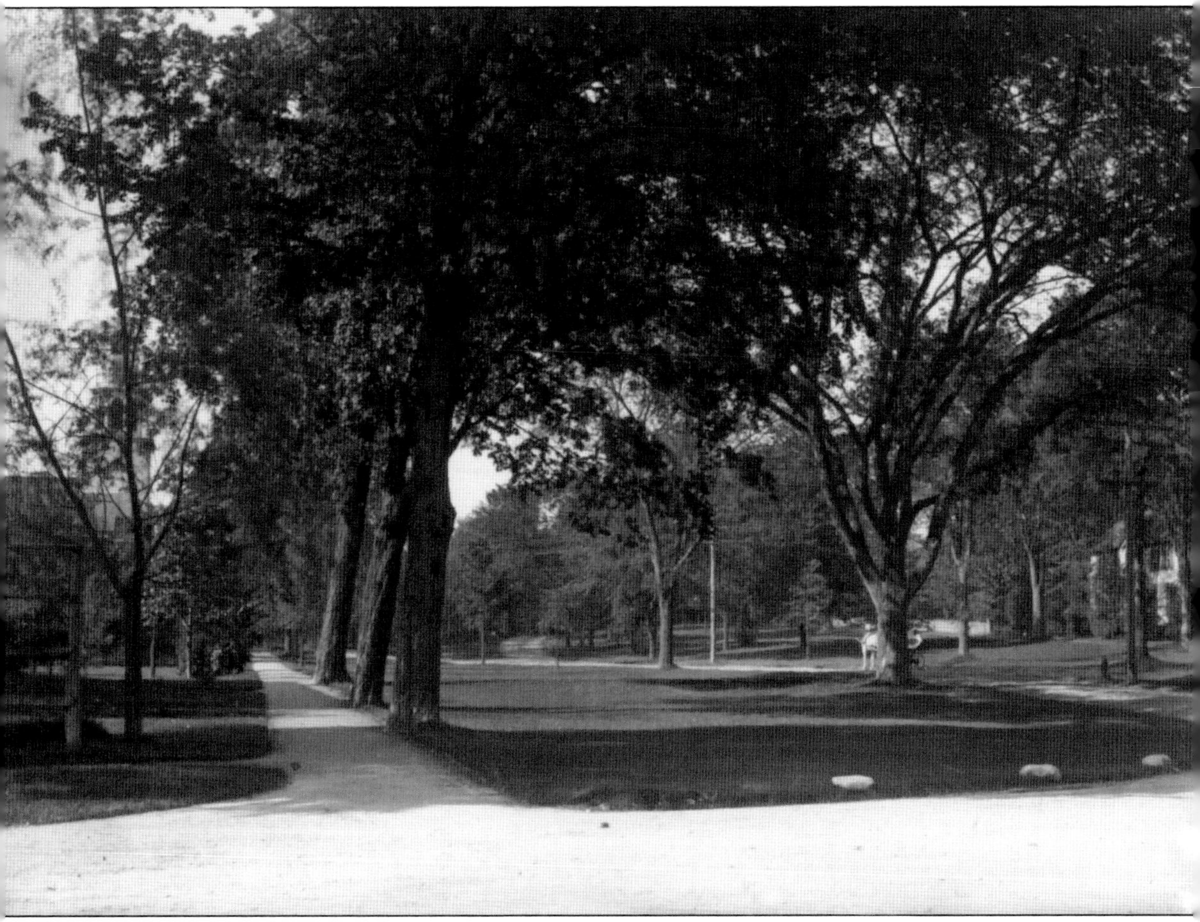

This shows the Sharon Green looking north from the porch of the Sharon Inn, on the southwest corner of Main Street and what is now Route 343. Note the "U" shape of the end of the Green and the narrow roadway that graces the trunks of the famous elms of Sharon. The sidewalks that residents are so fond of today are absent in this early photograph, which probably dates to 1900 or earlier. When sidewalks were first created, they were simply hard-packed dirt. A diary kept by Lawrence Van Alstyne for the Poconnuck Historical Society (now the Sharon Historical Society) had an entry from April 6, 1912, that noted, "Cement sidewalks laid on west side of Main Street from Van Rensellaer's place to Mrs. Prindle's."

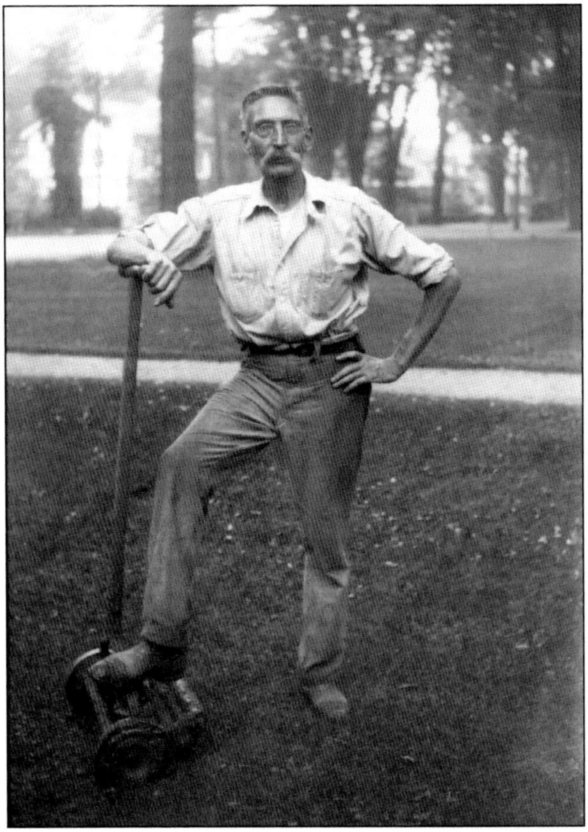

Before motorized lawn mowers, the grass on Sharon Green was tended by hand, first with clippers and then with hand mowers. James Way, pictured here, was an early groundskeeper of Sharon Green, responsible for cutting the entire Green (which continues on South Main Street) with a hand mower. (Photograph by George M. Marckres.)

William Pitcher is shown here riding a horse-drawn mower with a sickle bar on the Sharon Green, a practice that may have occurred well into the 1940s. Jack Ward took charge of mowing the Green in the 1940s with a push-style hand mower that had rotating blades. Horse-drawn equipment remained popular in Sharon for mowing large tracts and farming until well after World War II.

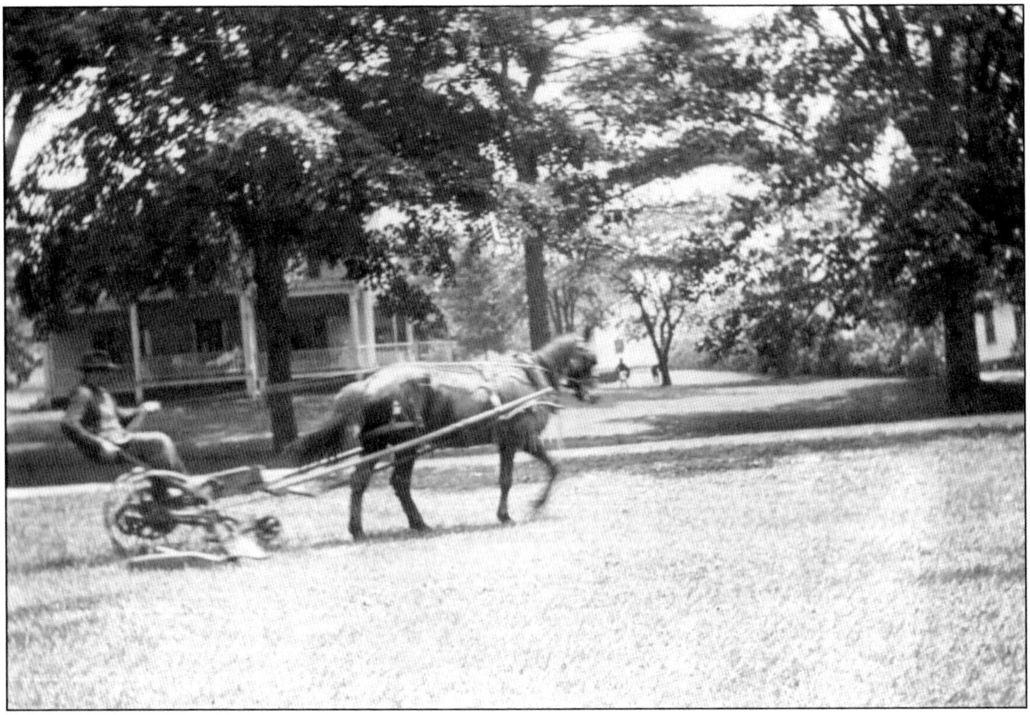

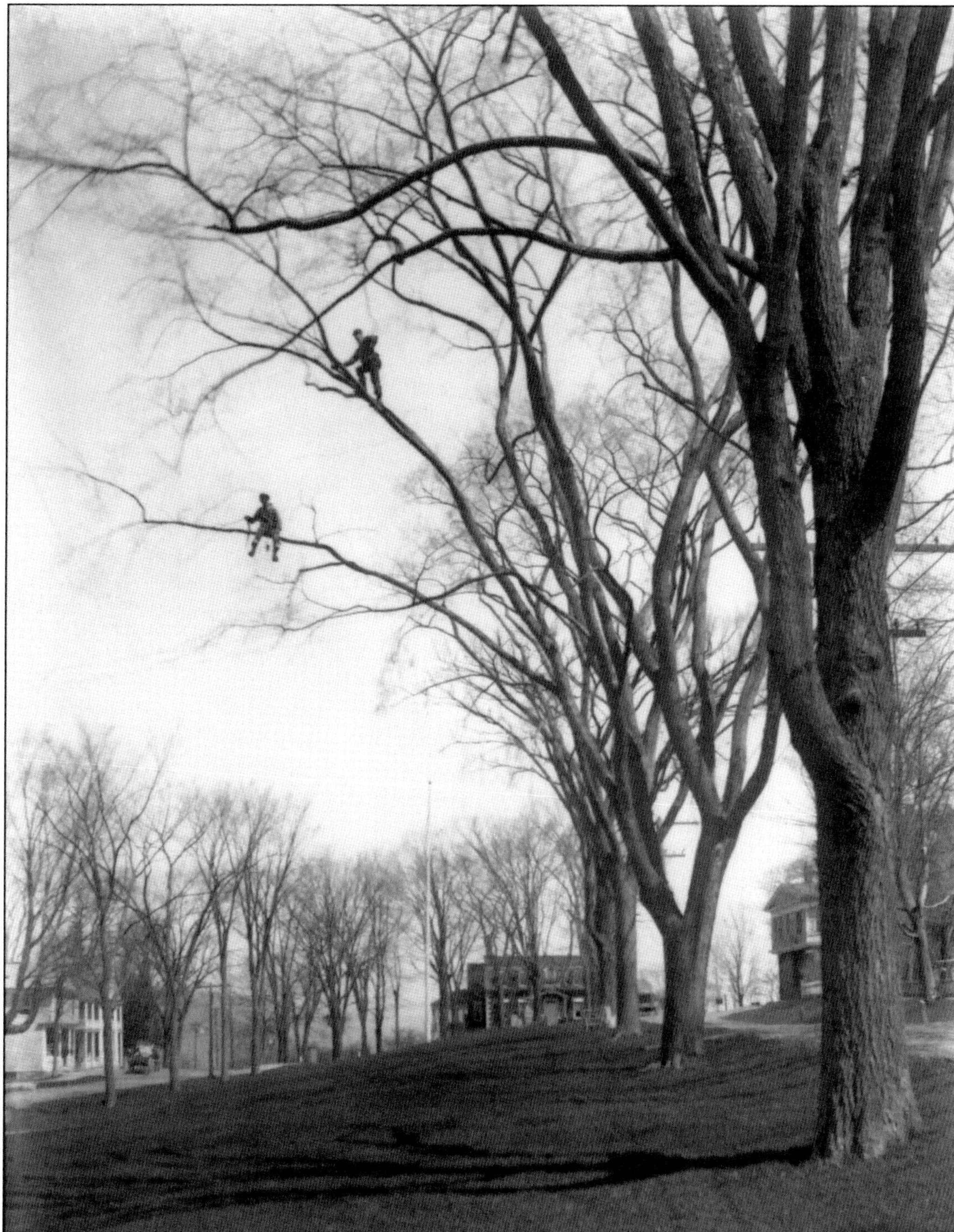

Young Joe Carberry and his brother Paul are pruning elms on the Green. The Carberry family was long known as the caretakers of Sharon's elm trees. This photograph was taken by George M. Marckres, a well-known Sharon photographer. Over 1,000 of his original glass-plate negatives are held in the Sharon Historical Society collection. (Photograph by George M. Marckres.)

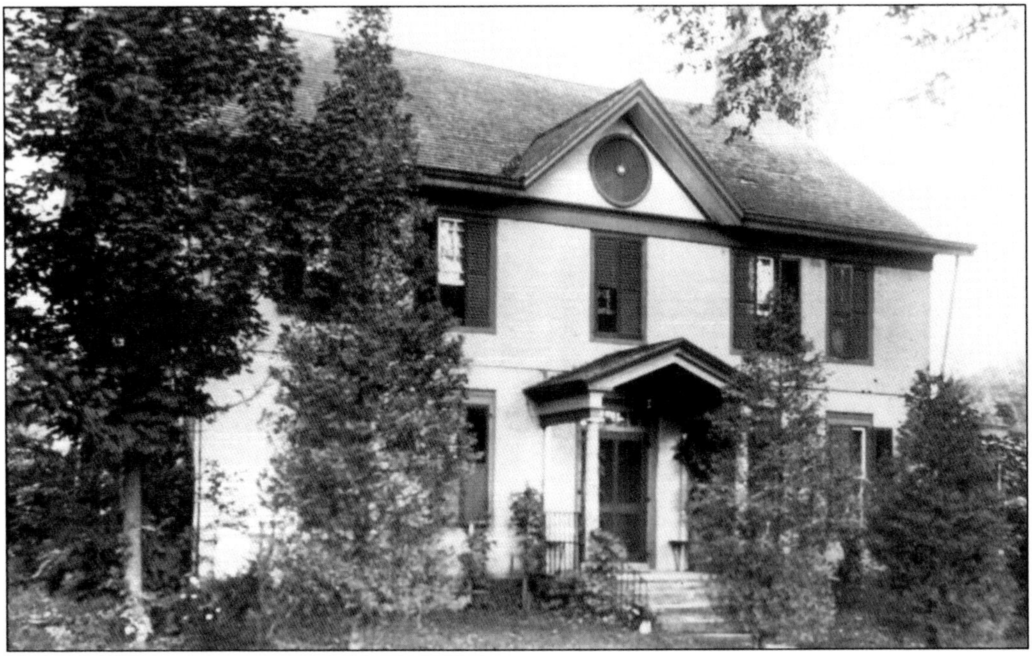

Located at 18 Main Street, the Gay-Hoyt House is home to the Sharon Historical Society. The original brick building was built in 1775 by Lt. Col. Ebenezer Gay of the 14th Regiment of Militia, formerly the North Trainband. Lieutenant Colonel Gay was active throughout the Revolution, mustering the Sharon militia at the time of the Battle of Danbury and marching south to Danbury in pursuit of the retreating British. The following year, he commanded the Sharon militia, which hurried north to fight Burgoyne's army and was in the engagement until the surrender. This photograph shows how the building was modernized in the Victorian style in the 19th century, like so many of the early houses on the Green.

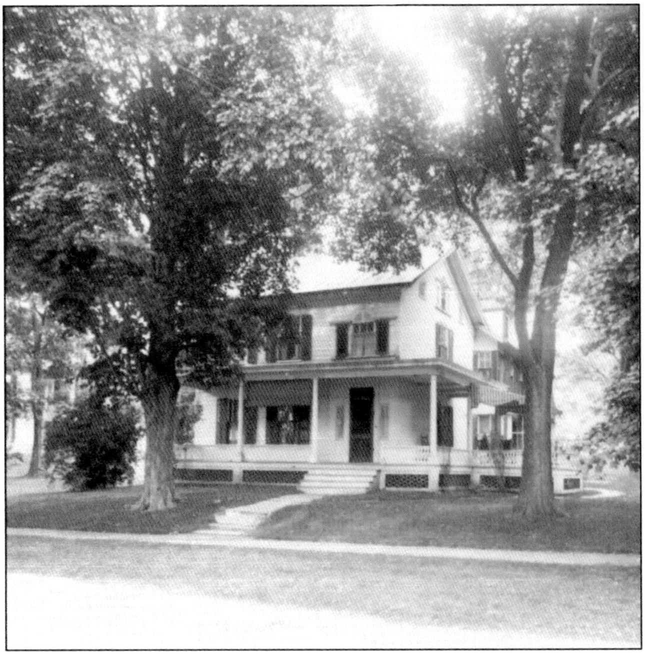

Known locally as the Vosburgh family home, the building at 22 Upper Main Street was long the home of the Sharon Clinic. It was purchased by four physicians who were also known as the four "founding fathers": Dr. Frederick Gevalt, Dr. Robert Fisher, Dr. George A. Fowler, and Dr. Robert P. Noble, all members of the 1940 graduating class of Columbia University's College of Physicians and Surgeons. They purchased the building in 1947 upon their return from service in World War II. Local resident (and violin maker) Al Stahovec renovated the building to become the Sharon Clinic, the first multi-specialist practice in Litchfield County.

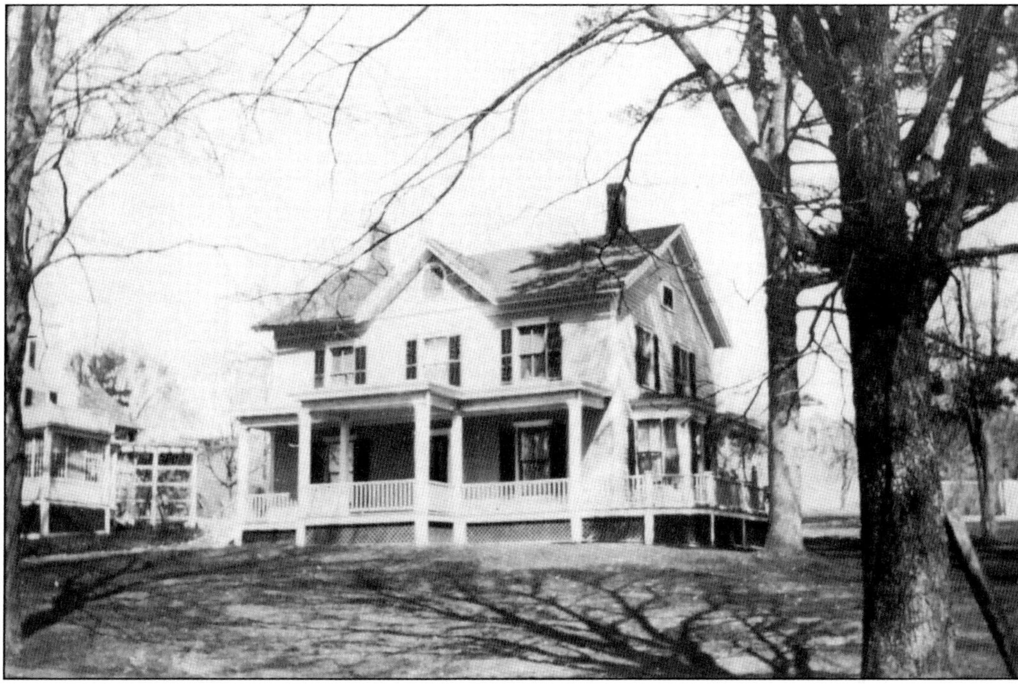

This home at 34 Upper Main Street was built in 1866, probably on a lot where the law office of Cyrus Swan once stood. Well-known author and playwrite Percival Wilde owned the house from 1935 to 1955. The expansive porch is now gone.

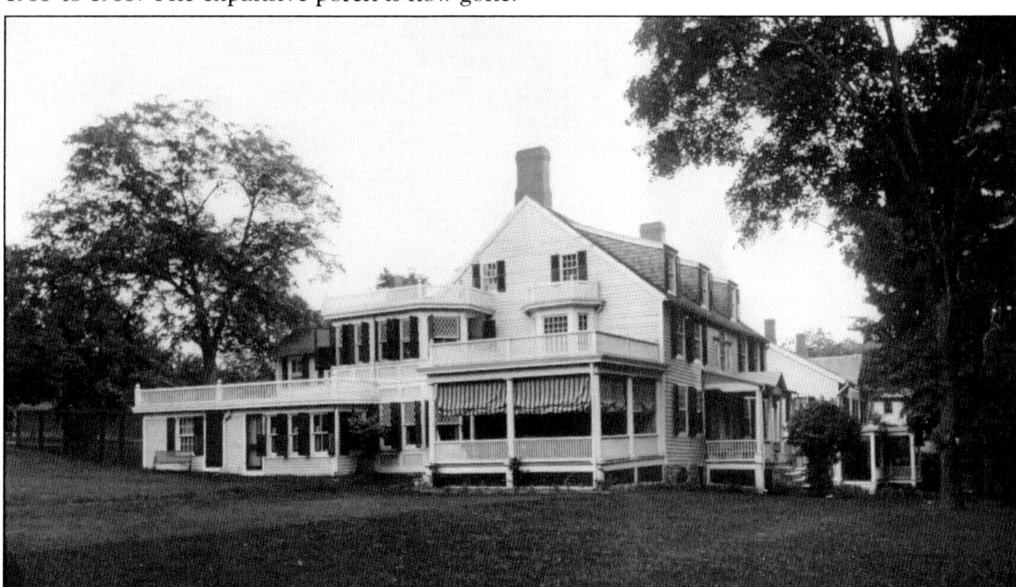

The stately Sedgwick House, at 42 Upper Main Street, was built in 1780 by Dr. Phineas Smith on home lot 28 and boasts a stone in the fireplace featuring that date. Smith was the nephew of Cotton Mather Smith and Dr. Simeon Smith, who built the Georgian-style mansion Weatherstone at 58 South Main Street. Judge Cyrus Swan and his son-in-law Gen. Charles Sedgwick made important additions to the house during their ownership, between 1801 and 1840. The south portion of the house burned in a fire in 1967.

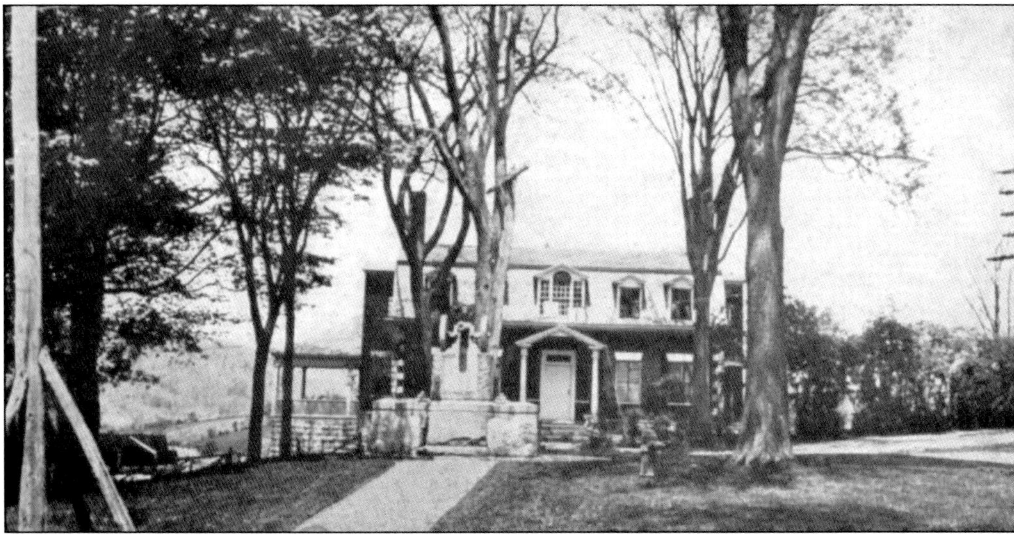

This gambrel-roofed brick building may enclose one of Sharon's earliest houses. The present dining room of the home is believed to have been a small brick home built in 1769 by John Pennoyer Jr. In 1783, Col. George King purchased it, and he made extensive additions in 1794. In 1924, Adm. Thomas C. and Caroline Brownson Hart purchased the home, which had once belonged to Mrs. Hart's great-great-grandfather, Col. George King. Admiral Hart was the commander of the ABDA (American-British-Dutch-Australian) naval forces in the Pacific in 1941–1942. Note the positioning of the Sharon Soldier's Monument, which was originally placed in a direct path from the front door of the King House and was later moved when the road was straightened mid-century.

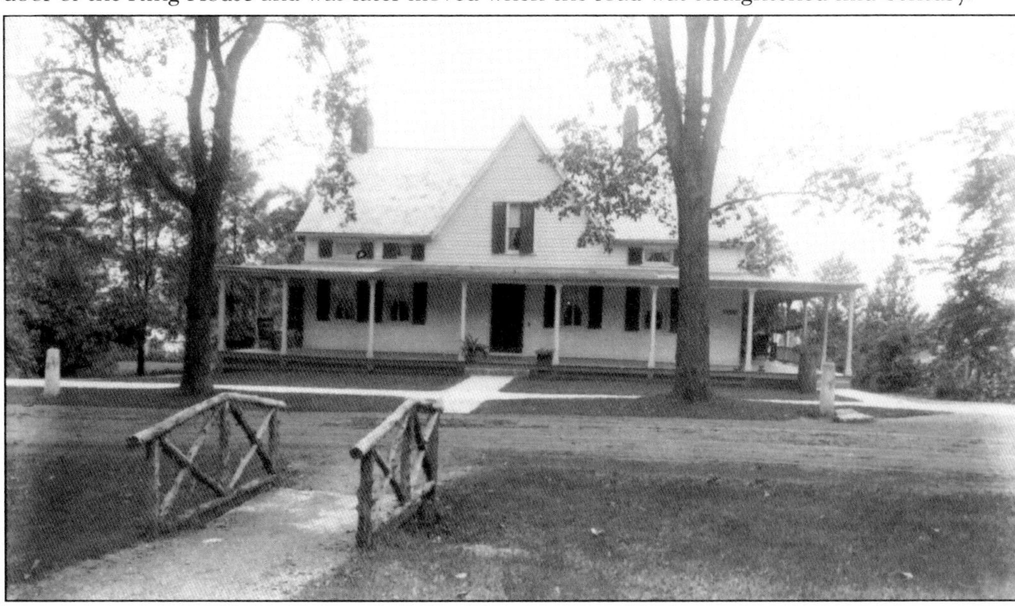

The Skinner House, at 99 Main Street, was so named because Nathaniel Skinner drew this 26th home lot, building one of the first homes in Sharon in 1739, the same year the town was founded. It is believed that the first town meeting was held on this site. Skinner was the first on the list of the proprietors of the common and undivided land, the first magistrate, the first town clerk, and the first deacon in the church. This became the home of Dr. Jerome Chaffee, founder of Sharon Hospital, in 1905.

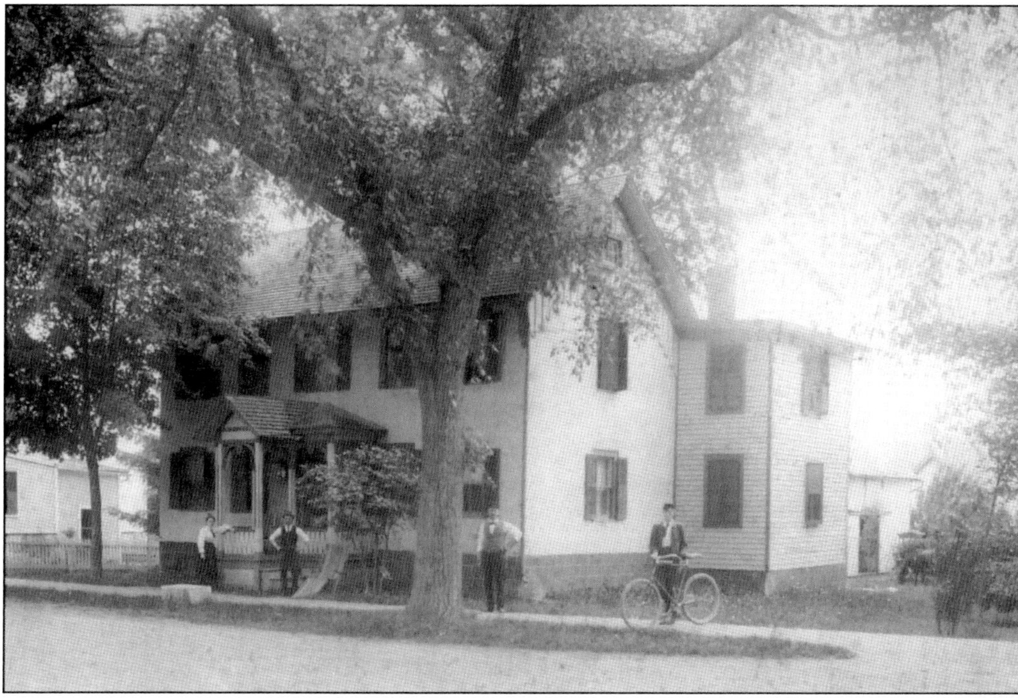

This building of white-painted brick is at 81 Main Street, on the corner of Main and West Main Streets. The family of Edward R. Middlebrook owned it from 1894 to 1959, and deeds filed in the town hall note that it was the home of a general store at one time. Today, the building houses offices, shops, and apartments. The unpaved street is easy to see in this photograph, as is the young man with his bicycle.

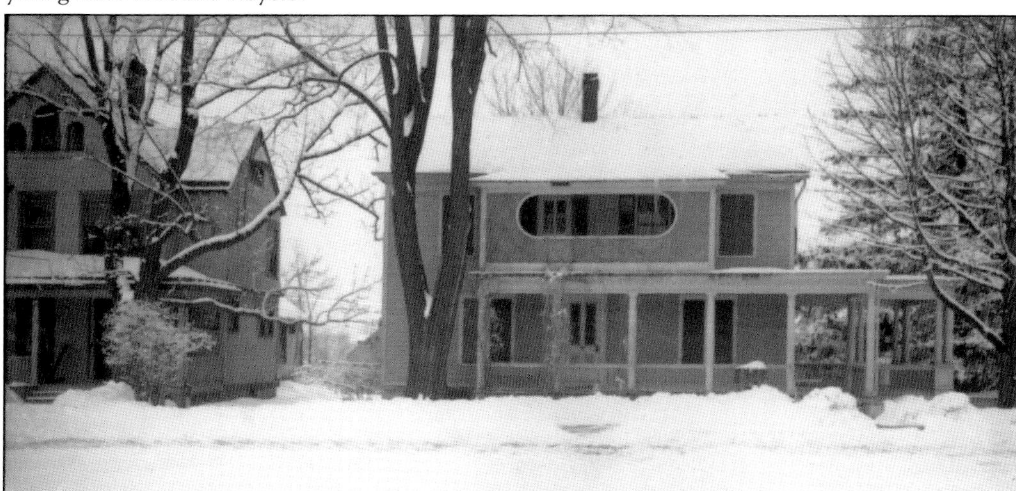

This photograph shows 73 Main Street, also known as Charles Sears's harness and trunk manufactory. Sears built it not long after 1836, and he made trunks, harnesses, and saddles and tanned leather right on the premises. It was converted to a house about 1880 and was home to Sharon historian and Civil War veteran Lawrence Van Alstyne from 1883 to 1937, and beloved Sharon physician Dr. Gaert Gudernatch and his wife, Anne, afterwards. It is rumored that the sleeping porch on the second story was built for a TB patient's recuperation.

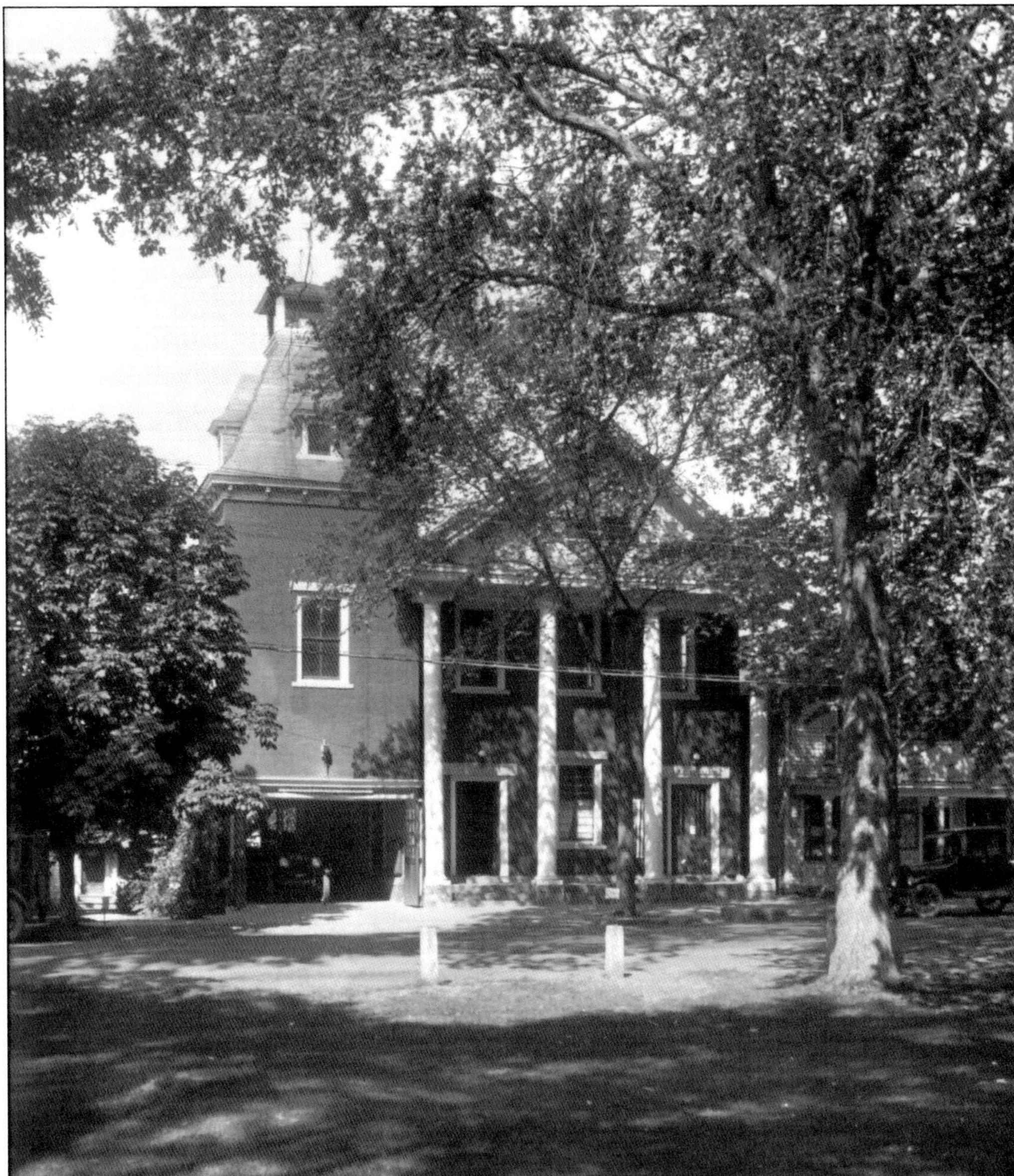

The "new" town hall was built at 63 Main Street in 1875. The brick building measured 45 feet by 30 feet. A lockup was built in the cellar and was frequently used to house overnight visitors. By 1876, busy offices and the regular use of the lecture hall made it necessary to correct an apparent building oversight, so indoor plumbing and a water closet were added. The tower was added in 1884 to accommodate an outside staircase. In 1924, a new facade of pediment, portico, and four columns was dedicated, and the Sharon Fire Department took over the lower room of the tower and part of the lockup to house their new fire truck. John Murtagh Sr. shared the following story about the new fire truck: for some time, he was the only one able to drive the new truck. Conveniently, he worked in the post office just across the hall from the fire truck. When there was a fire, he rushed across the hall to drive the truck to the fire. Someone would then drive him back to the post office and fetch him again when the fire was over so he could drive the truck back to its home in the town hall. This photograph dates to around 1925.

For many years, the second floor of the town hall served as a gym where Sharon's championship basketball teams practiced. The recruiting service had offices there during World Wars I and II, and plays and shows used the stage and auditorium. This area is now the Chapin Meeting Hall, where town meetings are held.

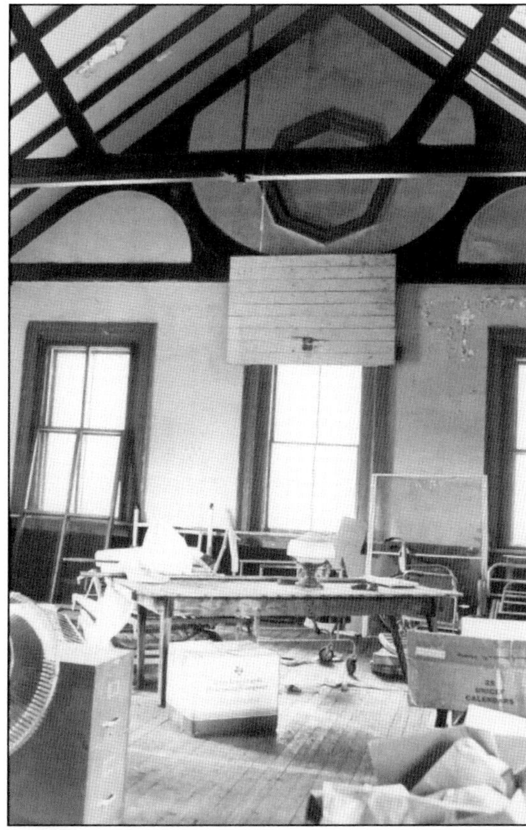

Victorian-era Sharon builder William Mow built George M. Marckres's home and store at 67 Main Street in 1888. A shopkeeper who ran a jewelry store, Marckres created a permanent place for himself in the historic record by being a photographer of some skill and note. Many of the photographs in this book were printed from his glass-plate negatives. The building is currently the home of WHDD, the smallest National Public Radio station in the United States.

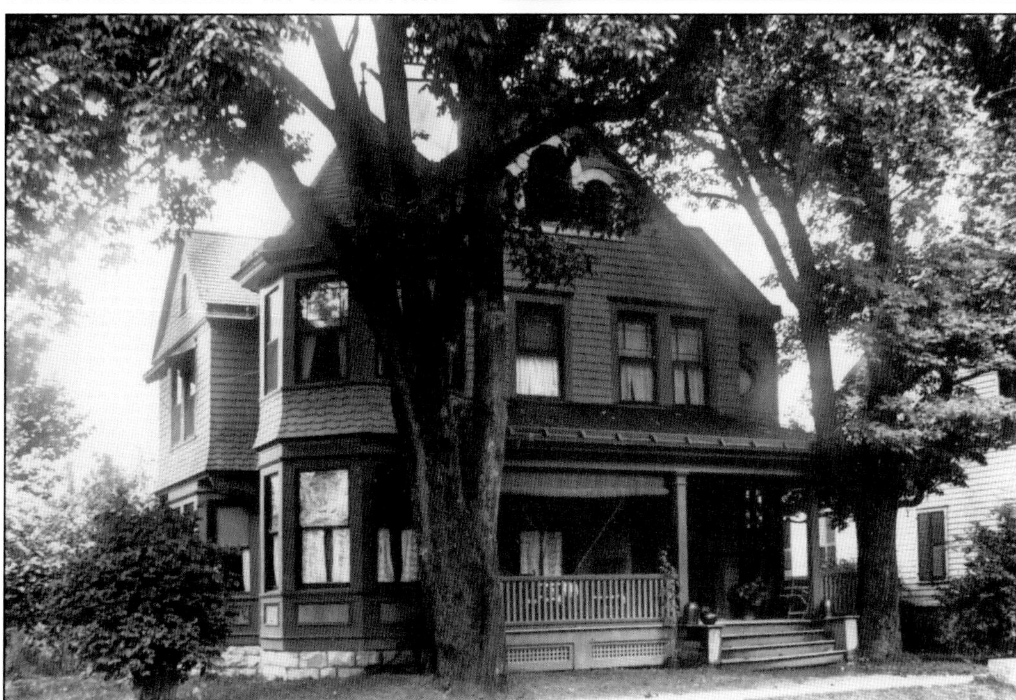

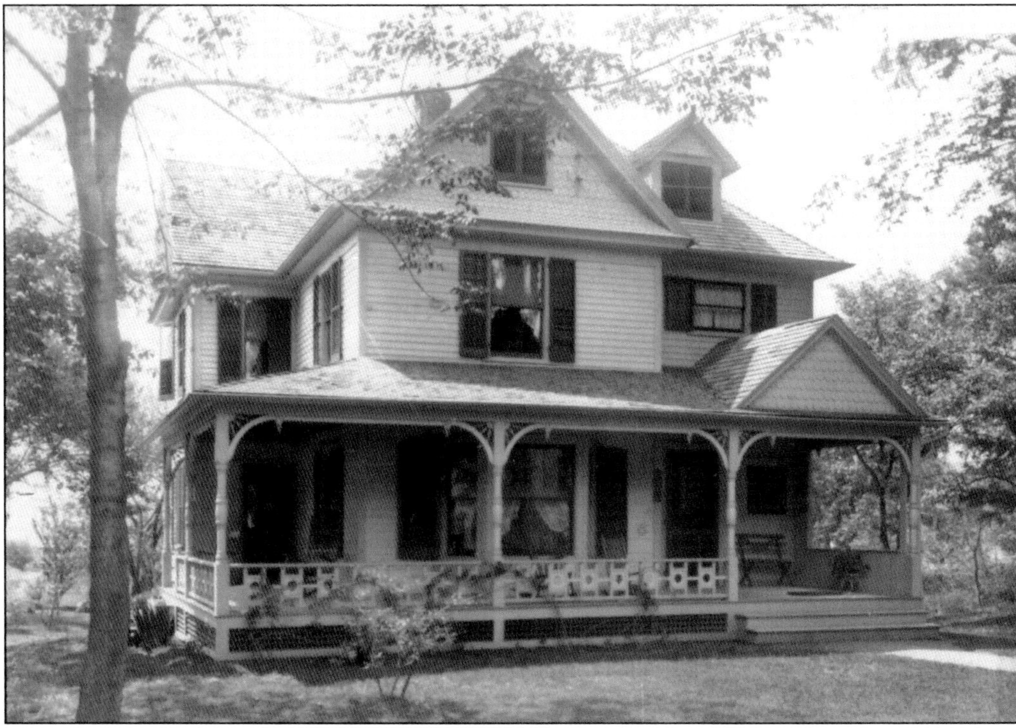

William Mow, a local builder who later built and resided at 113 Main Street, also built a number of Victorian-style houses around the Green. This home at 41 Main Street is currently the Kenny Funeral Home.

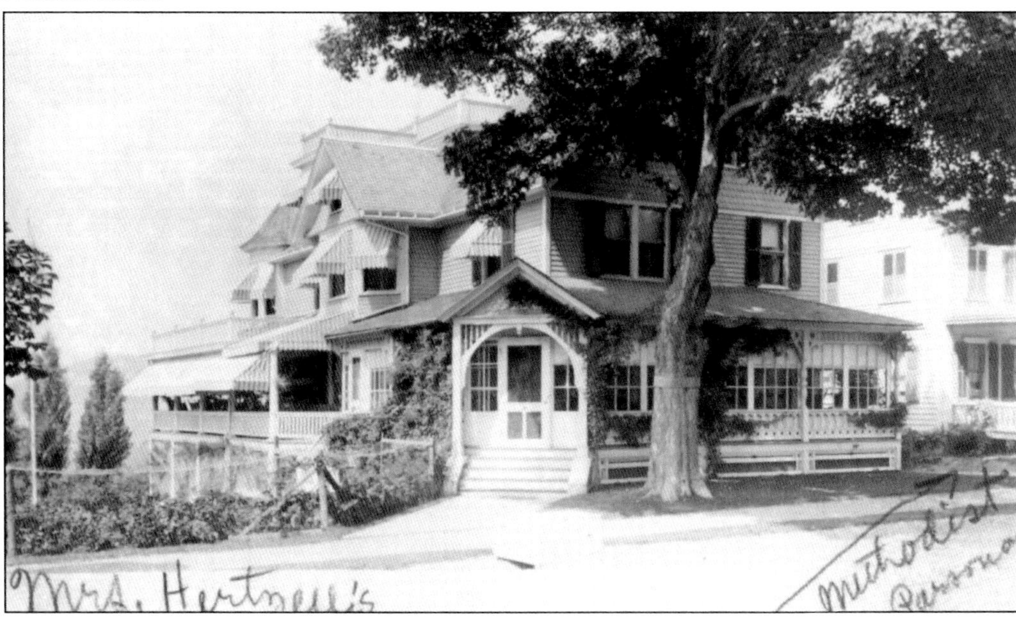

This exuberant Queen Anne–style three-story house at 22 North Main Street was owned by William Kenny Sr. and served as the first Kenny Funeral Home in 1914. Today, the Kenny Funeral Home is operated by Theresa and Brian Kenny, along with their daughter Meghan, at 41 Main Street, pictured above. The Methodist church parsonage is to the north.

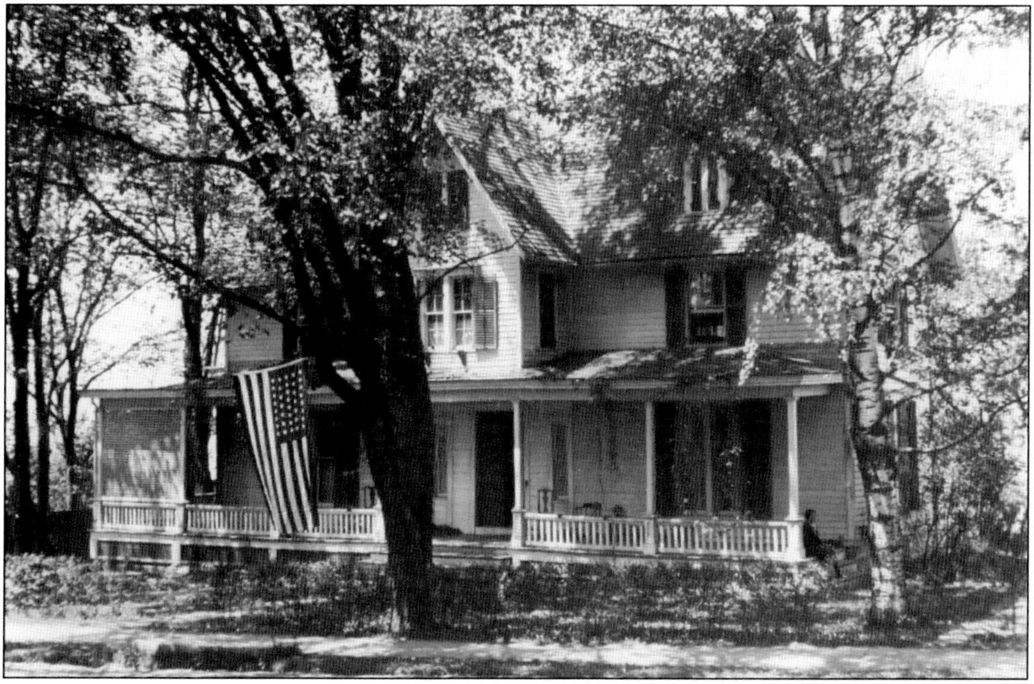

This home at 40 North Main Street was the farmhouse on the property of Arthur Waite, most of which was across the street. It is likely that later owners added the Victorian gable front and porch. Town resident Barbara Bartram says that as a child, she remembered Charlie Prindle and Andy Wheeler sitting on the porch in rocking chairs while smoking pipes.

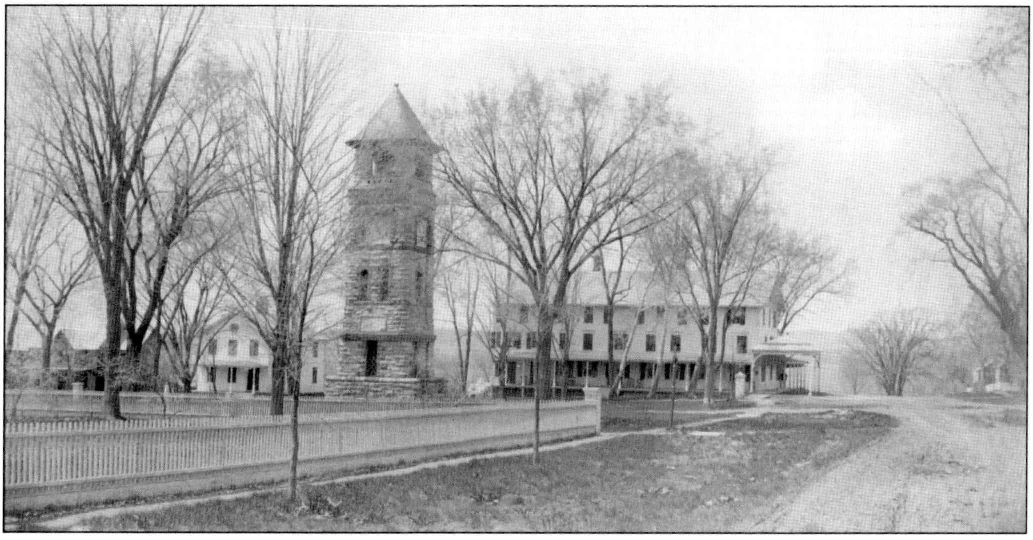

This photograph looks towards the southwest and was probably taken from the middle of Route 4, across from 3 Main Street. The clock tower, an icon in Sharon, was built between 1885 and 1886 and designed by New York City architects Lamb & Rich. It was donated in memory of Emily Butler Ogden Wheeler by her daughters Laura and Emily. Note the picket fence, the Sharon Inn, and the Episcopal church and rectory to the left. The modern road system, with Routes 4, 41, and 343, was finalized in 1909. In 1924, receipts from gasoline taxes were used for road construction and paving. Sharon's main roads were probably paved between 1924 and 1928.

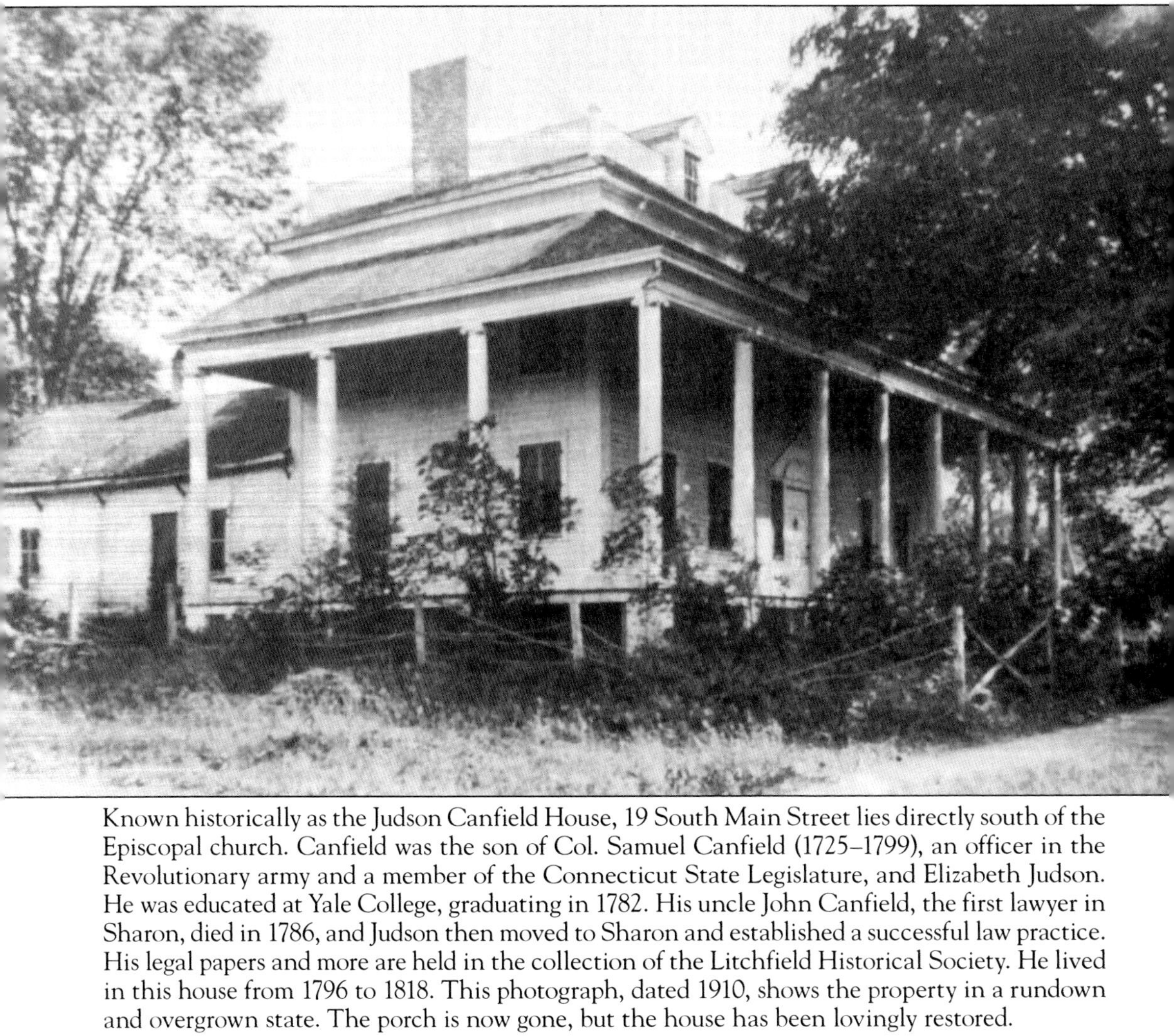

Known historically as the Judson Canfield House, 19 South Main Street lies directly south of the Episcopal church. Canfield was the son of Col. Samuel Canfield (1725–1799), an officer in the Revolutionary army and a member of the Connecticut State Legislature, and Elizabeth Judson. He was educated at Yale College, graduating in 1782. His uncle John Canfield, the first lawyer in Sharon, died in 1786, and Judson then moved to Sharon and established a successful law practice. His legal papers and more are held in the collection of the Litchfield Historical Society. He lived in this house from 1796 to 1818. This photograph, dated 1910, shows the property in a rundown and overgrown state. The porch is now gone, but the house has been lovingly restored.

Many new, stately homes were added to the landscape of South Main Street around the turn of the 20th century by prominent New York families. The late William F. Buckley Sr. named his home, fronting on South Main Street, Great Elm in honor of this huge elm tree, which had a circumference of 17 feet.

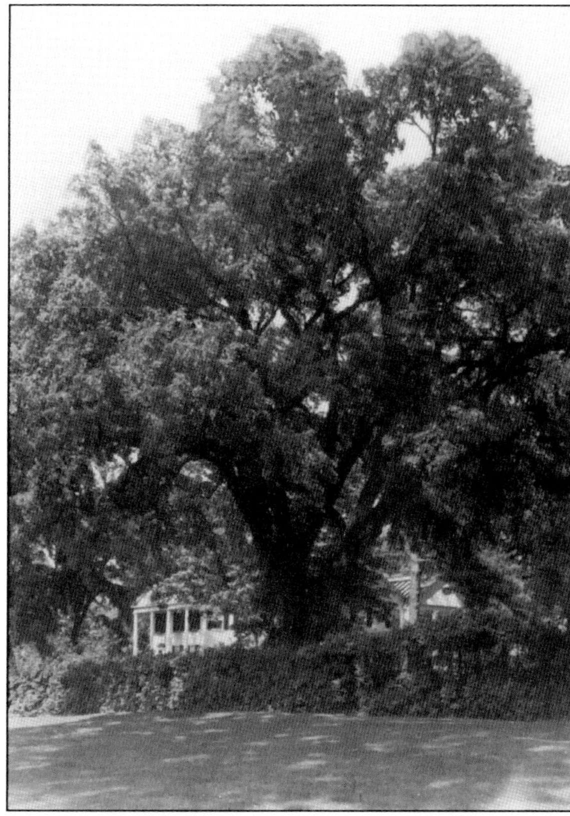

The original house at 36 South Main Street was built by Thomas Skinner between 1740 and 1741 and later became the home of Rev. Cotton Mather Smith. That home was demolished, and a new home was built sometime between 1808 and 1839. In the late 1880s, the property was purchased by Emily O. Wheeler and christened Nequitimauk, becoming part of a family compound on South Main Street that included the Wheelers, the Schwabs, the Herricks, and the Trowbridges. (Courtesy of Nancy Trowbridge.)

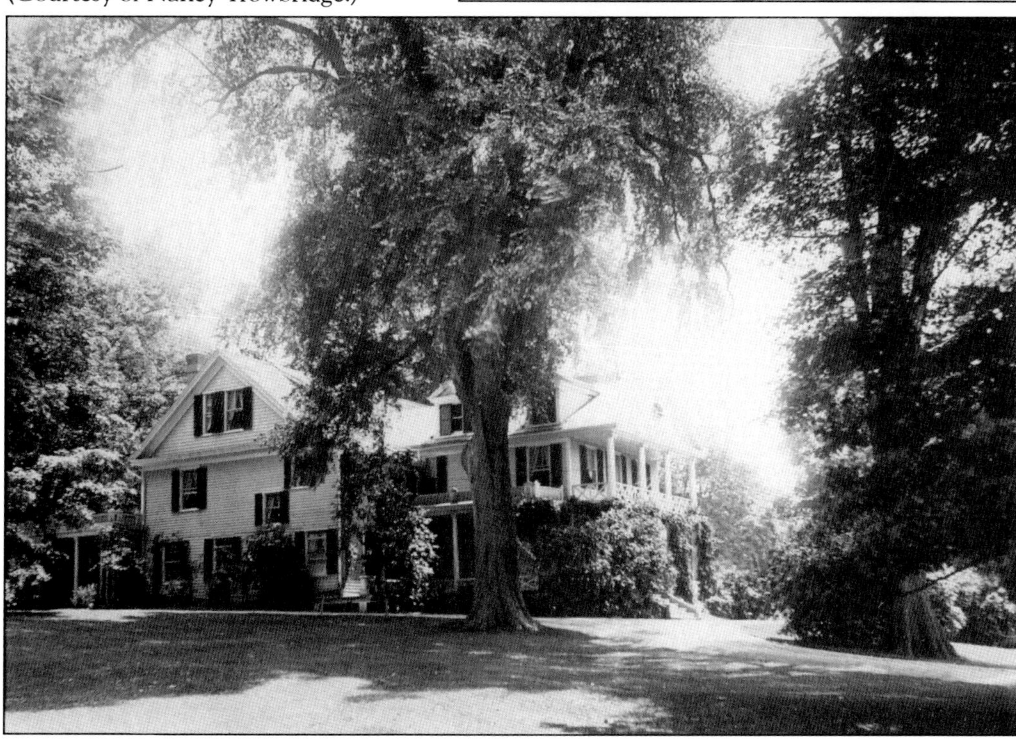

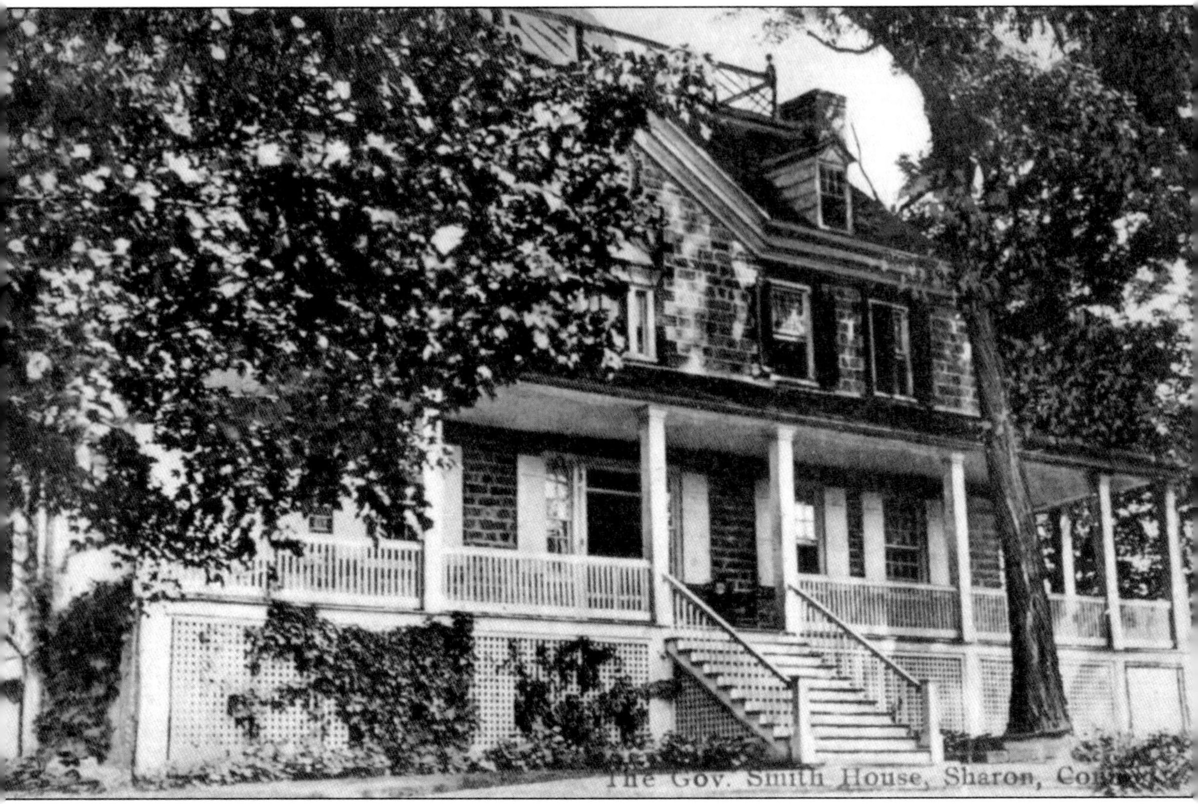

Acclaimed as one of the best examples of Georgian architecture in the state, the house known as Weatherstone is located at 58 South Main Street. The stone house was built by Dr. Simeon Smith between 1765 and 1775. John Cotton Smith, the last Federalist governor of Connecticut (in office from 1812 to 1817), the son of Rev. Cotton Mather Smith, lived here from 1794 until his death in 1845. Unfortunately, much of the interior of this house was destroyed by a major fire in 1998. The firemen were much impeded by the stone exterior and the slate roof, which is difficult to ventilate. The front porch is no longer there, but the house has been restored to its full glory.

This charming cottage at 95 South Main Street was home to Evelyn Pitcher, a lovely woman who was well respected in town and an inveterate gardener. It was probably built between 1808 and 1835, but it was demolished between 2000 and 2002. All summer long, Evelyn could be seen working in her lush garden. (Courtesy of Barbara Bartram.)

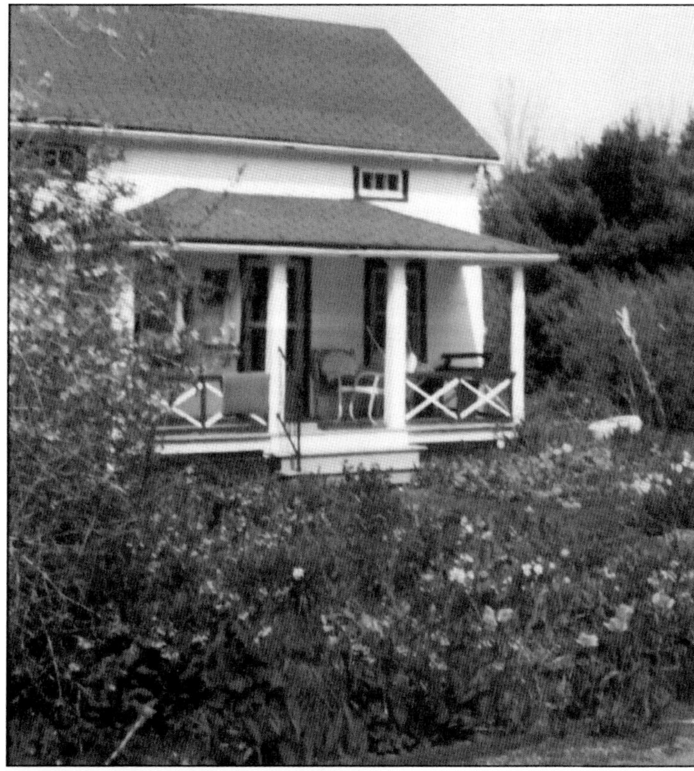

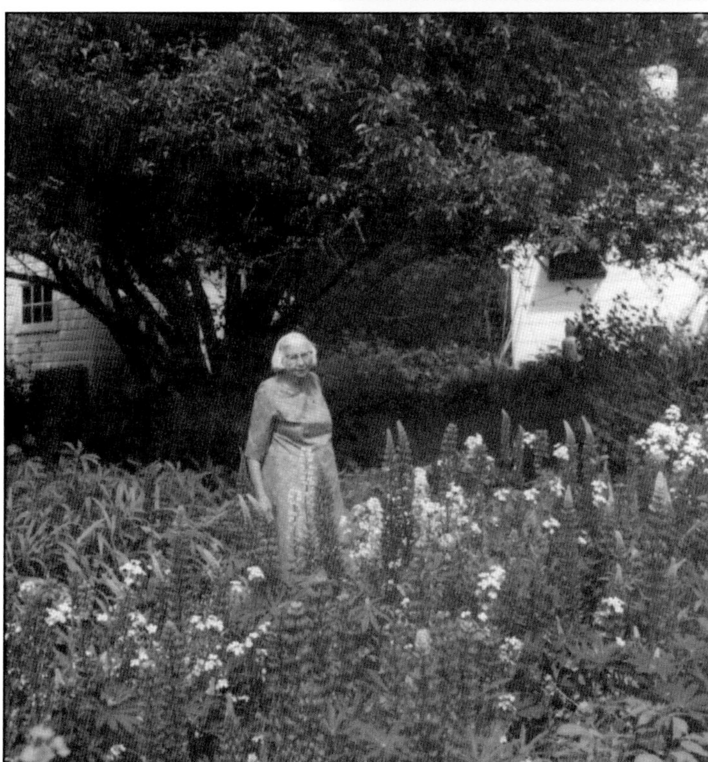

Evelyn Pitcher is pictured here in her later years, looking like a flower among the many blooms in the garden. Pitcher worked at the Sharon Hospital in the housekeeping department. She walked everywhere she went, including to Dakin's Store on West Main Street for her groceries. (Courtesy of Barbara Bartram.)

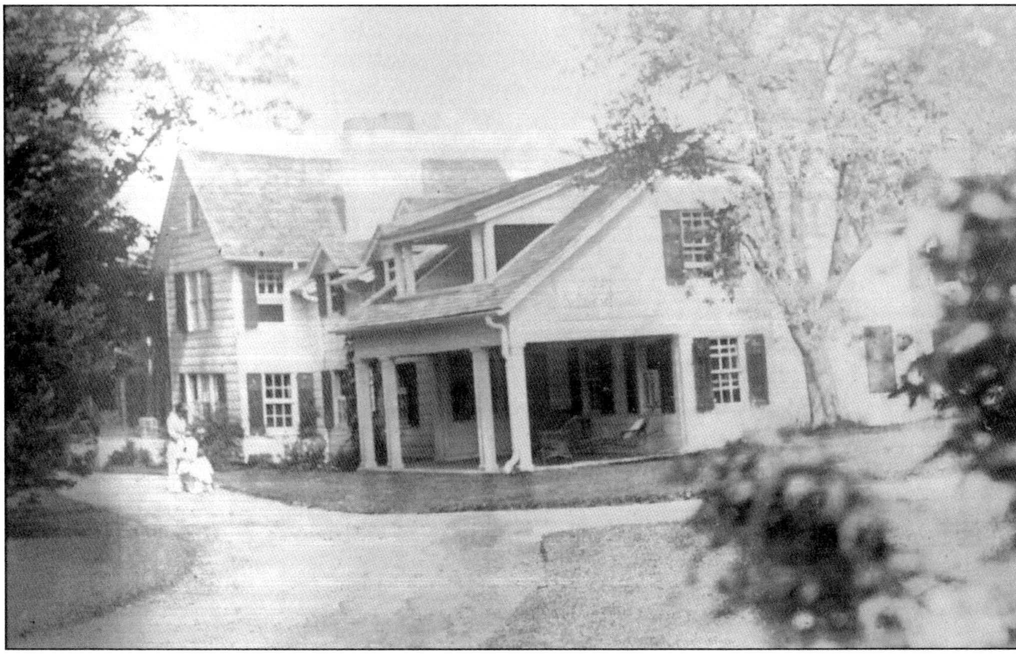

In 1910, Dr. William Herrick purchased this house for his family, along with 30 acres. A prominent New York physician, the family spent summers at the home, which included flower gardens on the exterior and a pipe organ and Steinway concert grand piano in the pine-paneled living room. The joys of the screened-in sleeping porch were extolled by Eunice Herrick Trowbridge in her charming book about growing up in Sharon, *Family Sketches*. (Courtesy of William Trowbridge.)

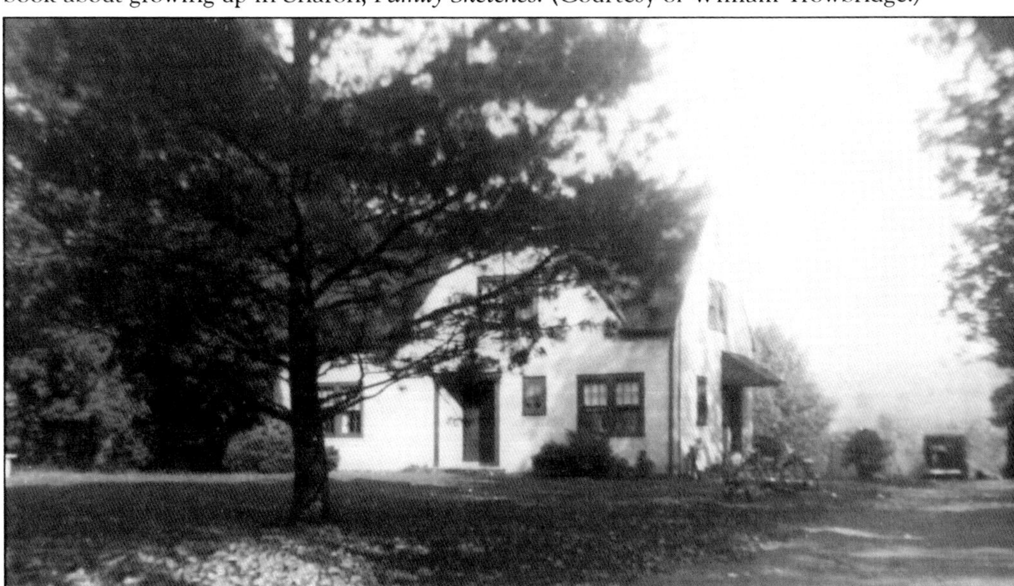

This Cotswold-style cottage at 24 Hilltop Road was built by William Riley Jr. for his family and their 11 children. It looks much the same today as it does in this photograph. Tom Riley, one of the children, is the owner of Riley Furniture, which is just across the state border in neighboring New York. It is still a family-owned business, and many of the Riley grandchildren work there. (Courtesy of Tom Riley.)

Two

Doing Business

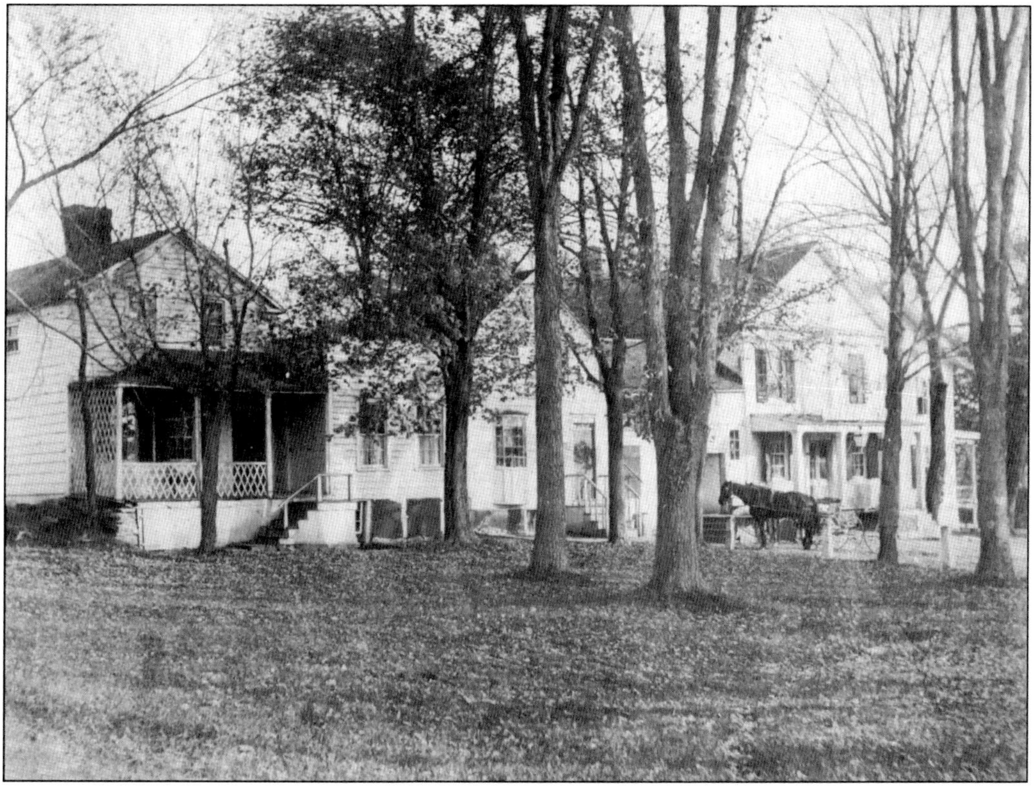

Today, the Sharon Green is a primarily residential area. It is a beautiful open space lined with rows of large trees and surrounded by well-kept historic homes. But it has not always been that way. For most of its history, the Sharon Green was the center of commerce for the town of Sharon and the nearby farms and industries. In this photograph, the only building that remains is now the private home at 2 Main Street, built around 1807 by Kellogg Berry across Route 4 from the clock tower (right side of the photograph). The house and the adjacent buildings were part of a complex of stores that included a millinery shop, a jewelry store, a general store, and a lumberyard originally run by Maj. David Gould. Later, Abel Woodward and Aaron Smith became the proprietors, and the complex was known as A.R. Woodward. The five buildings connected to form the A.R. Woodward Store, which sold a variety of merchandise, including lumber and hardware.

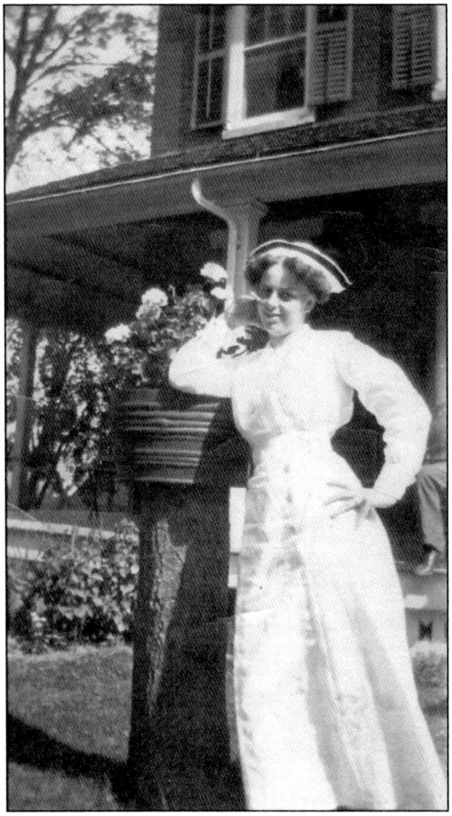

It is rare to find a photograph of a professional woman clothed in her work uniform, and this image of Frances Smith, wife of N. Collins Smith, a local music teacher and musician, is a treasure. Frances Smith poses in front of the first Sharon Hospital, located at 90 Calkinstown Road, which is now a private home (prior to becoming a hospital, it was the residence of Sharon iron man Hiram Weed). The hospital had four doctors, two nurses, eight beds, and a small operating room. (Courtesy of Ester Pollard.)

This photograph of the doctors at the Sharon Clinic was probably taken in 1972, the year the clinic marked its 25th anniversary. Each one of the faces would be familiar to every town resident. Shown here from left to right are (first row) George Longstreth, Richard Collins, and John Gallup; (second row) Frederick Gevalt, Robert Noble, George Haydock, W. Peter Reyelt, Malcolm Brown, Joseph Hajek, Martha Bennett, Robert Ryan, Robert Fisher, and Roger Moore. (Courtesy of W. Peter Reyelt Jr.)

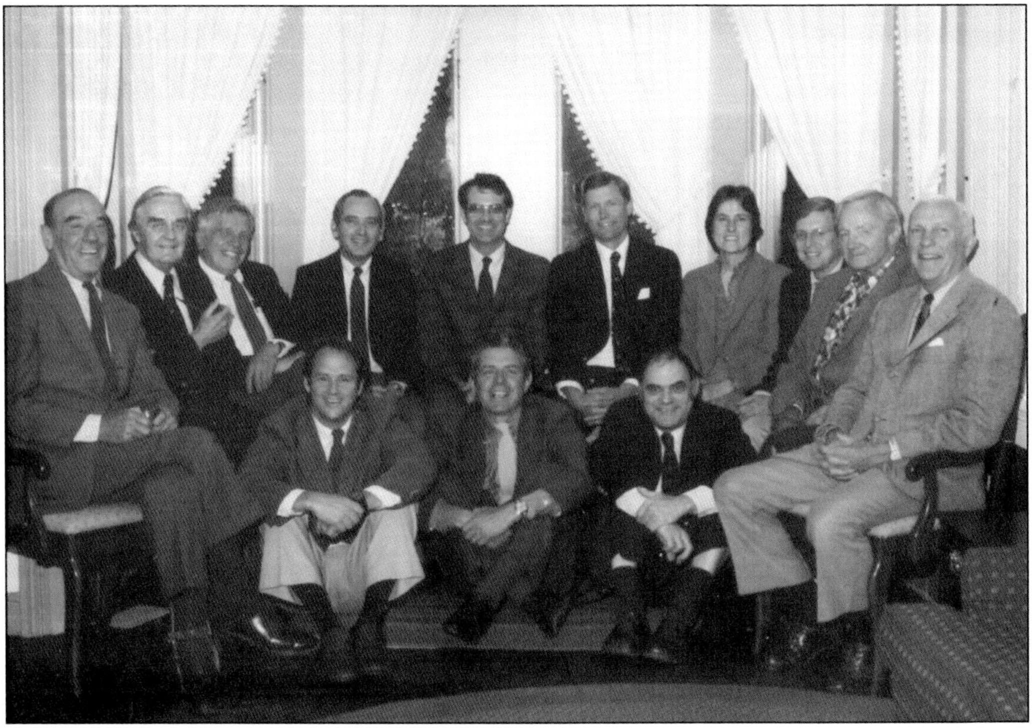

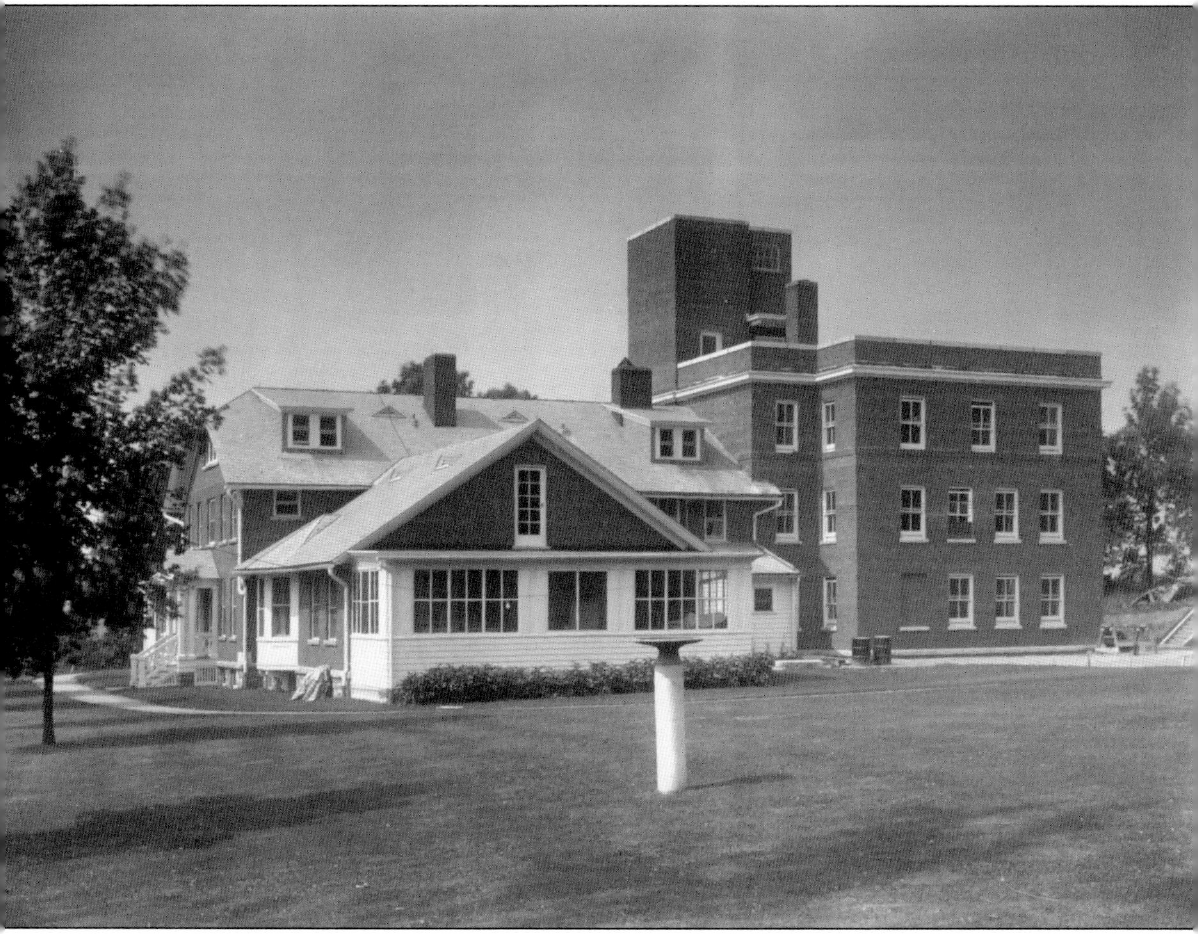

The new Sharon Hospital, at 50 Hospital Hill Road, opened in 1916, replacing the original hospital on Calkinstown Road. As community needs grew, a special fund for new construction was established with $10,700 raised in Sharon's first street fair, conceived and carried out by Mrs. Charles G. Kerley and associates in the Hospital Auxiliary. A second fair sponsored by Mrs. Plummer Schley and Mrs. Edward L. Pruyn was held later. Throughout the minutes and annual reports appear the names of hospital benefactors, such as Mr. and Mrs. R.R. Colgate; Augustus Van Cortlandt; Edward Thurston Jr. and his wife, Susan Hathaway Thurston; and Mr. and Mrs. Ward Belcher. Individuals contributed generously: Susan Colgate provided an elevator, Mrs. Ieuan Harris gave an oxygen tent, and the famous Dr. Charles Gilman Kerley, a Sharon resident, donated his professional services. This first three-story fireproof addition was added between 1928 and 1930 at a cost of $80,000, providing a waiting room, a nurses' room, an eight-bed ward, a full maternity department, and a new operating suite. (Photograph by George M. Marckres.)

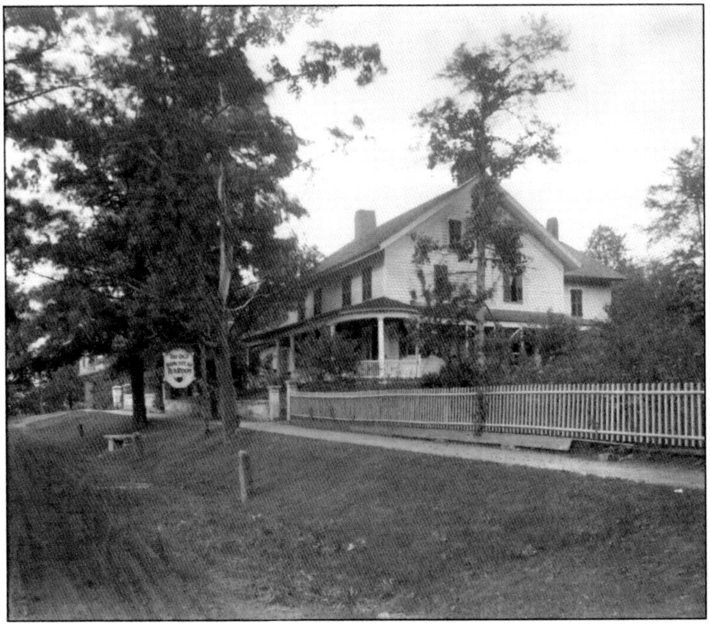

Tearooms, boardinghouses, inns, and all kinds of travelers' accommodations abounded in the early 20th century, as Sharon was a fairly easy trip by train—and, later, by motor car—from New York. The Old Homestead Tea Room, run by Mrs. Wiley, at what is now 96 Upper Main Street, was a popular destination. The sign in this photograph is said to have been the same sign, recycled, that was used at the Sharon Inn to advertise their tearoom. Later, it was also reportedly used by the Village Tea Room.

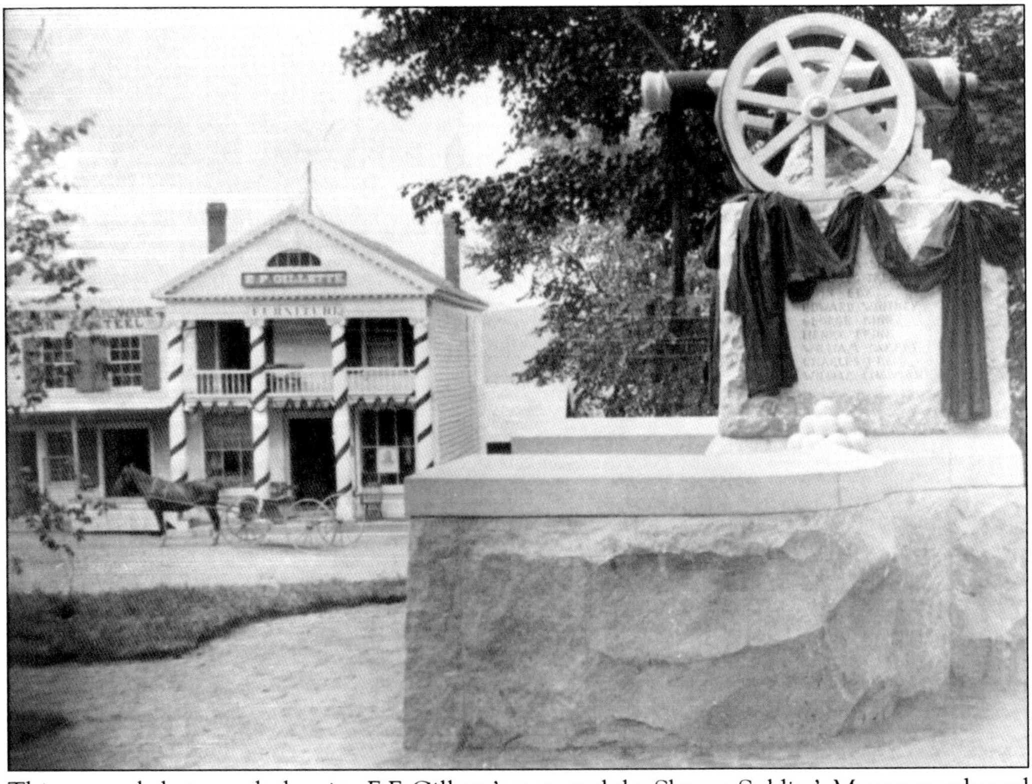

This unusual photograph showing E.F. Gillette's store and the Sharon Soldier's Monument draped in black bunting was taken in June 1909 on the occasion of Edward Franklin Gillette's death. The Sharon Soldier's Monument was erected in honor of Sharon men who enlisted in the Civil War. The Gillette Store was located at what is now 149 Main Street. The monument was moved from this site and now stands on the south side of the home at 12 North Main Street.

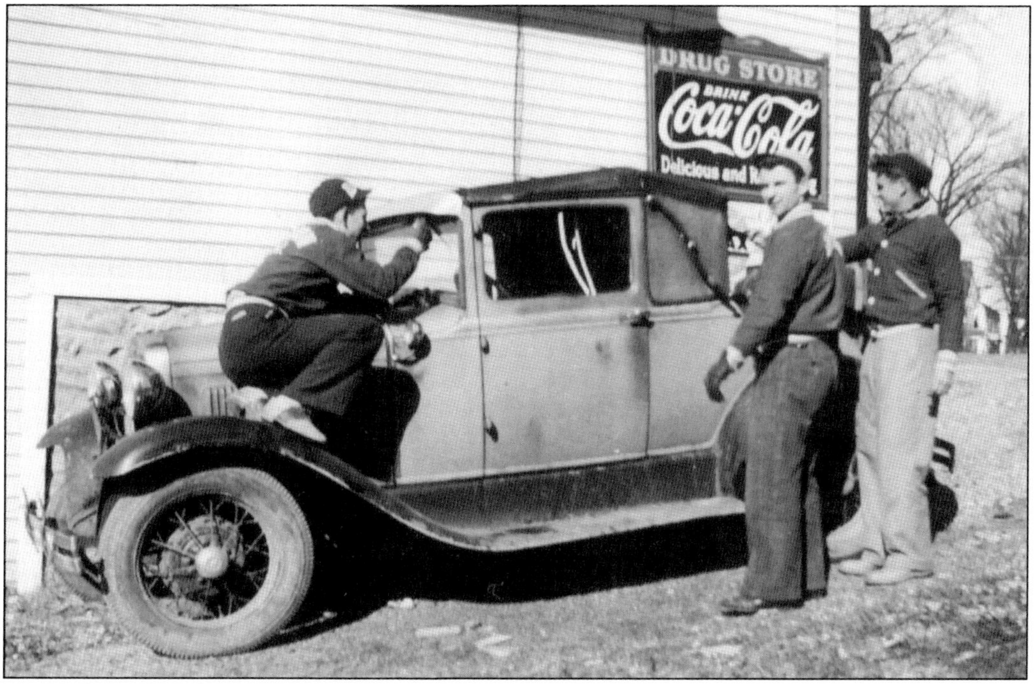

It was always handy to know something about cars, especially for young men looking to earn an extra nickel. Here, from left to right, Donald Carley, Everett "Bub" Pitcher, and Gaylord Eggleston collaborate on fixing a car beside the drugstore on Main Street. (Courtesy of Everett Pitcher.)

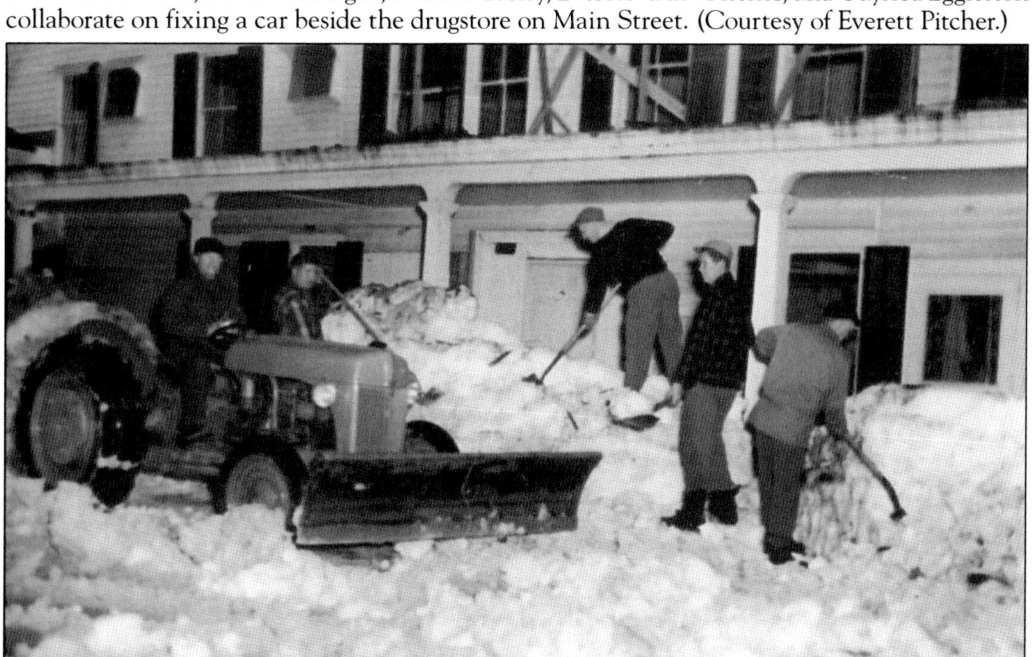

To the dismay of many in town, the Sharon Inn fell on hard times in the early 1950s and was put up for sale. No qualified buyers appeared, and the building was left to deteriorate. Even in this condition, people cared enough to remove the snow during a particularly hard winter. The inn was finally demolished in 1954. (Courtesy of William Trowbridge.)

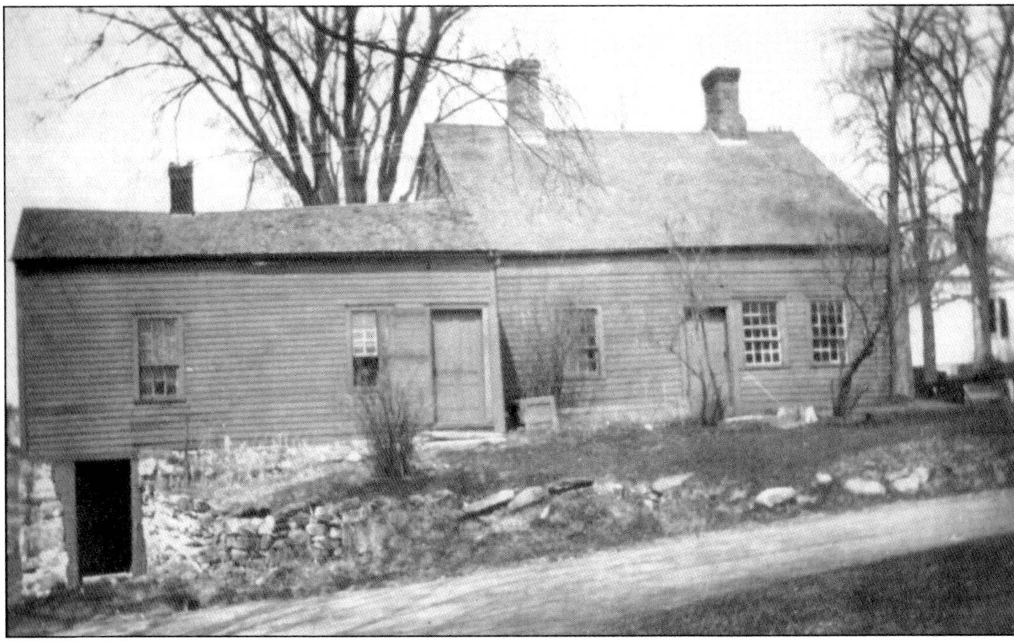

Daniel and Ruth O'Connell lived in this small Cape Cod–style house at 16 Amenia Road. Although the family owned the grander house at 1 Main Street, they lived in this home and rented the big house. Daniel had a car repair business next door to the house and Ruth served as the town treasurer and a state representative.

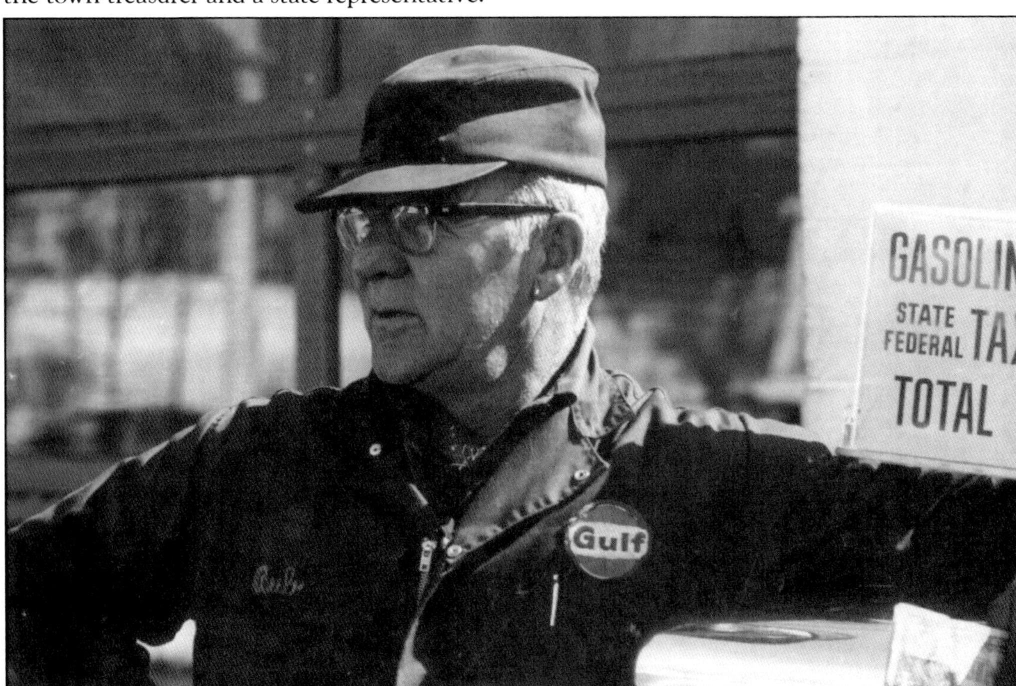

A well-known man born and bred in Sharon, Everett "Bub" Pitcher was the owner of the garage at 7 West Main Street (now Art's Automotive). When this photograph was taken in 1971, the price of gas in Sharon was 36¢ a gallon. (Courtesy of Everett Pitcher.)

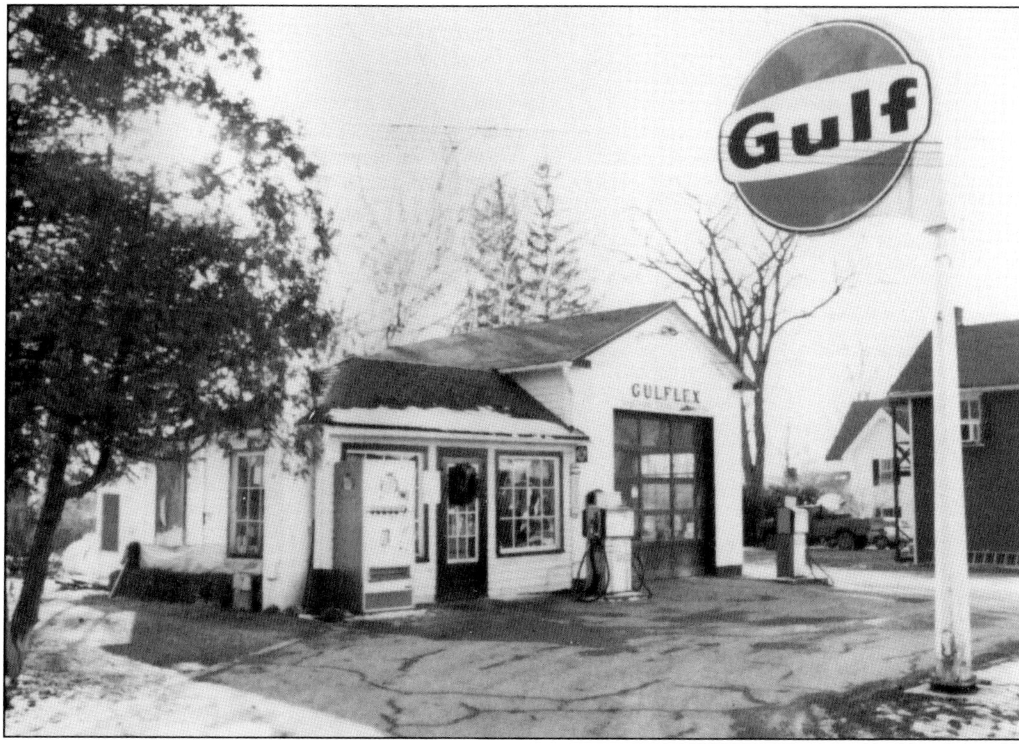

At one time, Sharon boasted at least 11 gas stations. Still easily recognizable, Bub's Garage, at 7 West Main Street, was operated by Everett "Bub" Pitcher from 1963 to 1980. Note the soda machine and the oversized Gulf sign. (Courtesy of Everett Pitcher.)

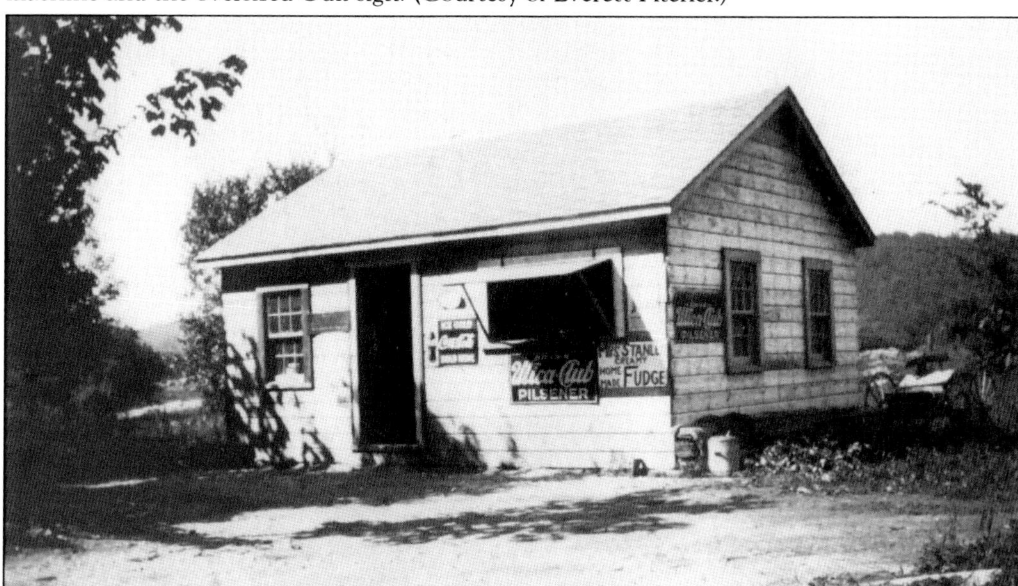

Because of the limitations of early automobiles, gas stations were located all across the town. This gas station at 206 Amenia Road, typical of small gas stations in Sharon, was run by Frank Marckres and sold ice cream and sodas in addition to gas. This building has been repurposed into the Greystone Nursery.

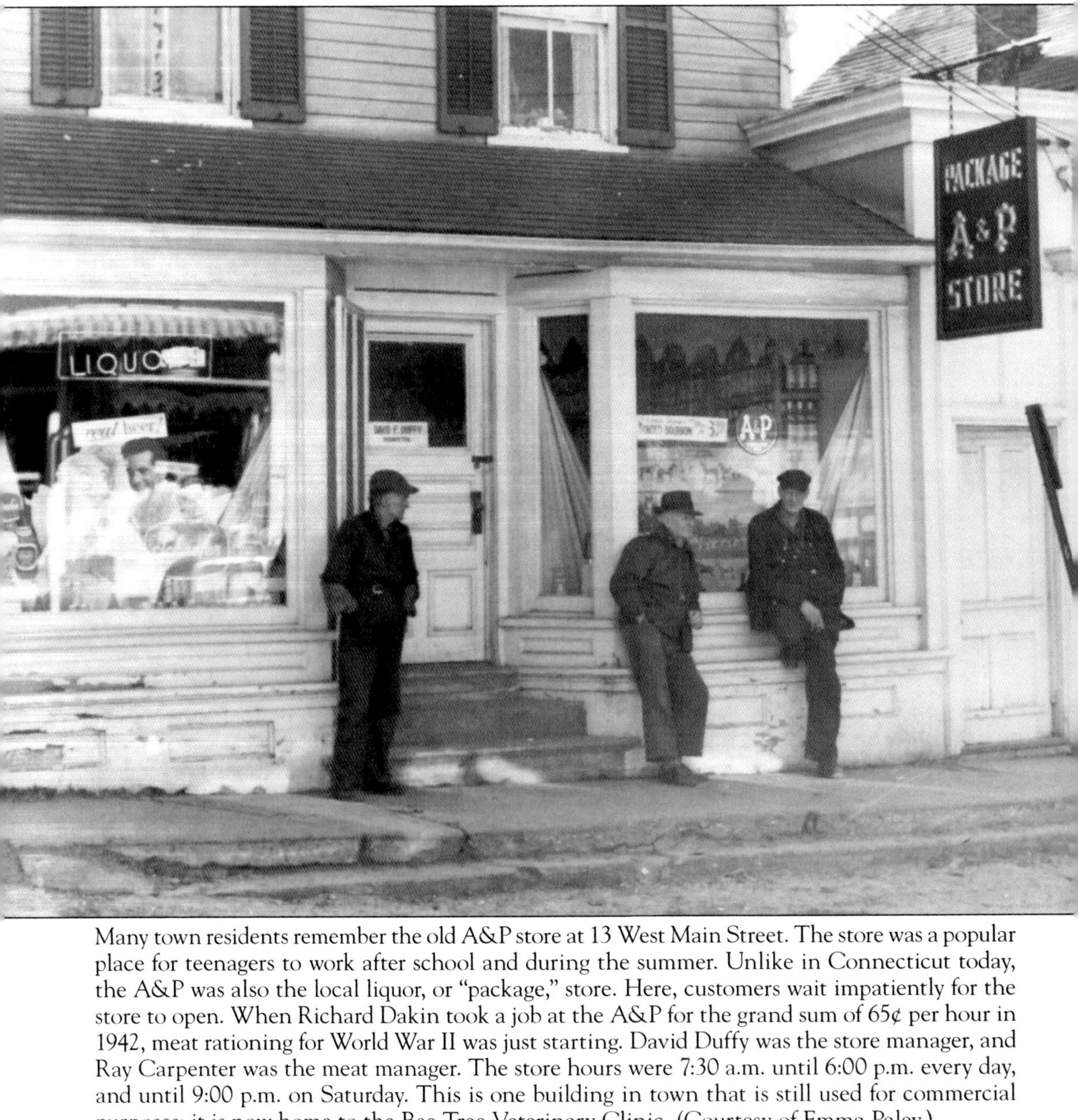

Many town residents remember the old A&P store at 13 West Main Street. The store was a popular place for teenagers to work after school and during the summer. Unlike in Connecticut today, the A&P was also the local liquor, or "package," store. Here, customers wait impatiently for the store to open. When Richard Dakin took a job at the A&P for the grand sum of 65¢ per hour in 1942, meat rationing for World War II was just starting. David Duffy was the store manager, and Ray Carpenter was the meat manager. The store hours were 7:30 a.m. until 6:00 p.m. every day, and until 9:00 p.m. on Saturday. This is one building in town that is still used for commercial purposes; it is now home to the Bee Tree Veterinary Clinic. (Courtesy of Emma Paley.)

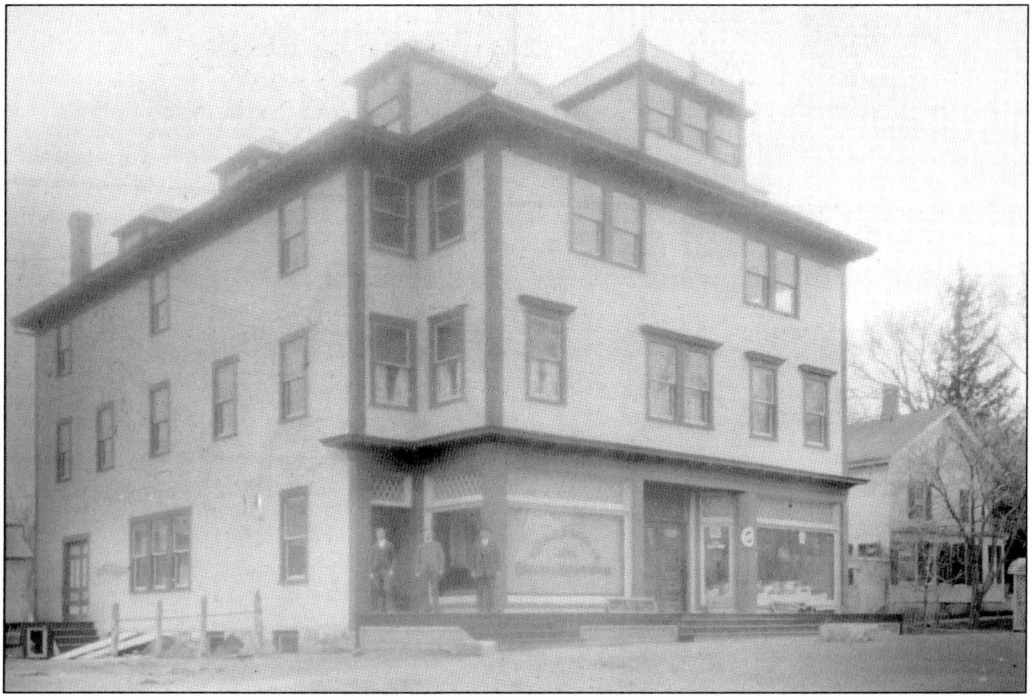

This large building at 16 West Main Street might be difficult to recognize today as the home of Roaring Oaks Florist. The Dakin Store, also known as H.B. Dakin Merchandise, was a general mercantile store. Note how the building seems to tower over the house next door. The top stories burned in a fire in December 1899.

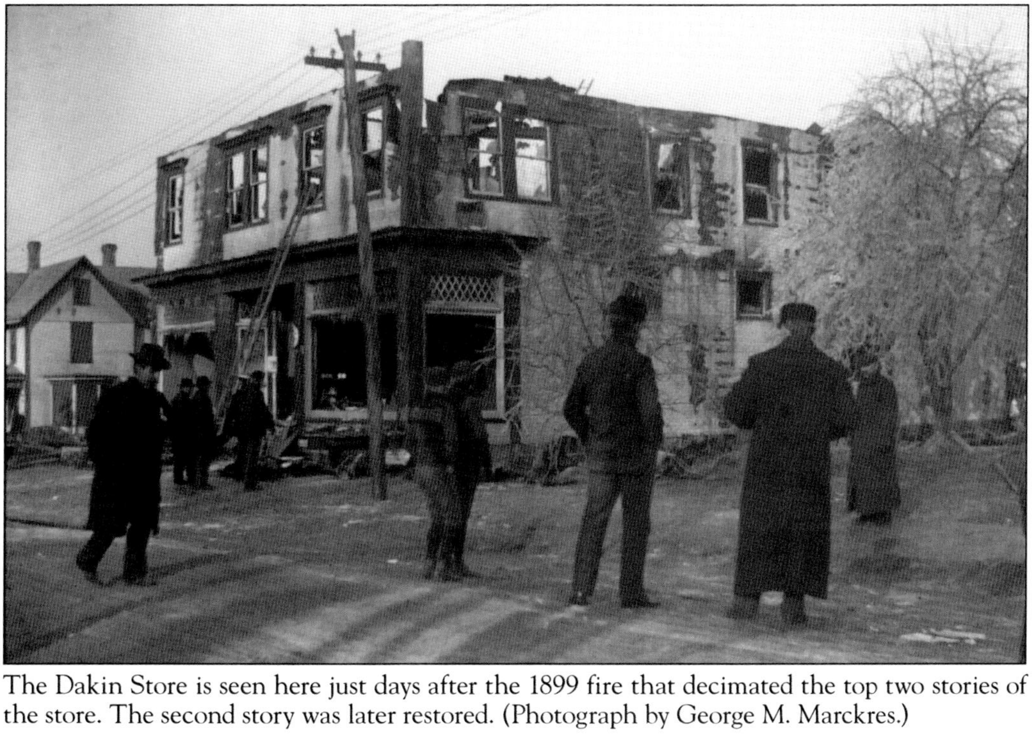

The Dakin Store is seen here just days after the 1899 fire that decimated the top two stories of the store. The second story was later restored. (Photograph by George M. Marckres.)

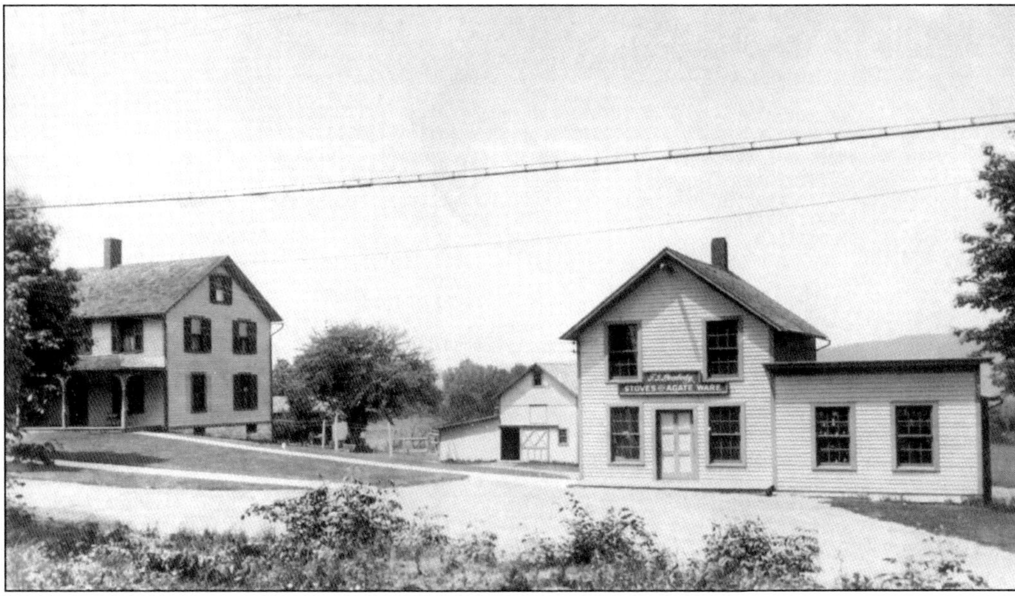

Whatever goods were needed could be purchased locally, as seen in this photograph of Peabody Stoves and Agate Ware. The house on the left is 42 New Street, currently owned by Jamie and Tom Casey. The house at 52 New Street belonged to the Peabody family, who ran the business pictured here. It is now the Catholic rectory and sits just north of St. Bernard Church, which was built on New Street in 1915 between numbers 42 and 52.

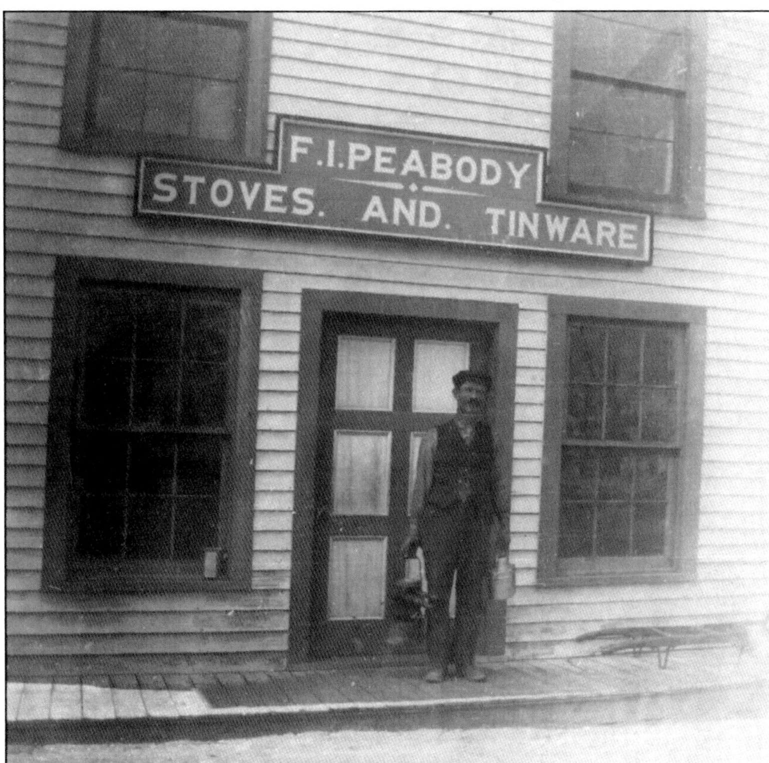

William Riley Sr. stands in front of the door to F.I. Peabody Stoves and Tinware, also pictured above. It is believed that this building was moved slightly to the north to make room for St. Bernard Church. It is now the garage for the rectory.

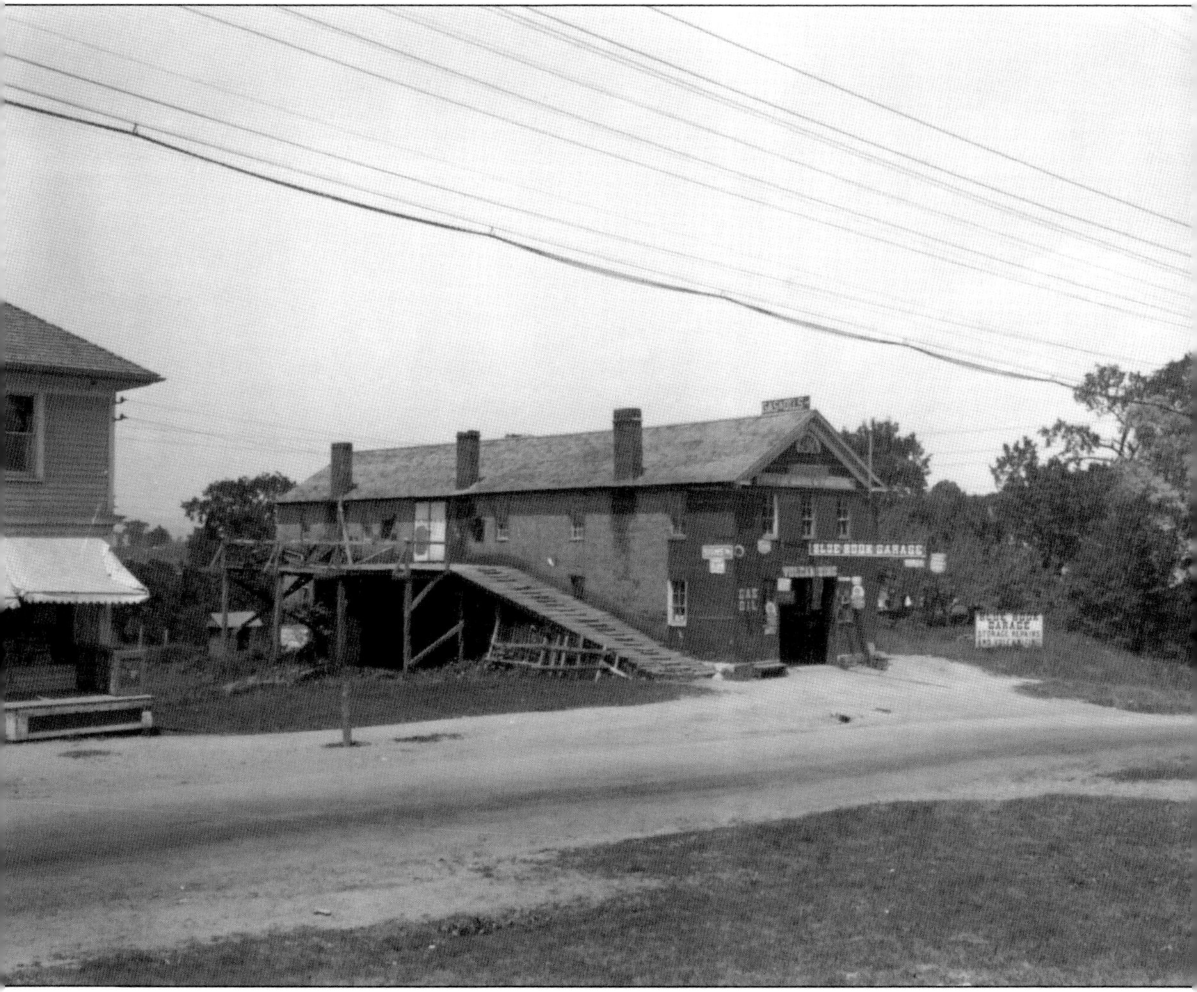

A few buildings in Sharon still house businesses that are nearly identical to their historical predecessors. This building at 130 North Main Street was home to the Blue Book Garage, which was later known as Lamb's Garage, run by George Lamb. Still later, it housed the Peder Aakjar Garage, from 1966 to 1975. The ramp was used to bring clients and their repair jobs to the wagon repair shop on the second story. Although it is hard to place this building on the current landscape because of the dingy dirt road, it is the current home of AutoSport, on Main Street across from the Sharon Center School. (Photograph by George M. Marckres.)

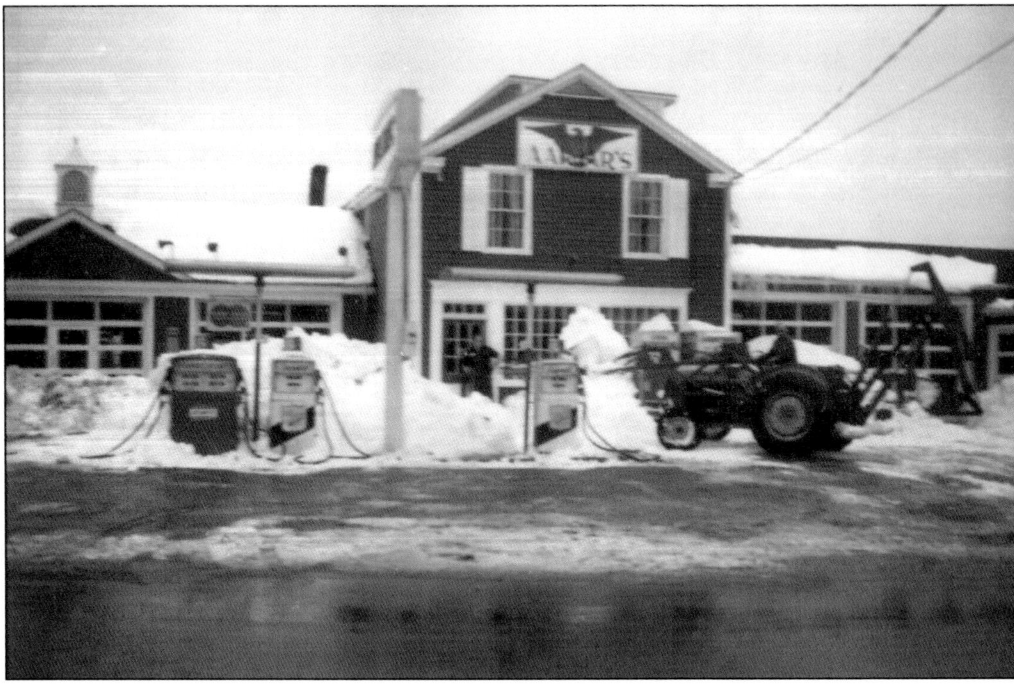

Many photographs in the collection at the Sharon Historical Society show the joys of living through winter in Sharon. This photograph is a much later image of the Peder Aakjar Garage, at 130 North Main Street, after a major snowstorm. It would be challenging to fill a tank when the pumps were buried to the top. (Courtesy of Bonnie Aakjar.)

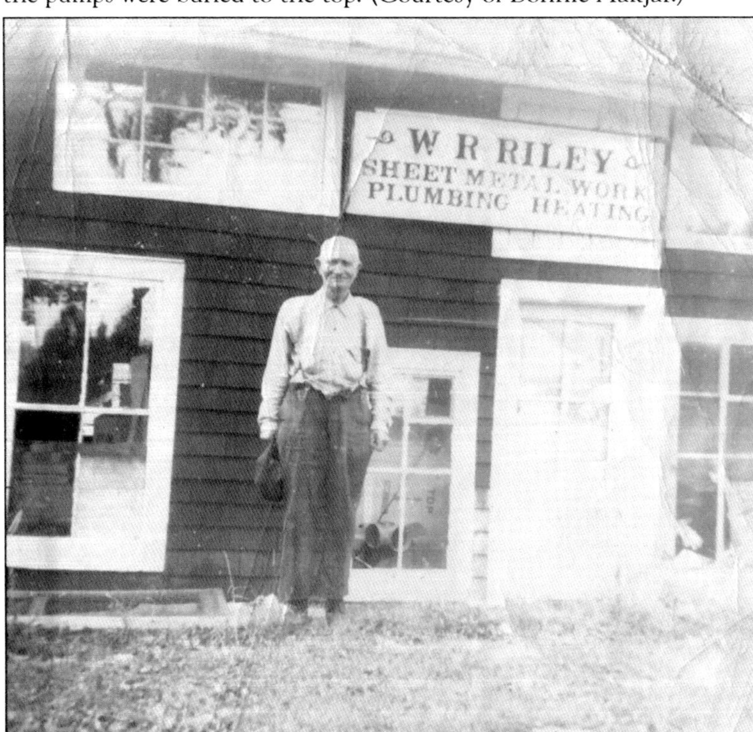

Some of the town's modern-day businesses have long roots in Sharon. William Riley Sr. started his sheet metal work, plumbing, and heating business in this building on Calkinstown Road in the early 1900s. William Jr. went out on his own in the 1950s, and, later, William III inherited the business. Today, Sharon residents can still call a William Riley to fix their plumbing. (Courtesy of Tom Riley.)

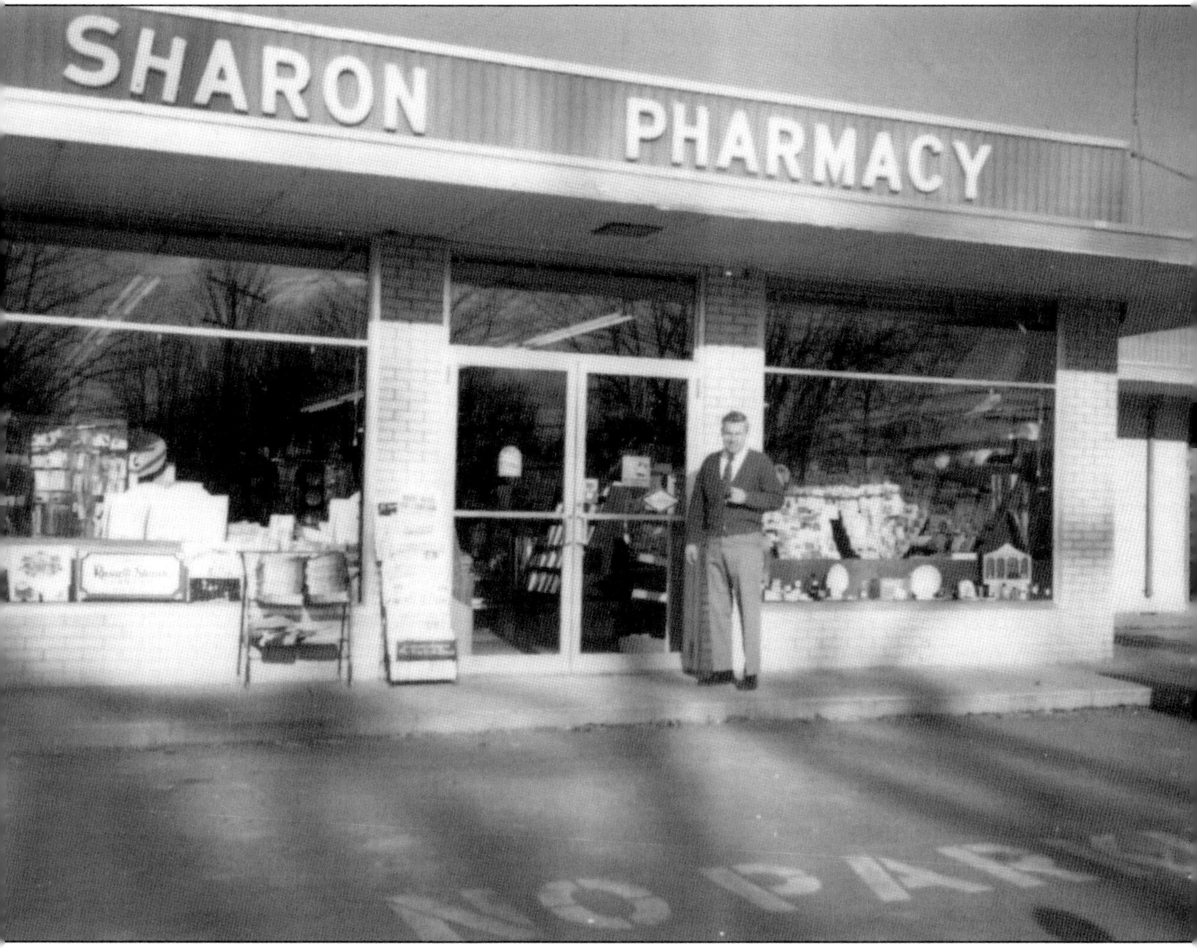

The Sharon Pharmacy, at 8 Gay Street, was the first store to open in the Sharon Shopping Center. Ray and Roberta Donovan purchased the Duplessis property on Gay Street and moved the existing house to Still Meadow Road to make room for the center. Edward Heacox Sr., age 28, is standing in front of his new venture in 1961. The pharmacy is still a much-beloved local business. Although some say that the shopping center drove retail businesses from Sharon's Main Street, the current lack of storefronts along the Green is partially responsible for the serene and unchanged nature of that section of town. Parking spaces and modern signage would interrupt that expansive natural space. (Courtesy of Kathryn M. Heacox.)

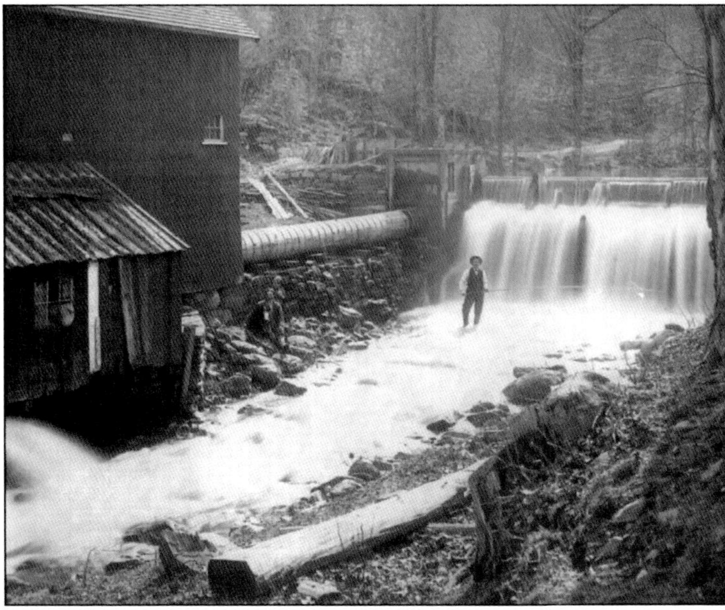

This is a rare photograph of two men fishing in Mill Brook (or Guinea Brook), which ran past Studley's Saw Mill on Route 4 near the Lovell House, at 519 Cornwall Bridge Road. The long pipe in the photograph shows that a turbine had replaced the waterwheel as the primary power source. The mill was still operating in 1900. The south portion of this picture, towards the bottom of the image, is now buried under Route 4.

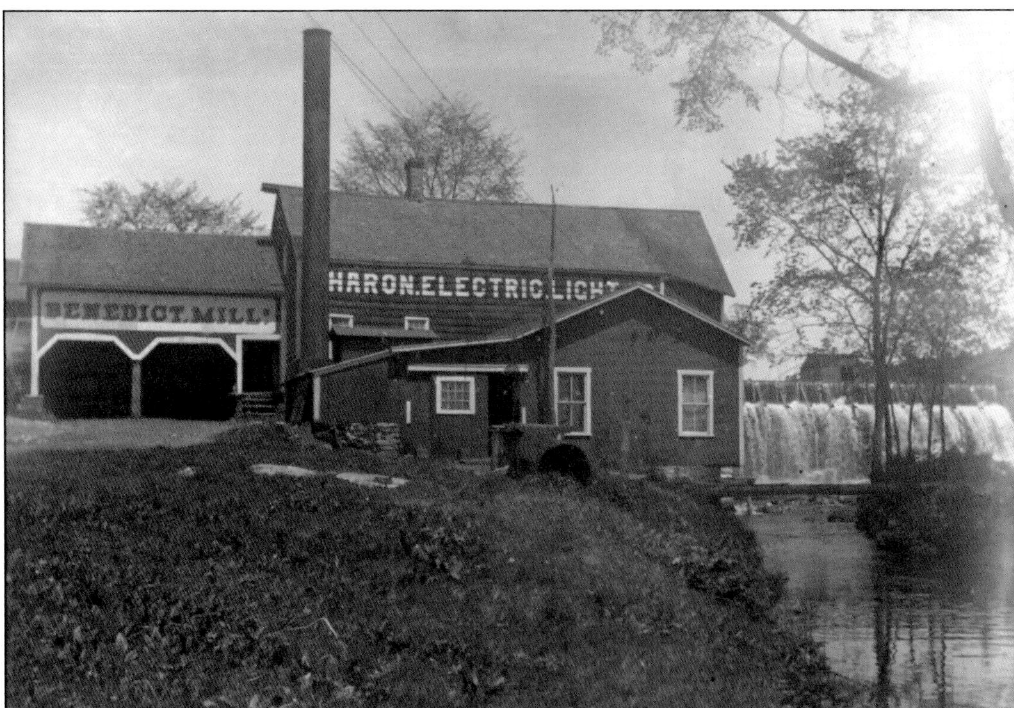

An intricate system of little rivers that maintained a good water flow through four seasons was integral to the growth of industry in town, from the very beginning up to the 20th century. The Benedict Mill was a gristmill that was once run by "Honest" Abel Benedict, local resident Barbara Bartram's great-grandfather. The mill was taken over by the Sharon Electric Light Company prior to 1911, when the milldam burst. The millpond backed up to the Mudge Pond dam. This building no longer stands, but it was located on the northwest side of Millerton Road where it meets Mudge Pond Road.

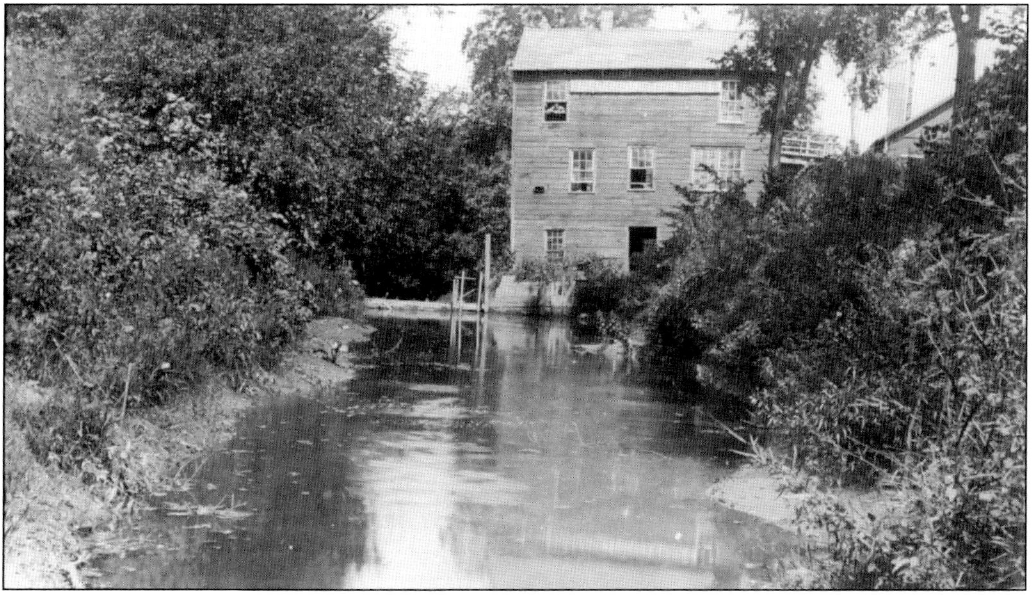

Even in today's world, Lover's Lane in Sharon does not seem to have been designed for road traffic. A very private thoroughfare, the stream, also known as Beardsley Pond Brook, flows into Sharon Falls and was dammed and harnessed for power at this three-story mill. The gristmill was owned by Judson Bostwick and ground grain into flour. It was probably powered by a breast waterwheel.

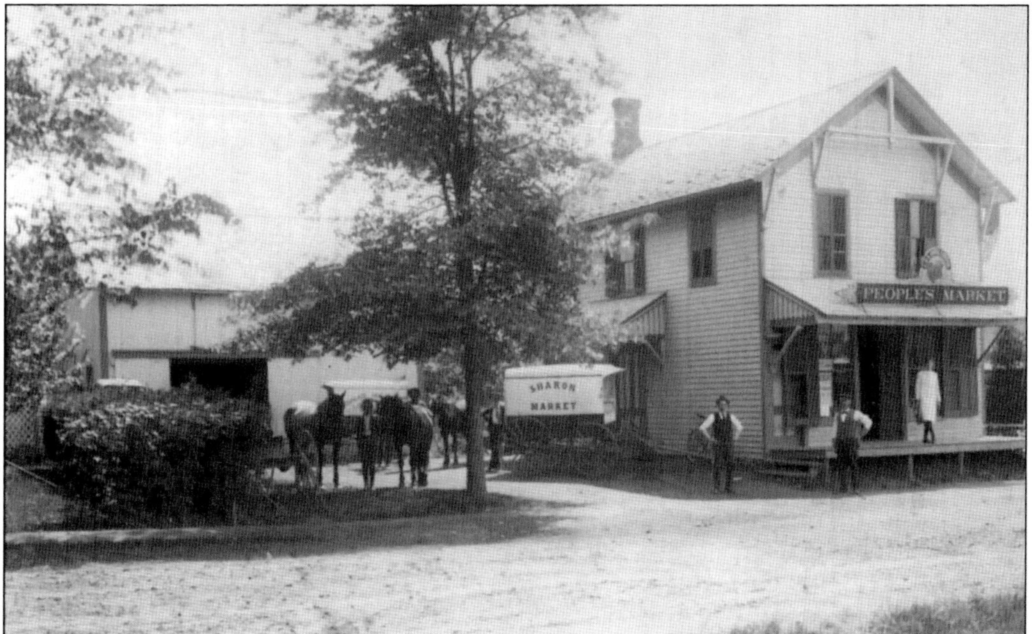

People's Market, at 1 Sharon Station Road, on the southwest corner of the intersection of Sharon Valley Road, was originally built by the Hotchkiss & Sons' Company as the company store. Workers at the factory would be paid in company script to be used for purchases at the company store. People's Market was later operated by Alanson Middlebrook Sr. and his wife, Ruth Bristol Middlebrook, as the Middlebrook Store. Ruth also served as Sharon's town clerk. The building remains in the Middlebrook family and is now used as rental apartments.

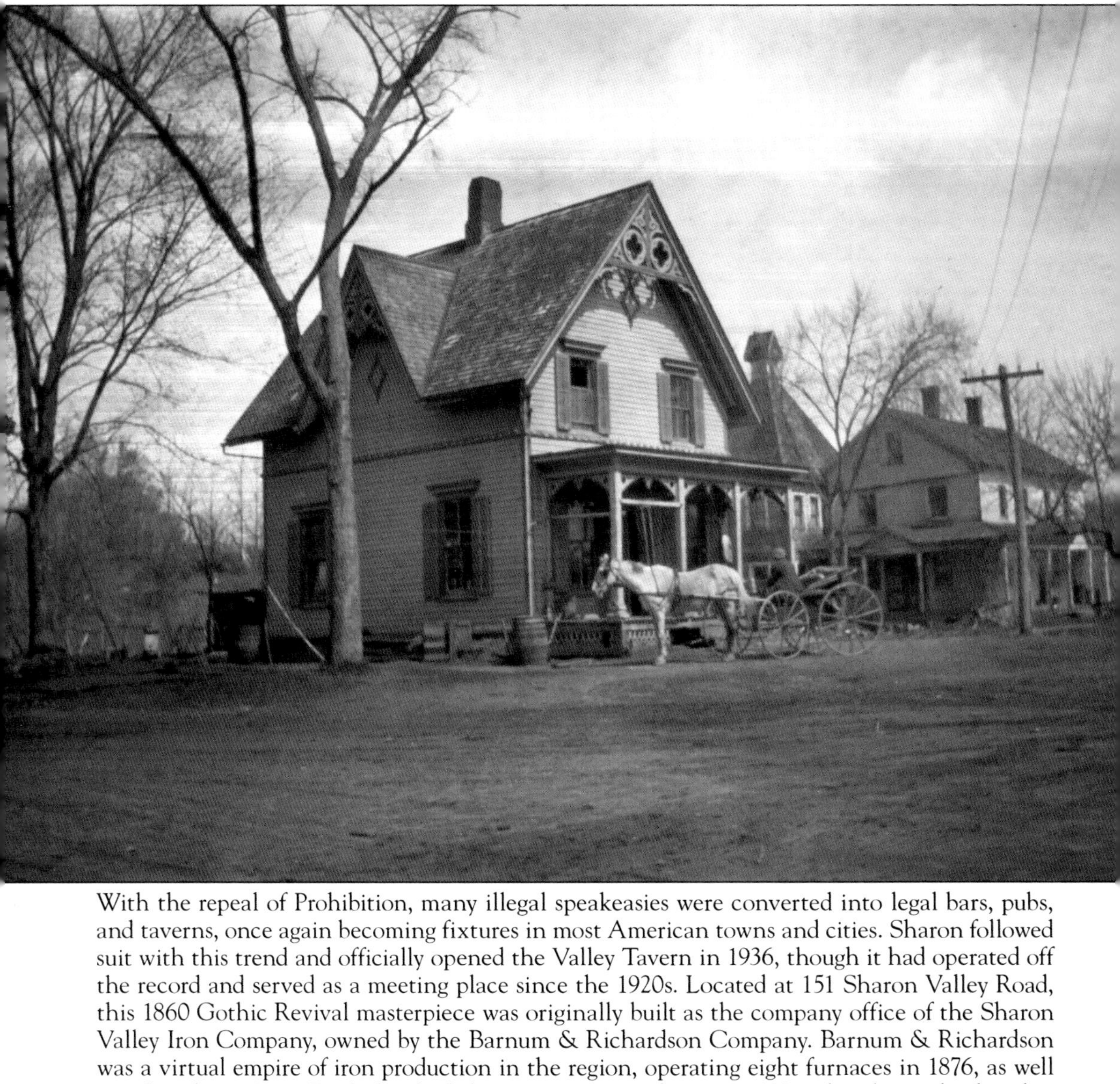

With the repeal of Prohibition, many illegal speakeasies were converted into legal bars, pubs, and taverns, once again becoming fixtures in most American towns and cities. Sharon followed suit with this trend and officially opened the Valley Tavern in 1936, though it had operated off the record and served as a meeting place since the 1920s. Located at 151 Sharon Valley Road, this 1860 Gothic Revival masterpiece was originally built as the company office of the Sharon Valley Iron Company, owned by the Barnum & Richardson Company. Barnum & Richardson was a virtual empire of iron production in the region, operating eight furnaces in 1876, as well as a foundry in Lime Rock that had the capacity to produce over 100 railroad car wheels a day. (Photograph by George M. Marckres.)

Three

EDUCATION, ARTS, AND WORSHIP

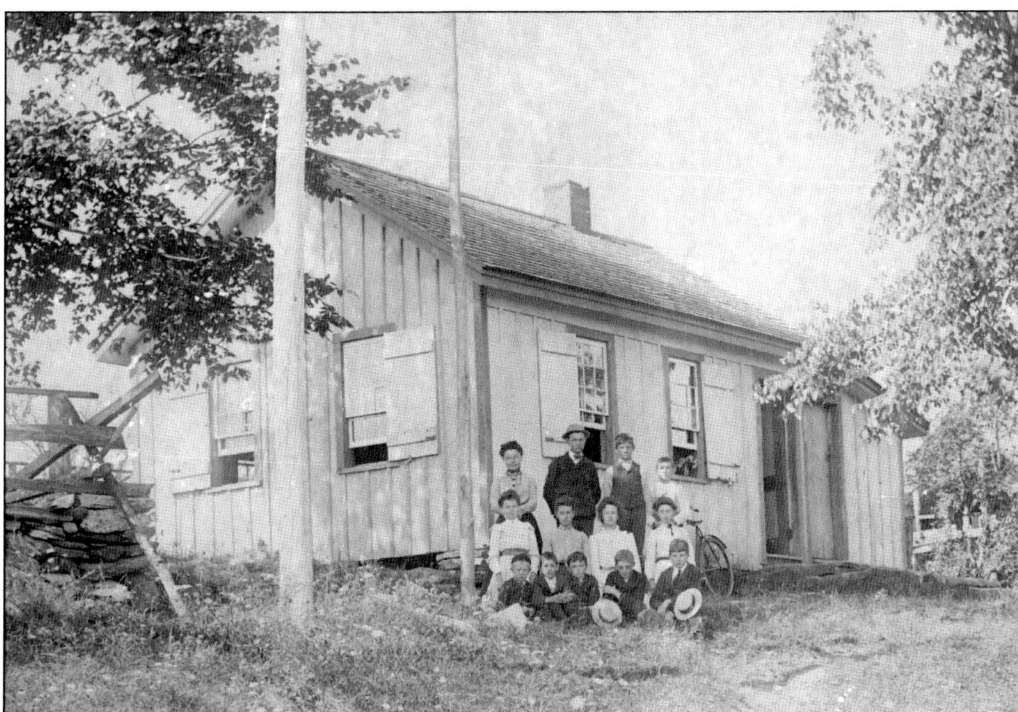

By 1873, the town of Sharon was divided into 17 separate school districts and one fractional district. The fractional district, on the west side of town, did not have a schoolhouse, and students probably went across the bridge to school in Cornwall. The Ellsworth section of Sharon had three districts alone. This is the Hartwell School, in District One. All of the schools were similar in appearance, and none survive today that have not been drastically changed.

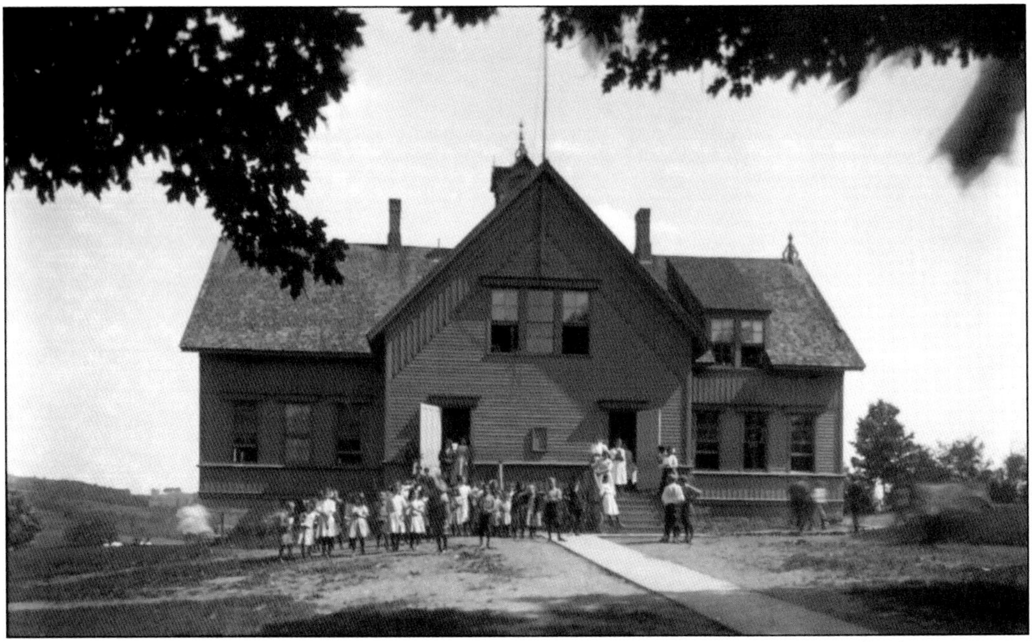

The first Sharon High School was built between 1886 and 1893 on approximately the same site as the current school. By 1910, there were plans for most of the district schools to be closed and consolidated. In 1912, eight of the district schools closed, and students were sent to the high school, which became the consolidated Sharon Center School. By 1915, the town had added on to the high school, but it was still overcrowded and poorly lit, and the town felt that the building should be condemned. Perhaps fortuitously, the school burned nearly to the ground in 1918. (Photograph by George M. Marckres.)

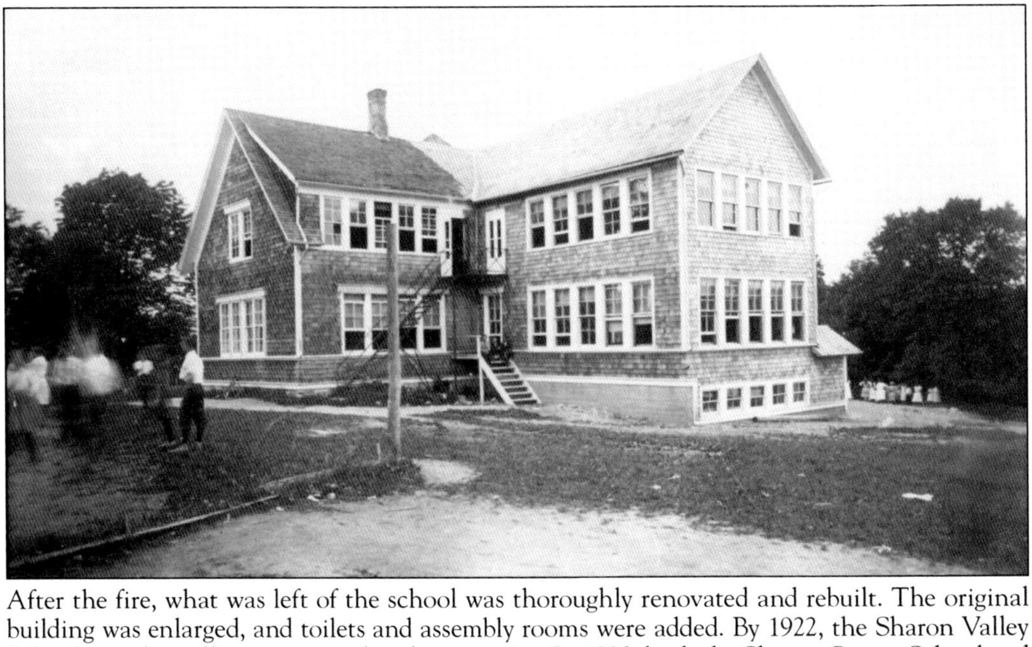

After the fire, what was left of the school was thoroughly renovated and rebuilt. The original building was enlarged, and toilets and assembly rooms were added. By 1922, the Sharon Valley School was also still in operation, but deteriorating. In 1923, both the Sharon Center School and the Sharon Valley School were destroyed by fire.

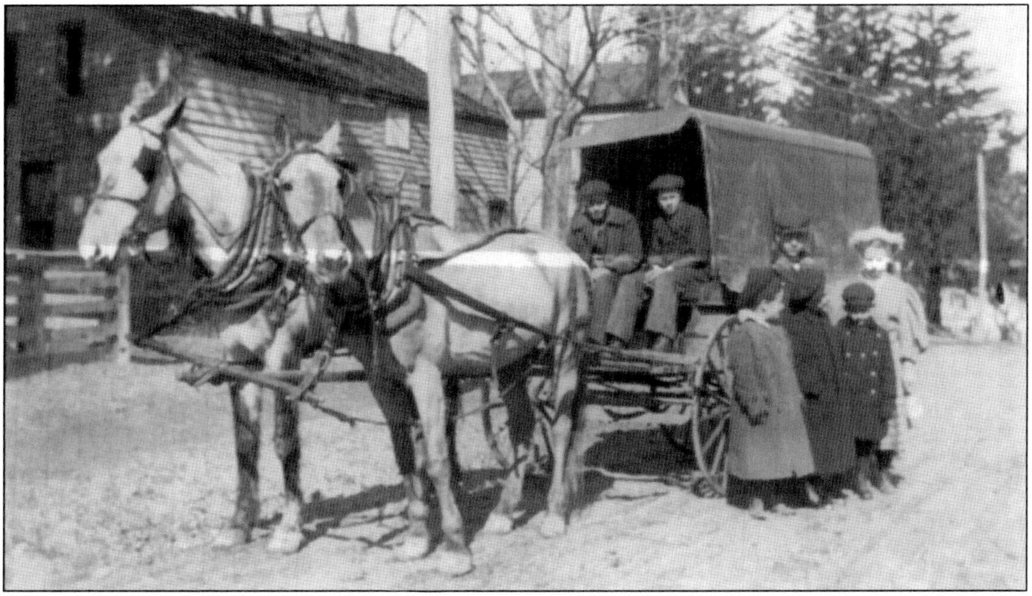

School buses ran in the early days of Sharon schooling. This photograph, taken in 1910, shows the school "bus" to the Amenia Union School, on Knibloe Hill Road. Pictured from left to right are (seated) Bertram Beyer and Charles Peck; (standing, first row) Edith Peck, Colar Austin, and Chester Keeler; (standing, second row) two unidentified children. The wagon and team, with horses Harry and Buck, were owned by William H. Conklin.

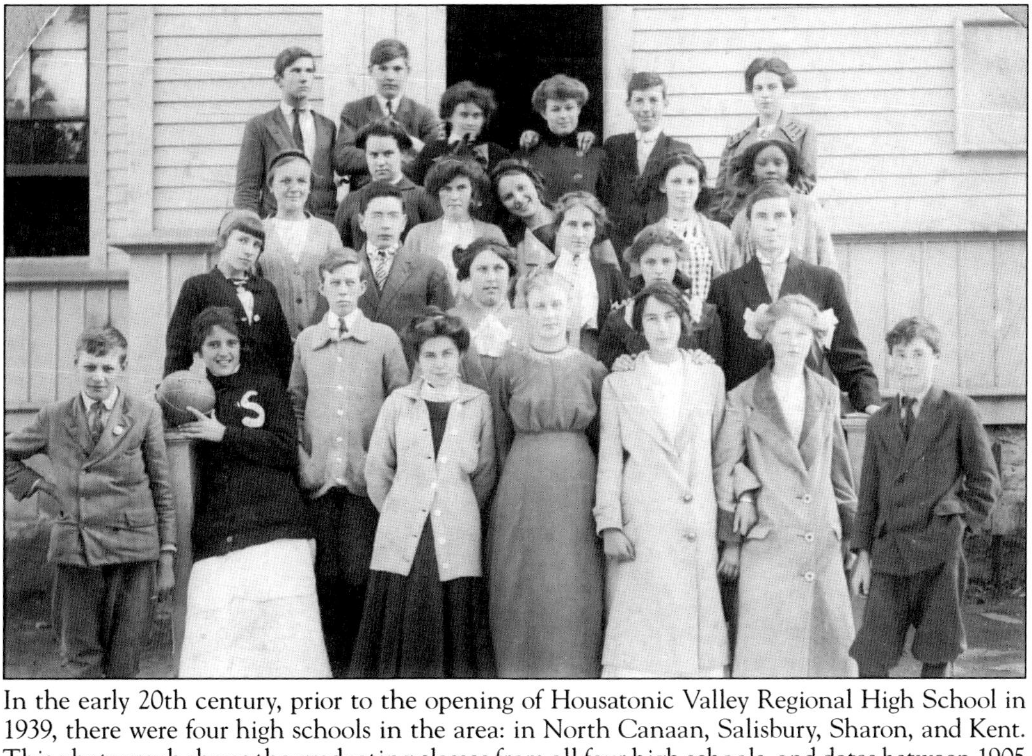

In the early 20th century, prior to the opening of Housatonic Valley Regional High School in 1939, there were four high schools in the area: in North Canaan, Salisbury, Sharon, and Kent. This photograph shows the graduating classes from all four high schools, and dates between 1905 and 1915. (Courtesy of Tom Riley.)

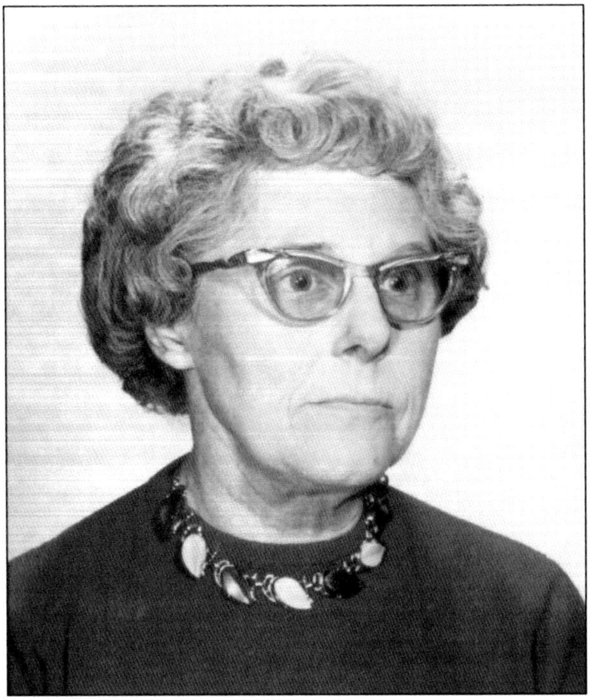

Evelyn Hamlin was an institution at the Sharon Center School, teaching for nearly 40 years. After graduating from the school in 1923, she attended Danbury Normal College, returning to teach in Sharon in 1925. She taught most elementary grades during her career, but she spent most of her years with the third grade, although her last assignment was fourth grade. Hamlin had a special interest in local history, and she taught the subject to all her third-grade students. Many residents share memories of the infamous Miss Hamlin, and when old-timers get reminiscing about their school days, the line heard most often is, "Miss Hamlin! I had her for a teacher."

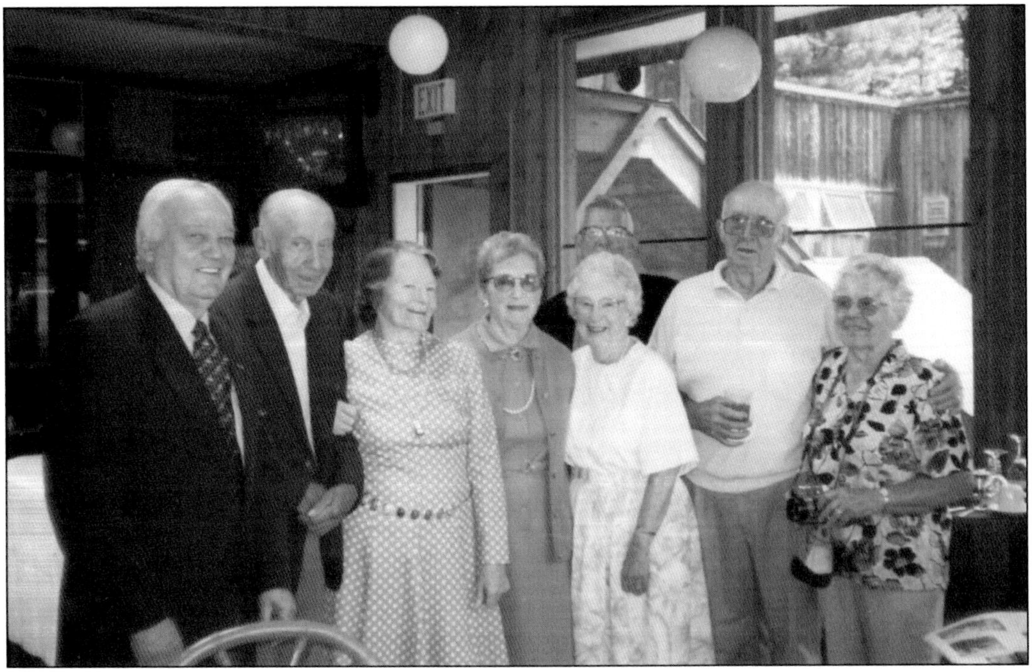

Sharon High School graduated its last class in spring 1939, as Housatonic Valley Regional High School opened in fall 1939. A reunion of the Sharon High School class of 1938 was held at Housatonic Valley Regional High School in the 1990s. Pictured from left to right are Jake Shoifet, Ken and Margaret Bartram, Mary Weinstein, Margaret Downey Hayne and John Hayne, and Donald and Helen Humeston. Jake, Ken, Mary, Margaret, and Donald were all members of the class. (Courtesy of Helen Humeston.)

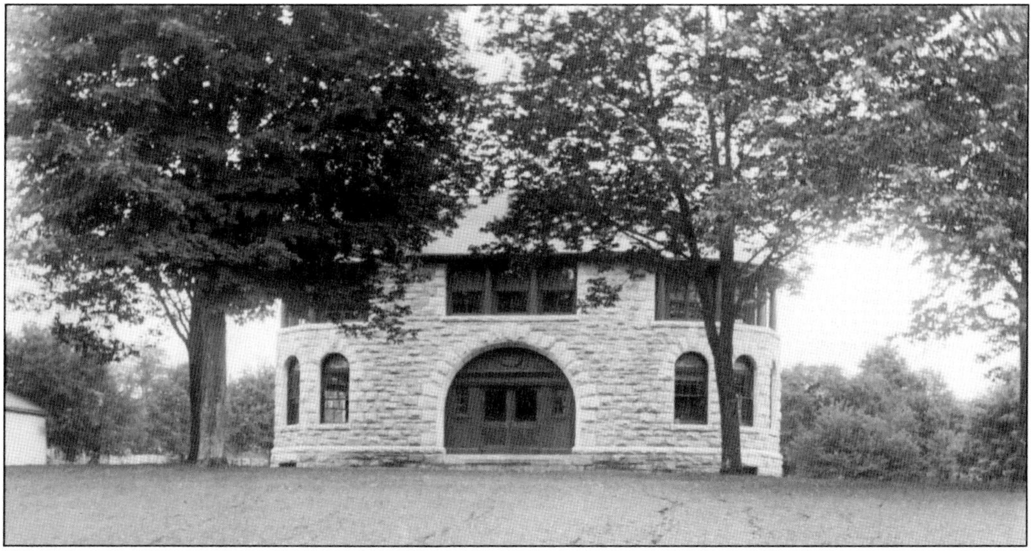

The Hotchkiss Library opened in 1893. It was a gift to the town from Maria Bissell Hotchkiss, who inherited the estate belonging to her husband, Benjamin Berkeley Hotchkiss, when he died. Built at a prominent site on the Sharon Green, much of the design of the building was supervised by Maria Hotchkiss herself. An unsubstantiated story says that Maria, a former teacher, wanted to build a training school in the town, and so she offered the town leaders the choice of a library or a school. Sharon chose the library, and the Hotchkiss School was instead built in Lakeville.

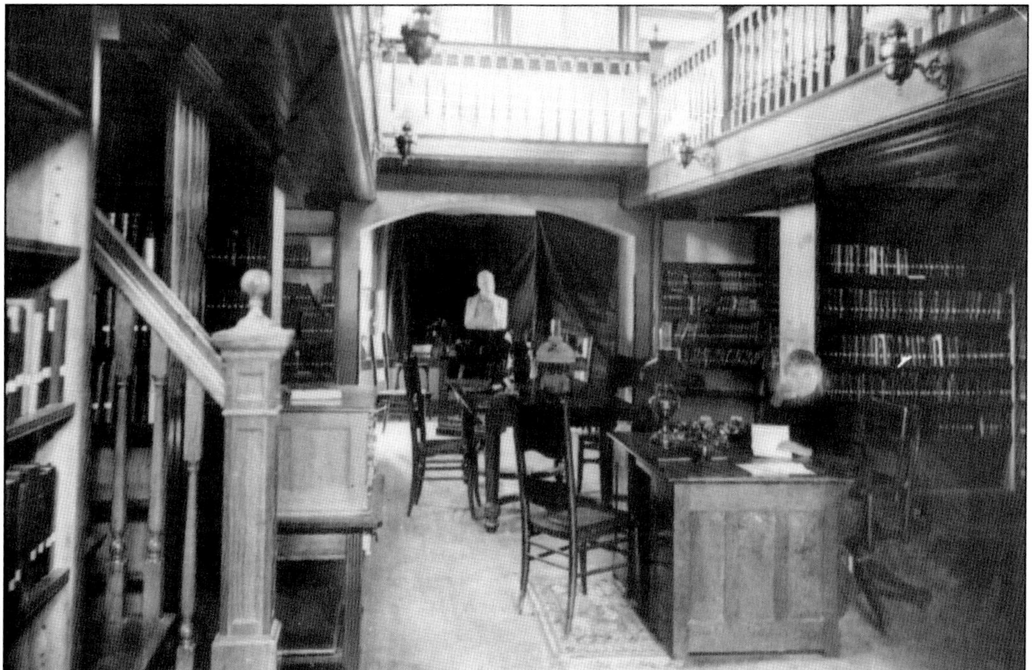

Hotchkiss librarian Mary Mackey was another town institution, the head librarian from 1916 to 1962. The interior of today's library would be easily recognizable to Mackey, although the gas lamps attached to the library balcony are no longer in place. The marble bust in the middle of the photograph is of Benjamin Berkeley Hotchkiss, commissioned by his wife.

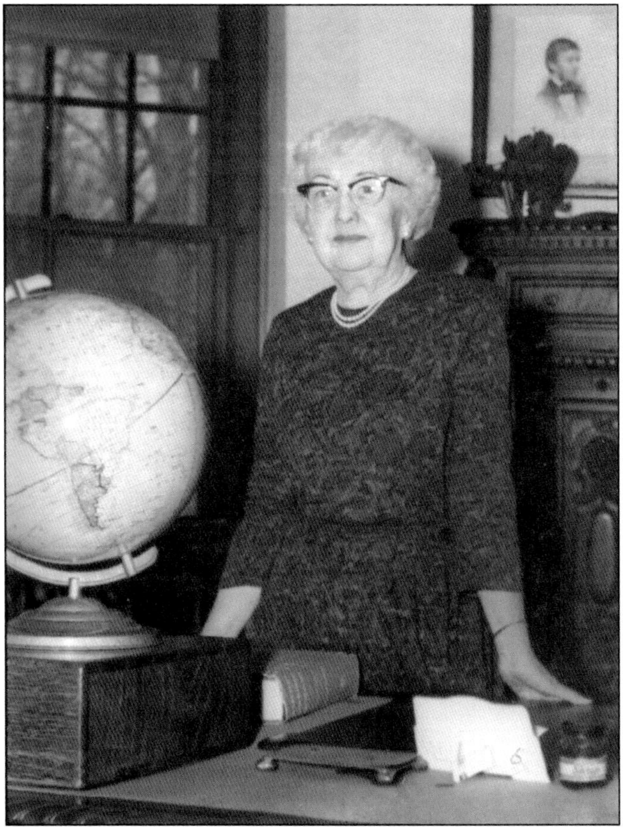

In his book *Seldom Told Tales of Sharon, Book Two*, Ed Kirby described Mary Mackey as "a small, white haired elegant lady with sparkling eyes behind magnificent silver rimmed glasses." Always a wonderful resource for people in town, Mackey was known for her insistence on the use of quiet voices and appropriate behavior in the library.

The imposing public building at 133 Main Street was Sharon's early community center, known as "the Casino." Activities held there included movies, plays, dance classes, and dances. Meetings of organizations like the Masons and the Order of the Eastern Star were also held there. An apartment was in the basement.

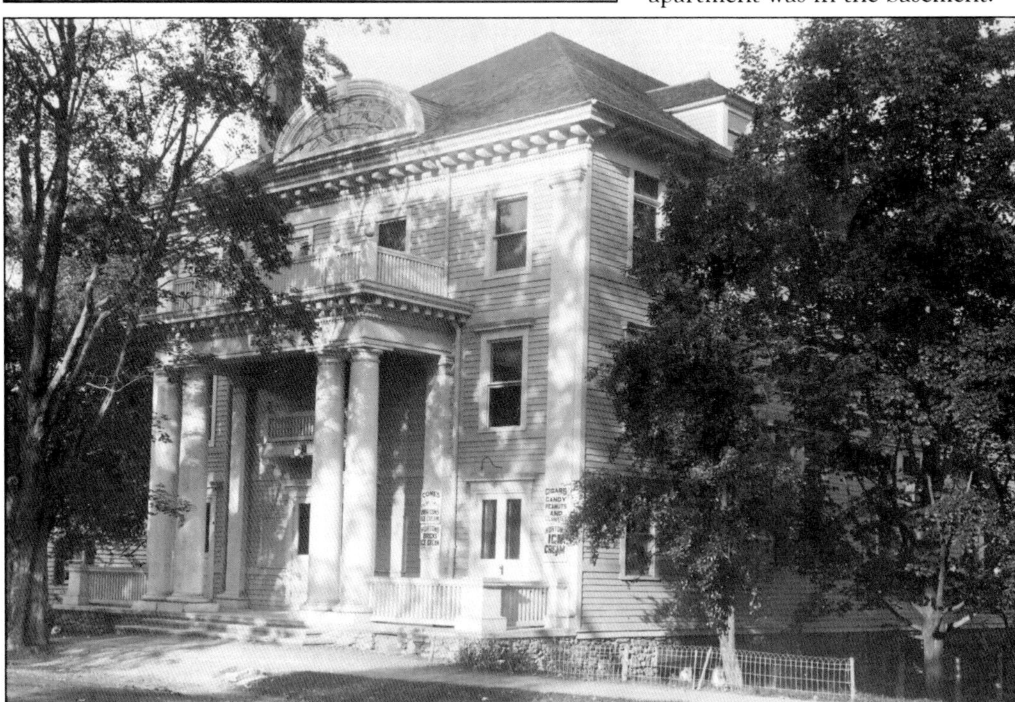

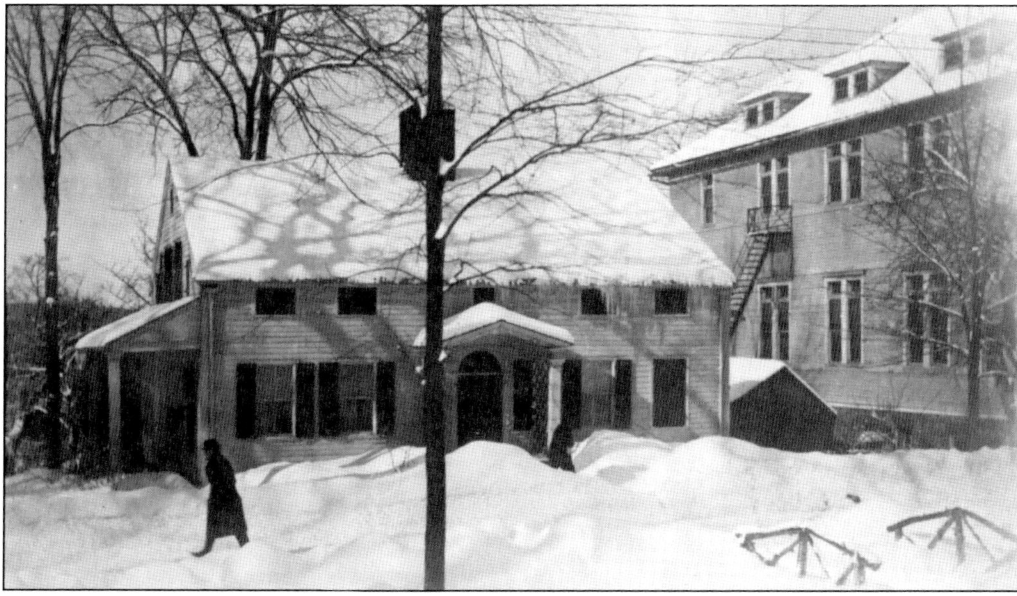

Known as the Abner Burnham house, the home at 125 Main Street was built between 1811 and 1813 by Burnham, a well-known clock maker. In 1817, Burnham defaulted on his mortgage, and the house, barn, and other buildings were sold. The house later became a tavern and, after that, a dame school. In 1865, it was purchased by Redwill St. John Boughton and Jeanne Johnson, who opened what became a prosperous millinery shop. Ladies came from as far away as Poughkeepsie to buy hats in the "latest Parisian style." Notice the south side of the Casino next door. This proximity became very important in 1925 when the Casino suffered a serious fire and the house was badly damaged.

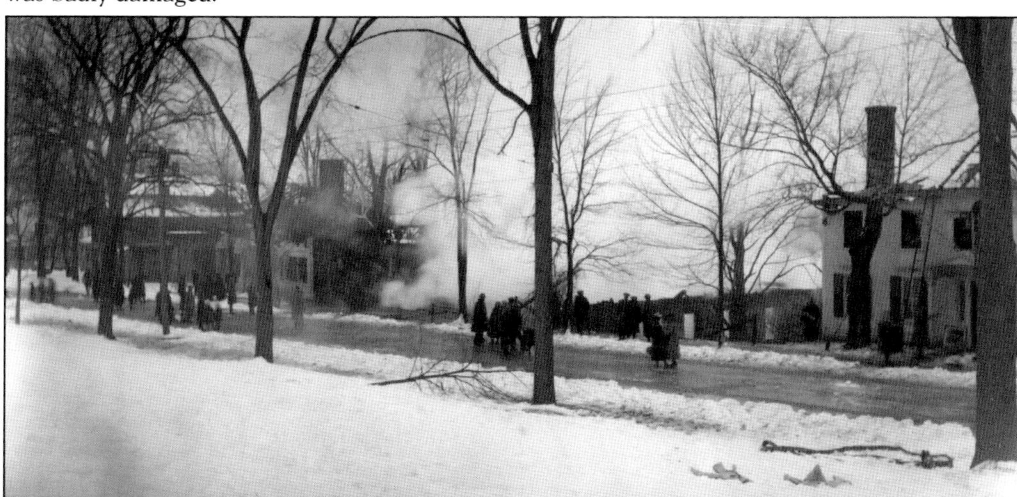

The large, smoking, empty spot is all that was left of the Casino after the fire in winter 1925. The building burned to the ground, and houses on both sides suffered serious damage. Frank Dakin, a builder, bought the Casino property after the fire, building a house on the old foundation between 1927 and 1929. It was lived in by George and Florence Wheeler and has the distinction of being the second "newest" house on the Green. The 1927 deed restricts future building on the site to residential only, perhaps due to the greater chance of fire associated with mixed commercial and residential buildings. (Photograph by George M. Marckres.)

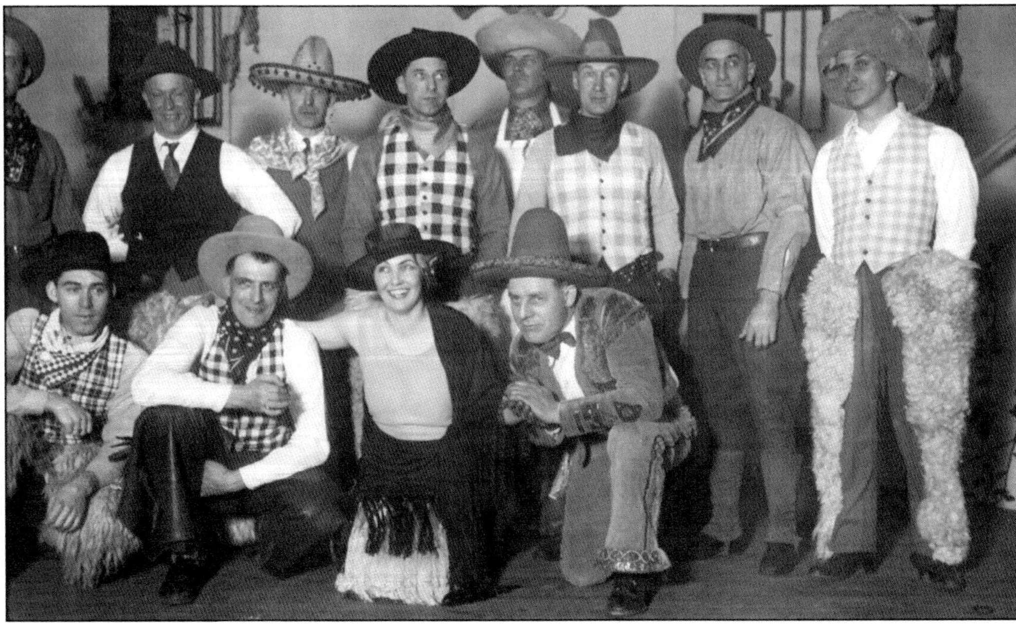

Based on the sheer number of photographs in the historical society and private collections, "Putting on a Show" was a frequent occurrence in town. Sharon folks liked to perform. Local talent in this Wild West review included, from left to right, (first row) Whitney Vosburgh, Al Jenkins, Blanche Byron, and Thomas McKee; (second row) Rex Manley, Adolph Anderson, Charles Adams, Clayton Walter, William Williams, Floyd Laird, David Duffy, and Alanson Middlebrook.

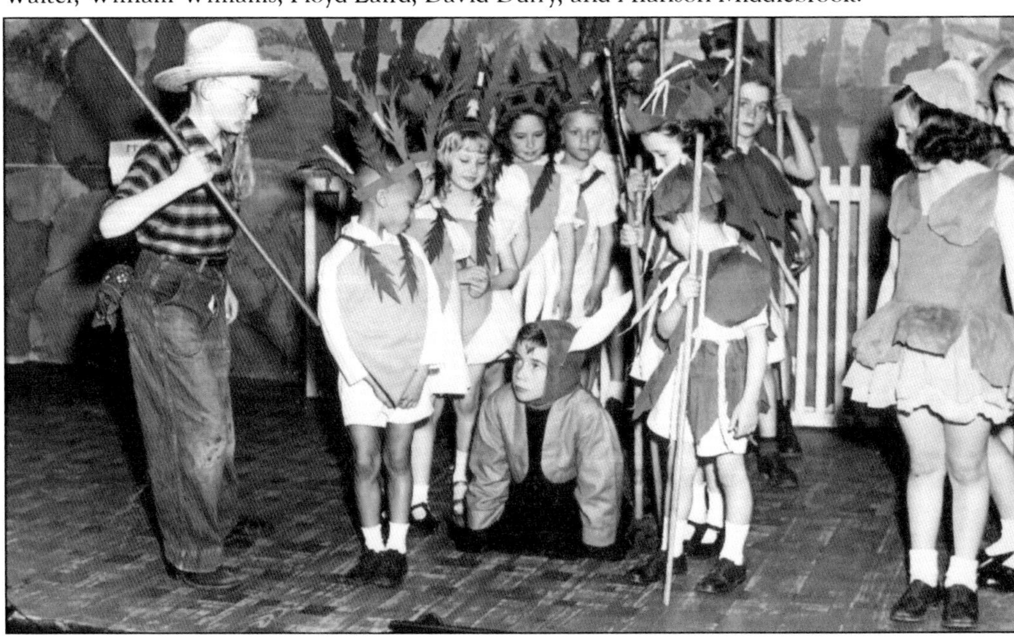

Performing was clearly an activity that cut across all ages in town. Here, a school play reenacts the popular tale of Peter Rabbit. And because even in grammar school there is human drama, the child originally cast as a carrot was so disappointed in her meager role that she was absent from school that day. Jack Perone played Mr. McGregor, Michael Carley was Peter Rabbit, Tom Riley played a string bean, and Connie Gilderdale portrayed a cabbage. (Courtesy of Jayne Larsen.)

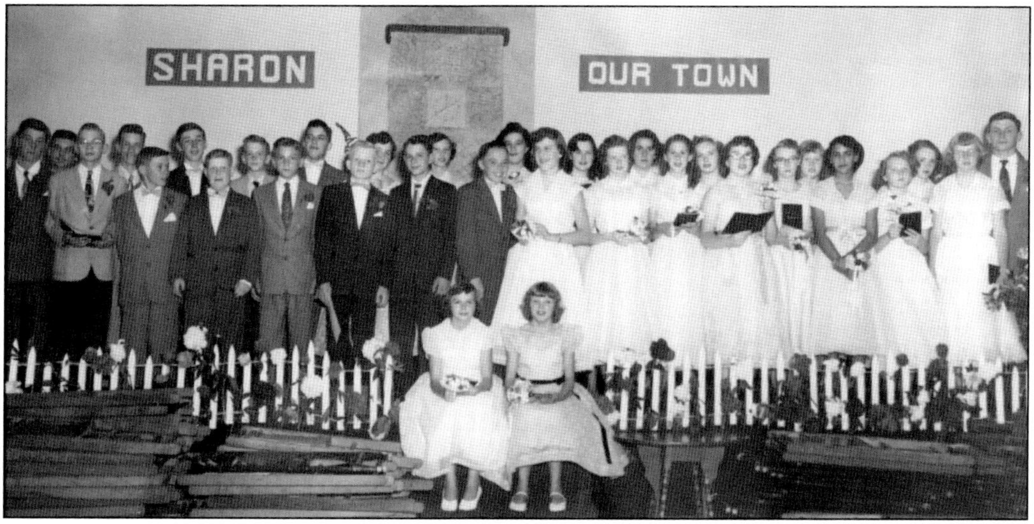

Mr. Nickerson's eighth-grade graduating class at the Sharon Center School presented a program on the history of Sharon to admiring parents and guests in 1954. In front are Dorothy Ammerman and Jayne Peterson. Standing from left to right are (first row) unidentified, John Russell, Ralph Peterson, Wally Pond, Ed Wilbur, Bing Irving, Dick Neil, James Gobillot, Elizabeth Stapleton, Gladys O'Dell, Sharon Gavel, Shirley Course, unidentified, Madeline Carroll, Virginia Drake, and unidentified; (second row) Gerald Magilio, Perry McNeil, Brent Prindle, Dan O'Connell, George Drum, Barbara Carberry McEnroe, Glennis Metcalf, Judy Prindle, Mona Hutchinson, Connie Gilderdale, Lois Sturman, unidentified, Dawn Prindle, and Philip Waugh. (Courtesy of Barbara McEnroe.)

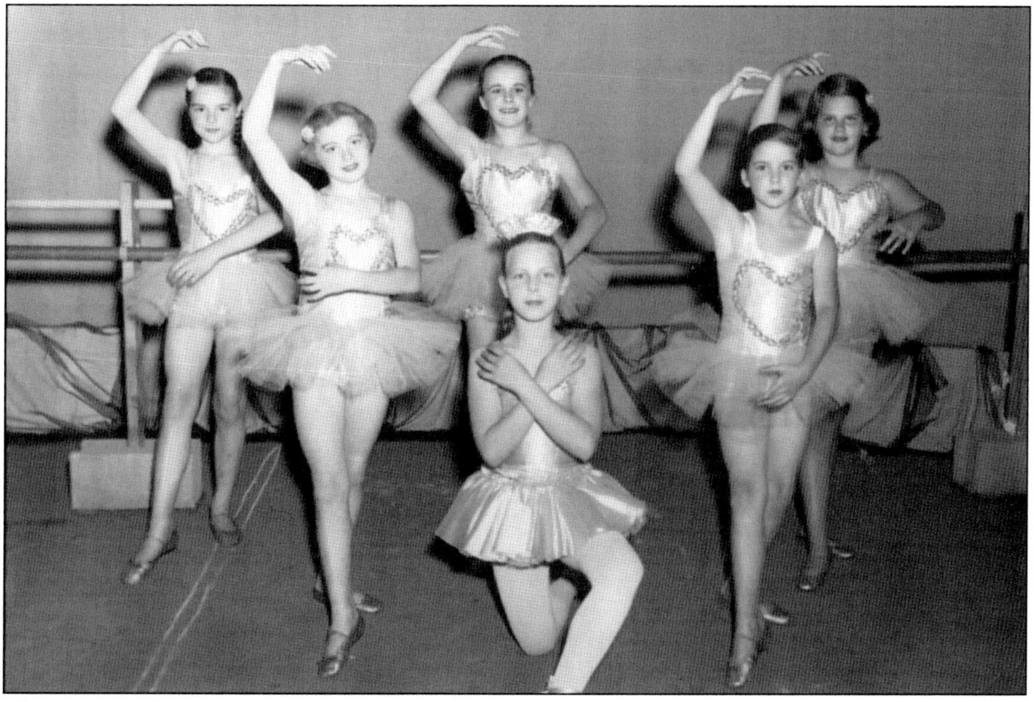

There was no shortage of culture and the arts in Sharon. Students from Helen Hain's dance class are shown here in a recital at 110 North Main Street in the 1970s. Hain was a professionally trained ballet dancer and an excellent teacher, preparing her students thoroughly. (Courtesy of Tom Riley.)

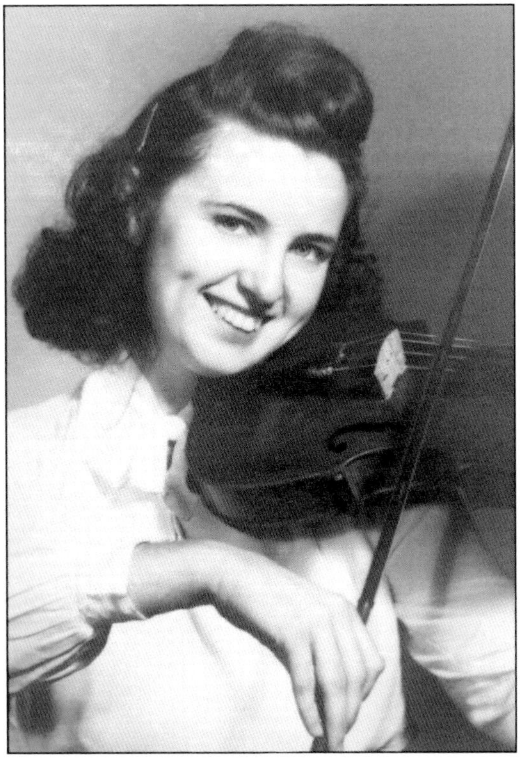

Myrtle Maddox Hayden is seen here about 1950. Myrtle was beloved in Sharon for her talented fiddling. She received national recognition twice from the Daughters of the American Revolution for her research and performances of Colonial music. She was an avid and talented composer, writing "The Rose of Sharon Waltz" to honor her love of the town she lived in. Myrtle performed with her band, Country Spice, in Sharon and across the region until her death in 2013. (Courtesy of Harvey Hayden.)

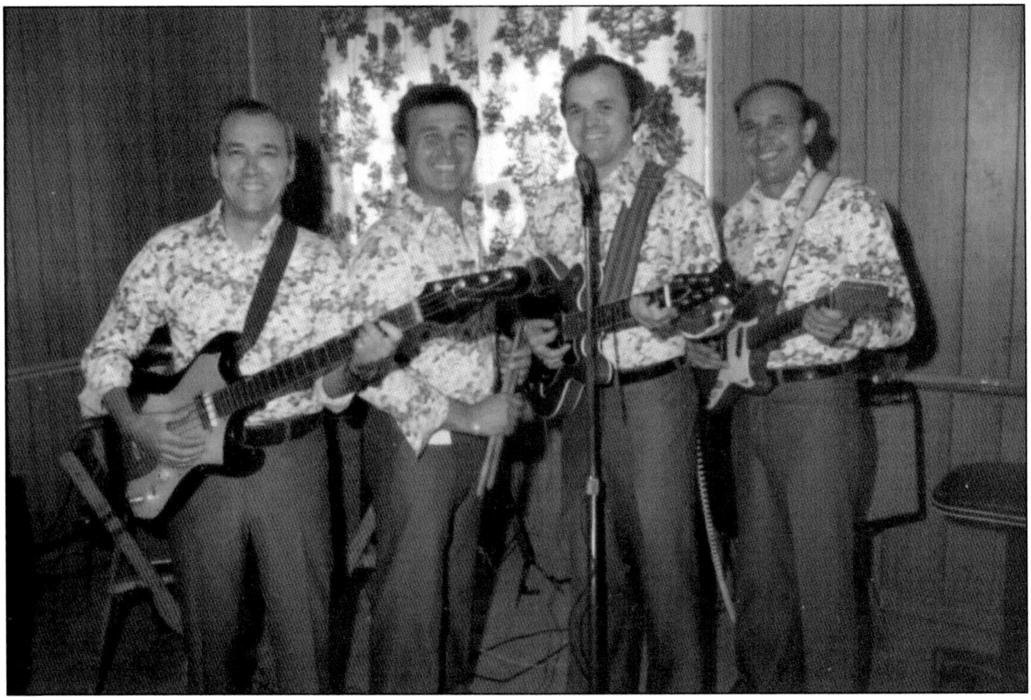

People in Sharon loved to dance. Very popular locally, the Cahill Brothers Band played in the 1950s, 1960s, and 1970s at square dances and weddings. They were much loved for their keen sense of fun. From left to right are Bob, Fritz, Pete, and Bill Cahill. (Courtesy of Maureen Cahill.)

Sandy and Caroline Paton moved to Sharon in 1967 and founded Folk-Legacy Records. They were well-known performing artists, often playing with their two sons, David and Rob. Their home on Sharon Mountain, formerly the model farm of philanthropist Albert Metz, called Fiddlestyx, was a gathering place for the huge folk music community in the Hudson River Valley, western Massachusetts, and northwestern Connecticut. (Courtesy of Caroline Paton.)

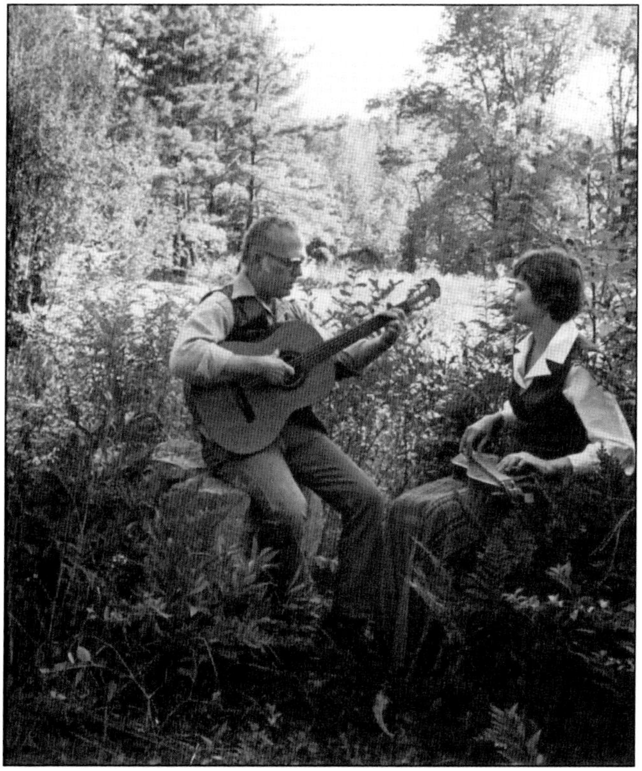

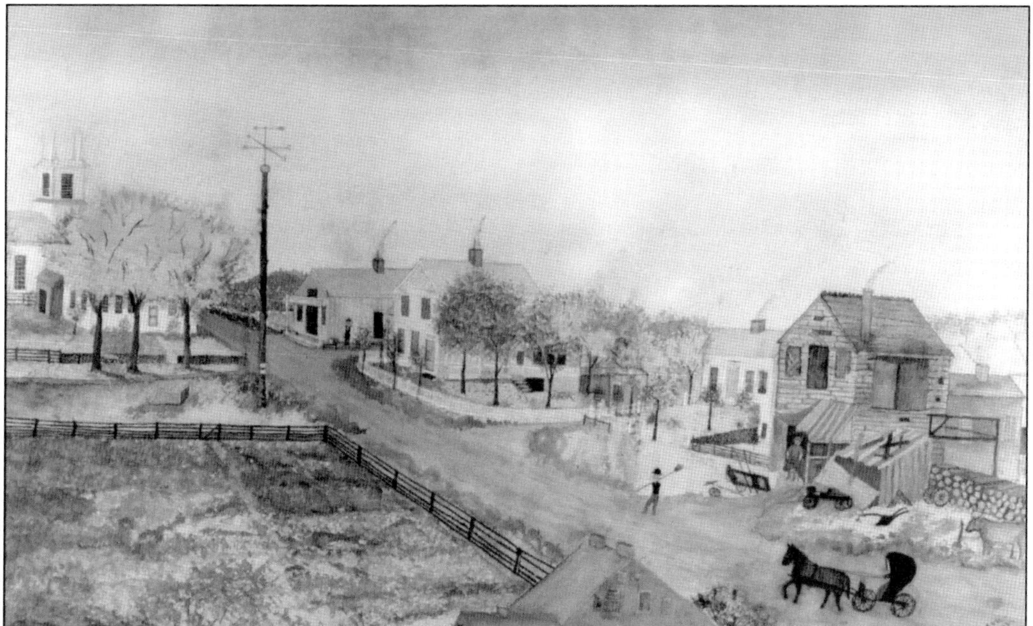

Because Sharon's hilly terrain made travel to the town center difficult, several smaller centers of commercial and religious life developed in Amenia Union (also known as Hitchcock's Corners), Calkinstown, and Ellsworth. This painting of the Ellsworth village center on South Ellsworth Road is a 20th-century rendition of the thriving village.

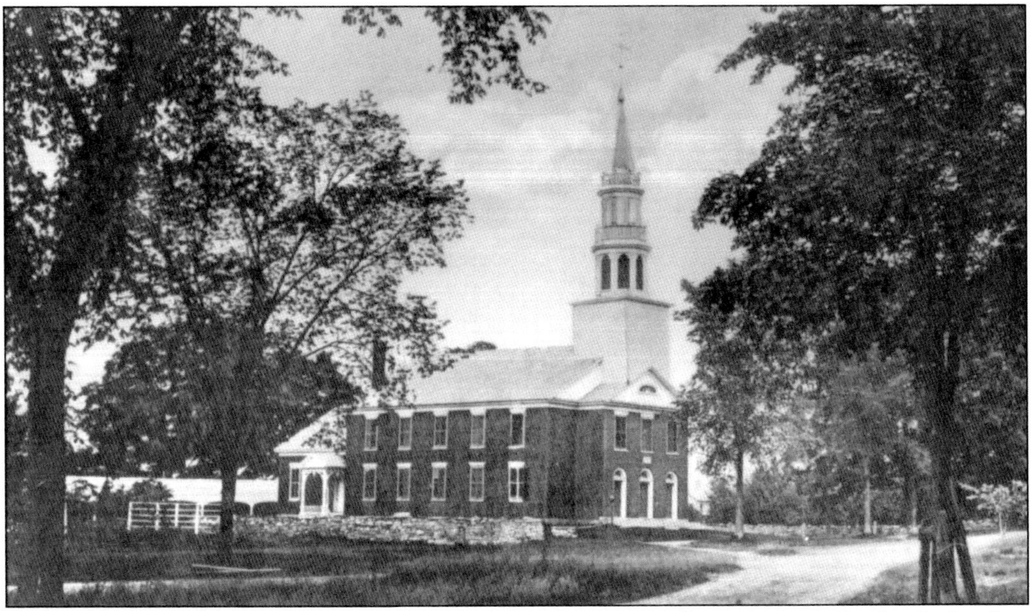

The community also came together to worship. As in most places in New England, the first meetinghouse built was home to the Congregational Church. This gracious building is the fourth meetinghouse in town, built in 1824. The first meetinghouse was built of logs, possibly towards the north end of the Green in 1741. In 1742, a larger church supplanted the log one and stood opposite the tavern. A much larger meetinghouse was built in 1768, and that site is marked by a boulder on the south end of the Green. The most important person in town between 1755 and 1806 was likely to have been the congregational minister, Cotton Mather Smith. In 1939, the interior of this church was restored to its original design. The exterior remains much the same, although the horse stalls to the rear of the building are long gone.

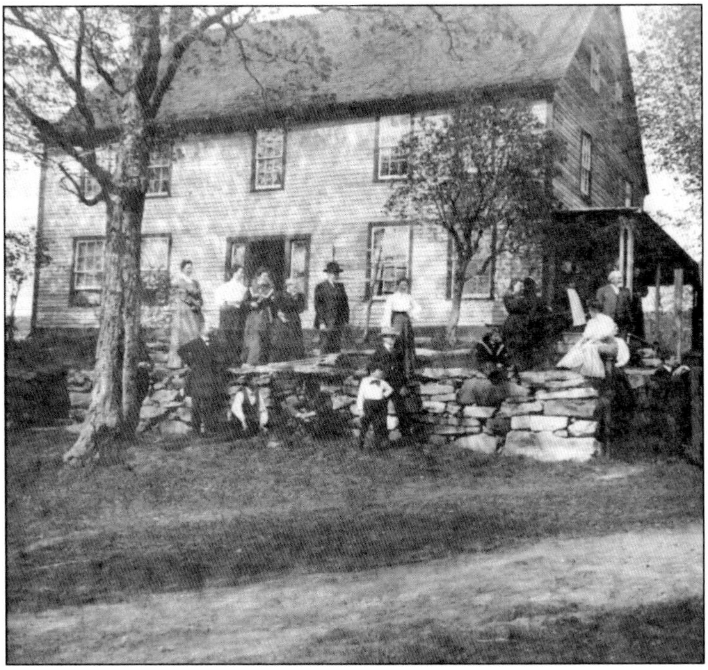

This house at 424 Cornwall Bridge Road was probably built before 1784 by Timothy St. John. By 1790, there was a thriving community in Ellsworth, and the St. Johns were some of the most prominent members. Before the Congregational meetinghouse in Ellsworth was built, congregants who could not travel to the center of town due to poor weather and bad roads met here. This picture was probably taken before the turn of the 20th century, when the Dean family owned the house. The house burned to the ground in 2009.

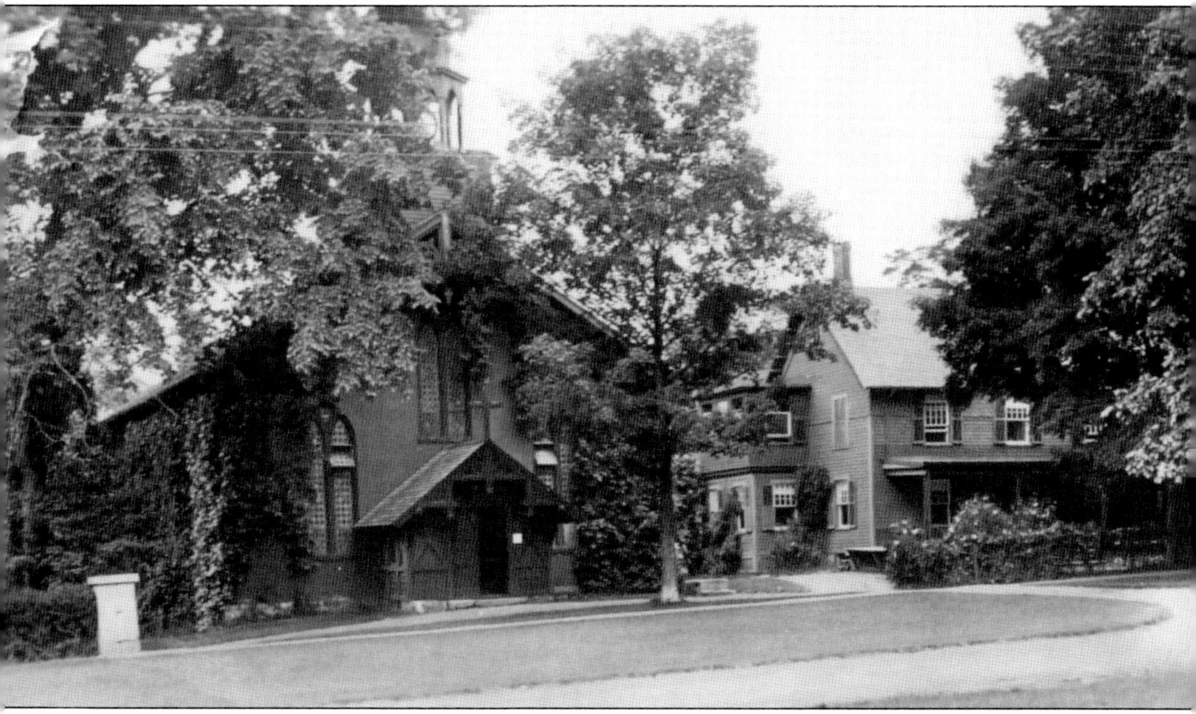

Christ Church Episcopal, at 9 South Main Street, built between 1813 and 1814, was the third Episcopal church to be sited along the Green. In early 1811, decisions were made to build with brick and to make the building either 40 feet by 45 feet or 30 feet by 50 feet. The first full-time minister was hired about 1844 for $400 per year. In 1866, a meeting was held to consider building a parsonage. The year before, a horse shed with stalls had been erected on the parsonage lot for the use of families attending services. In 1882–1883, improvements were made to the church, including the addition of "16 feet to the west end of the church" and "cushions for the pews." The organ was donated in memory of Eleanor Wheeler McClurg by her sisters in 1905, and, in 1908, new pews, a new pulpit and font, and new chandeliers were added in preparation for the church's centennial festival, held on May 27, 1909. In 1929, the paint covering the exterior of the church was removed, and, in 1933, the old overhanging church porch was replaced. The church is noted for its stained glass windows, the oldest of which date to around 1882. The steeple was restored to its original beauty in 2012–2013.

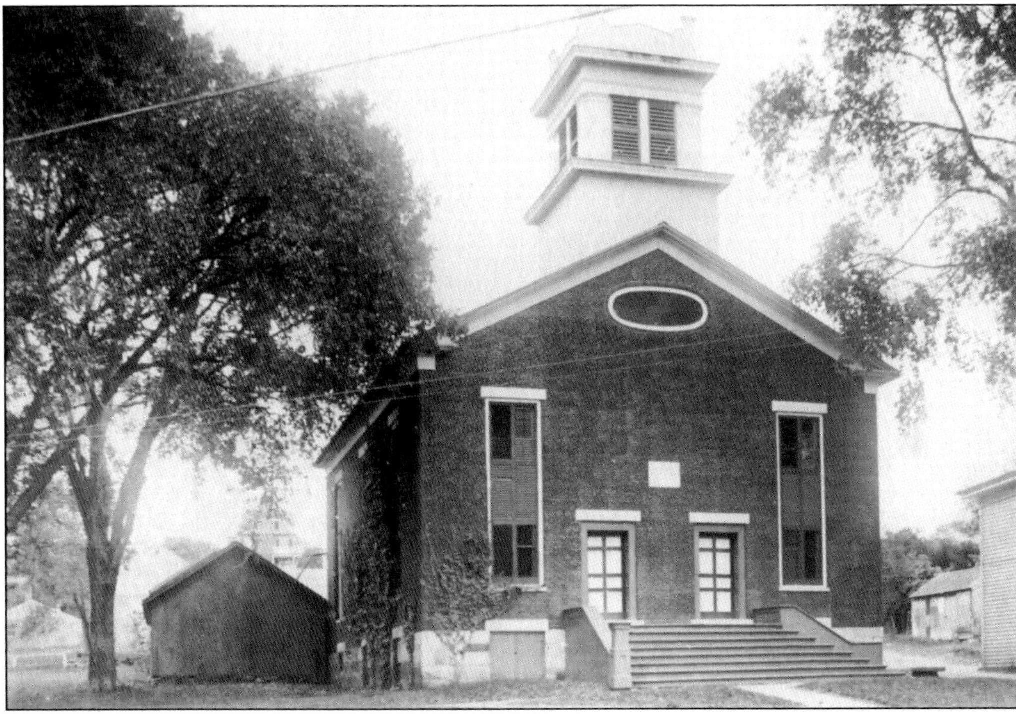

The first Methodist church in Sharon was built on the west part of Calkinstown Road in 1808. It served the community until this church was built at 112 Upper Main Street in 1835. Contemporary accounts speak of the 1835 church as the "costliest and most tasteful church of that denomination in Litchfield County." Alterations to the original building include new windows and changes in the aisles in 1882, and a chapel and Norman tower added in 1894 and 1904, respectively. The first Methodist sermon in Sharon was preached in 1788 by an itinerant preacher. His sermon greatly displeased townspeople, not due to its content, but due to its location—in the local tavern. This photograph dates prior to 1904, before the tower addition.

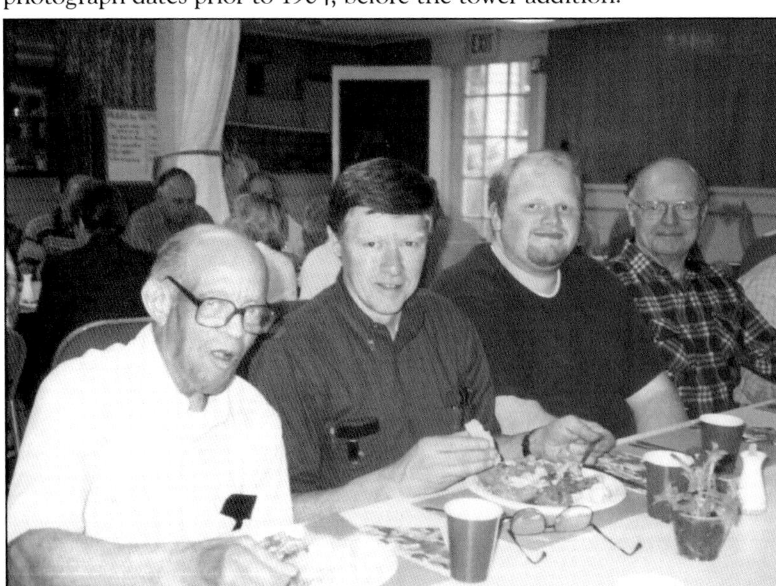

Churches in Sharon have always served community as well as religious functions. This photograph was taken at a birthday party held for Bob Outram, a yearly event held at the Methodist church. Outram died in 2009 at the age of 103. From left to right are Outram, Bob Loucks, Brian Pedersen, and Ed Pedersen. (Courtesy of Marian Chatfield.)

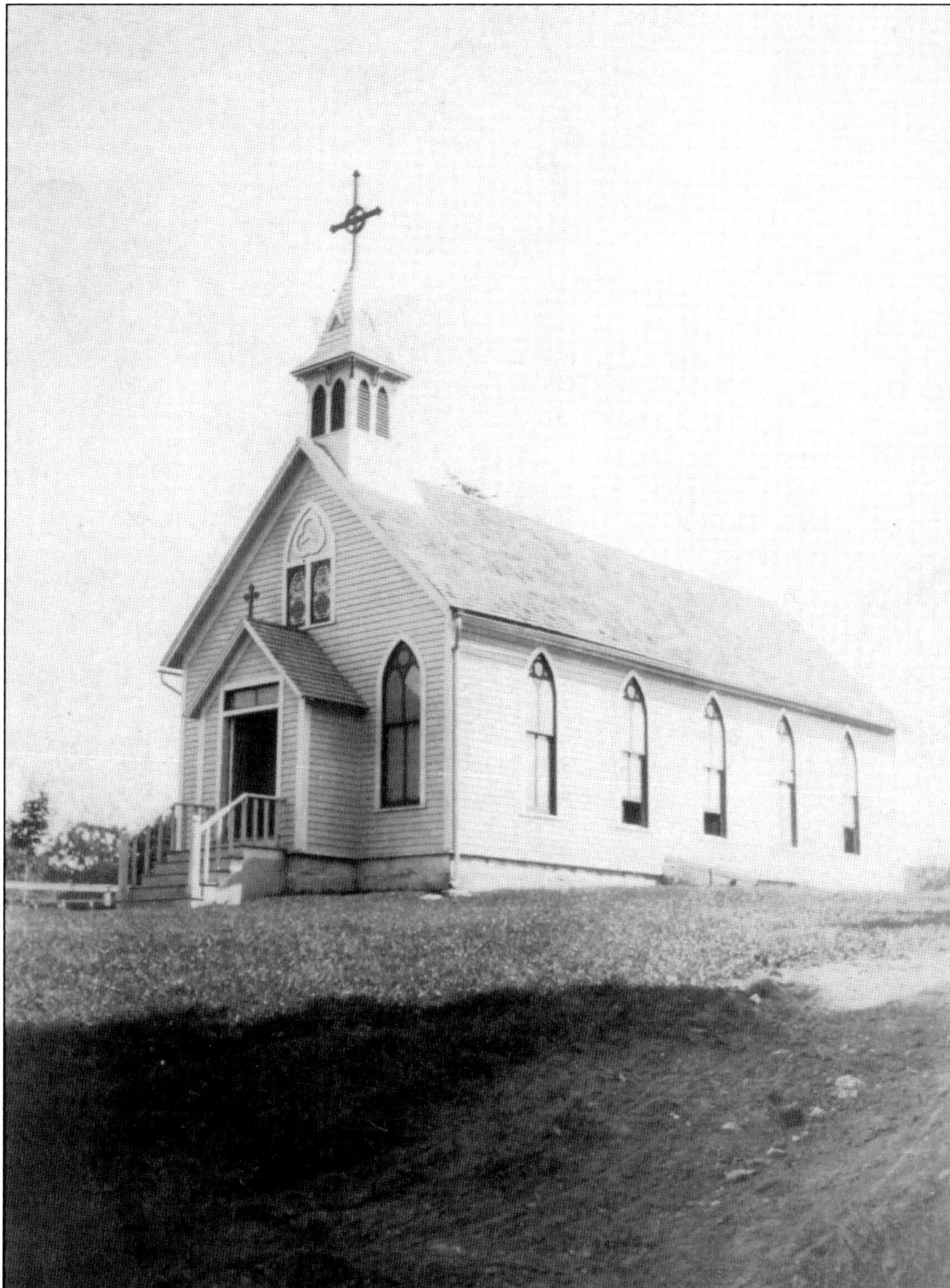

The first Catholic church in Sharon, St. Bernard Church, pictured here around 1900, was located at 65 King Hill Road, on the south side of the road about 300 feet west of the intersection with Sharon Valley Road. The church was built and dedicated in 1885 at a cost of $2,400, with an additional $91 paid for the lot. It seated about 50 people. When the congregation built a new, larger church, this building became a residence.

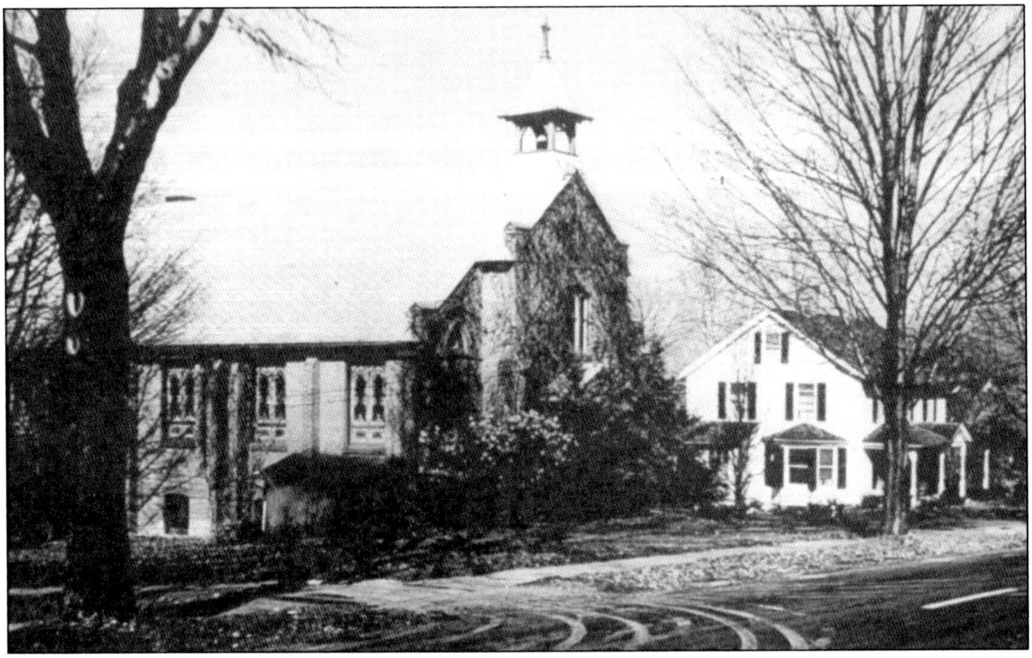

The new St. Bernard Church and rectory were suitably located at 50–52 New Street. Under the guidance of Rev. Dr. A.J. Plunkett, a piece of land located on the west side of "the highway leading from the Taghhannuck Inn to Millerton" was purchased from Gilbert L. Smith in 1914. The ground-breaking occurred on April 12, 1915, after architects Whiton & McMahon of Hartford were hired. The entire basement of the church was excavated using a horse-drawn scoop by Richard Murtagh Sr. and his son Richard Jr., Jack Murtagh's uncle. Work went quickly, with Reverend Plunkett an able fundraiser. The building was completed in September 1915, only a little more than five months after the ground-breaking.

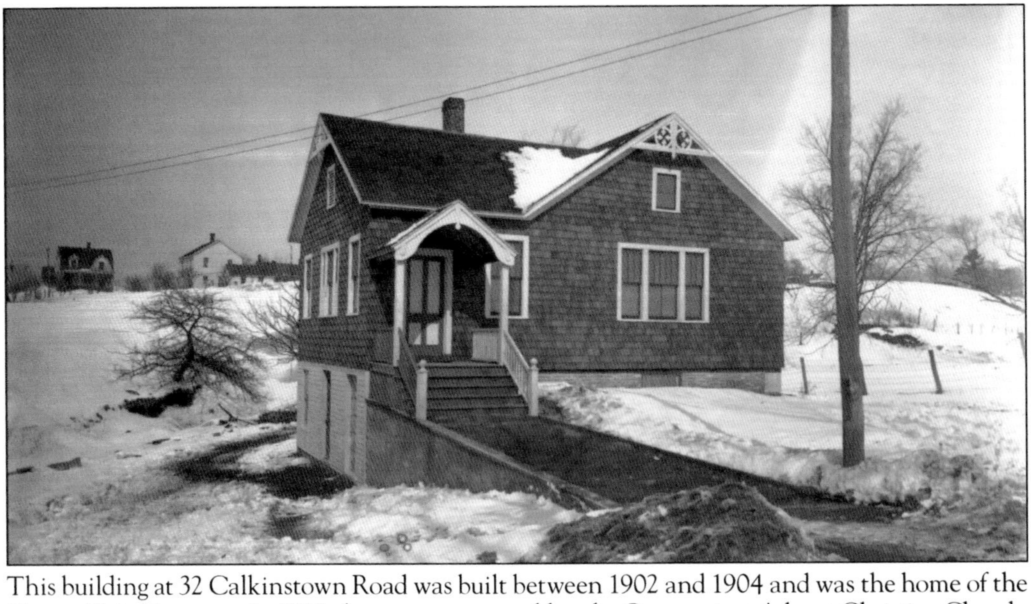

This building at 32 Calkinstown Road was built between 1902 and 1904 and was the home of the Sharon Elgin Creamery. In 1907, the creamery was sold to the Connecticut Advent Christian Church, which used it for 20 years. It is now a private residence. (Photograph by George M. Marckres.)

Four

On the Farm

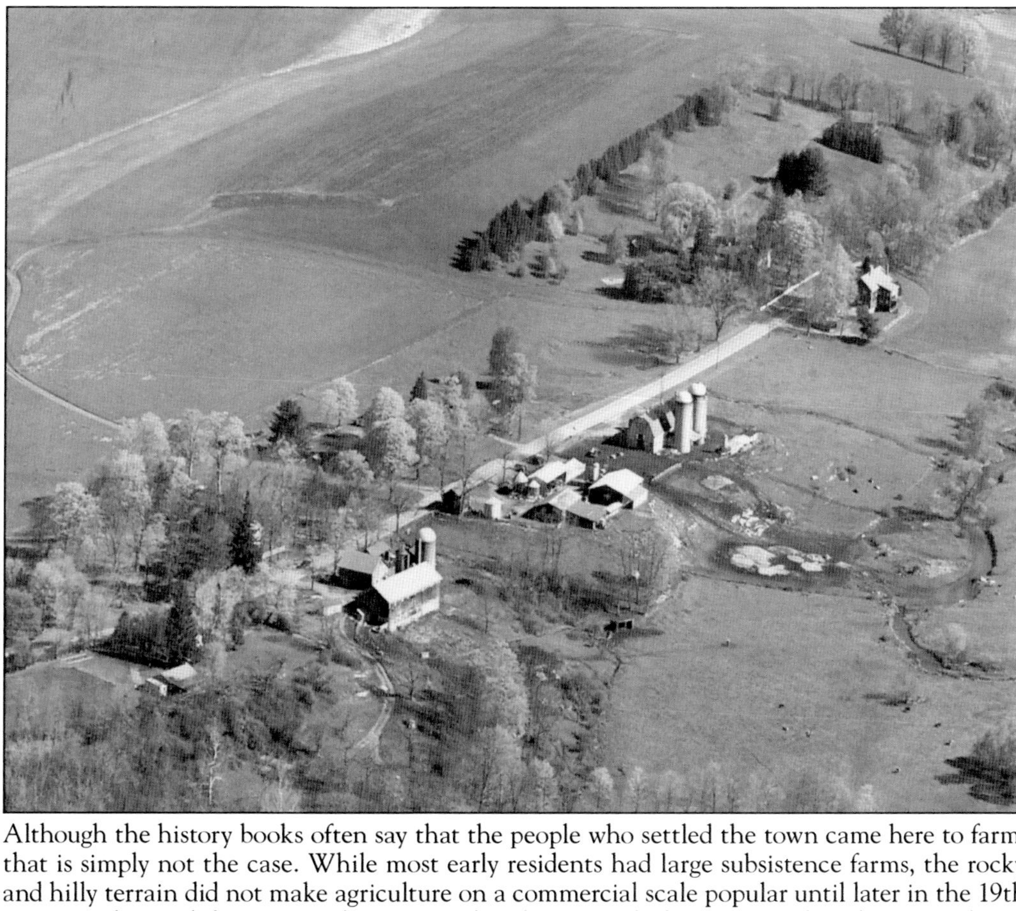

Although the history books often say that the people who settled the town came here to farm, that is simply not the case. While most early residents had large subsistence farms, the rocky and hilly terrain did not make agriculture on a commercial scale popular until later in the 19th century. That said, farms were always critical to the survival of a region, and, as the iron industry faded, the proliferation of larger-scale farms increased. This is an aerial view of four farms on Amenia Union Road. Seen from left to right are the Wilcox, Grindrod, Chapman (now Learsy), and Chase farms. The Wilcox farm is owned and operated by James Krissel, while Phil Grindrod still runs his dairy farm. The famous Oblong Valley is on the right side of the photograph, while the landmark four maples are at the top right, in front of the Chase farm pond. (Photograph by Brian Wilcox; courtesy of Catherine Wilcox.)

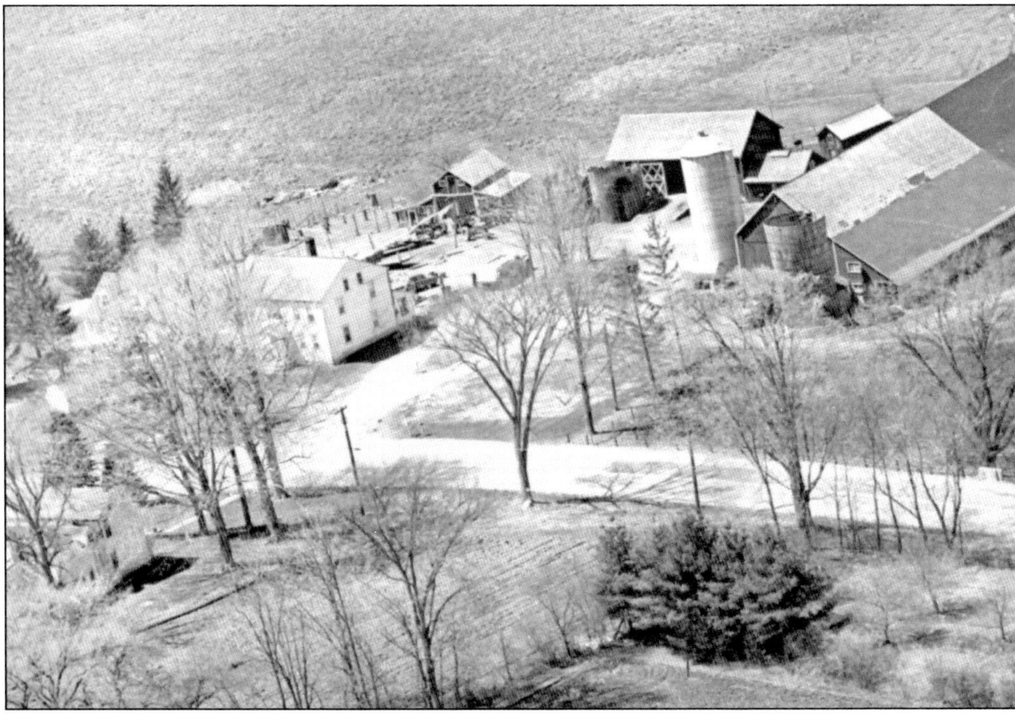

A working farm since 1915, the Chase farm, on Amenia Union Road, is seen here in 1965. The two-story house seen in the photograph is now a one-story structure; the smaller house in the lower left was the Loper farm tenant house and is now gone. The large barn on right still exists. (Courtesy of Dave Chase.)

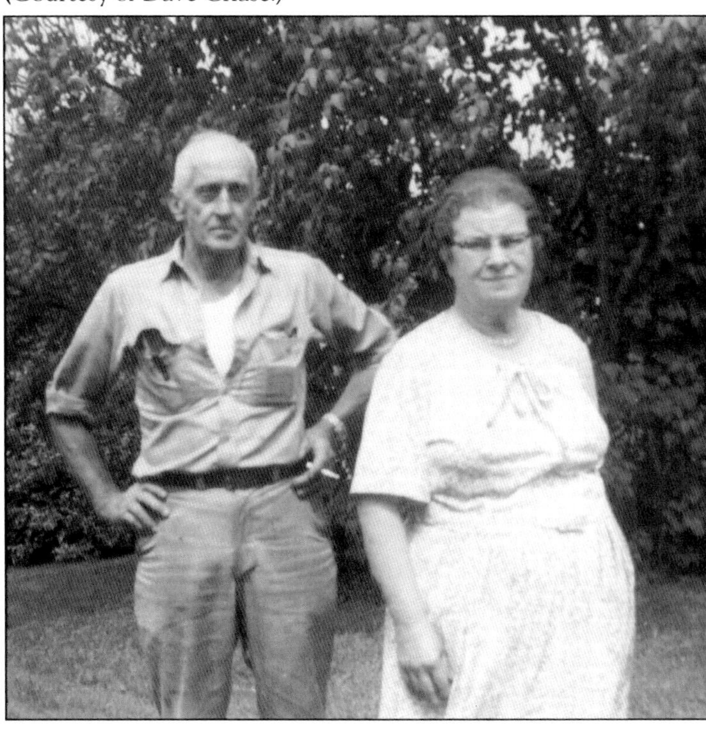

Howard and Winifred Loper owned two dairy farms on Amenia Union Road. They first purchased the farm on the east side of the road. When the barn burned down in 1946, they purchased the farm on the west side of the road. After they retired, their son Ralph ran the farm on the west side. (Courtesy of Wally Chase.)

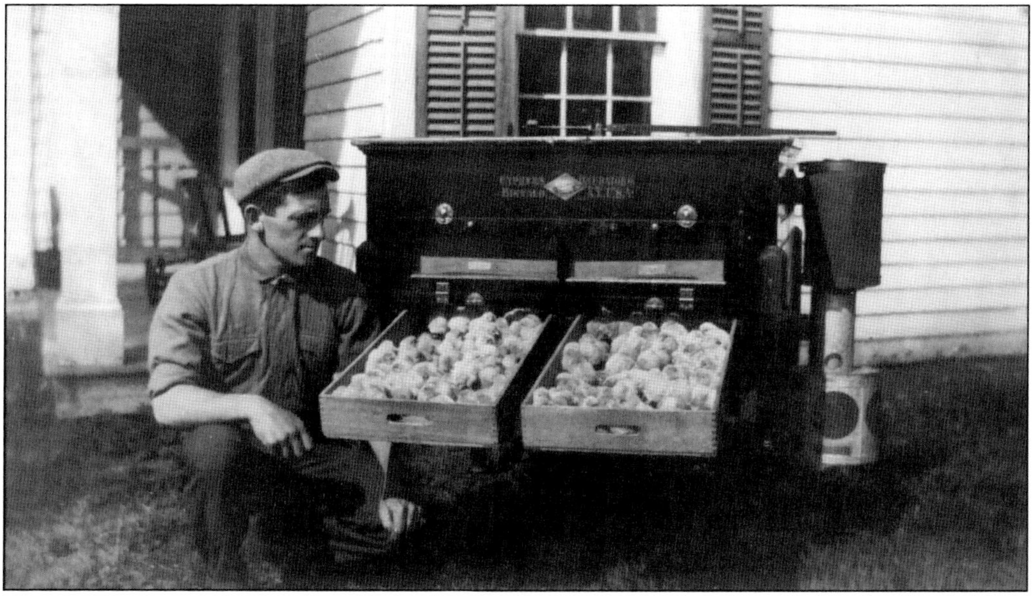

Not all Sharon farms were dairies. This 1915 photograph shows George Wilbur, the father of Charles, Bill, and Odge, with baby chicks in an incubator. These were the early days of Odge's Egg Farm, still a local supplier of eggs today. (Courtesy of Diane Monroe.)

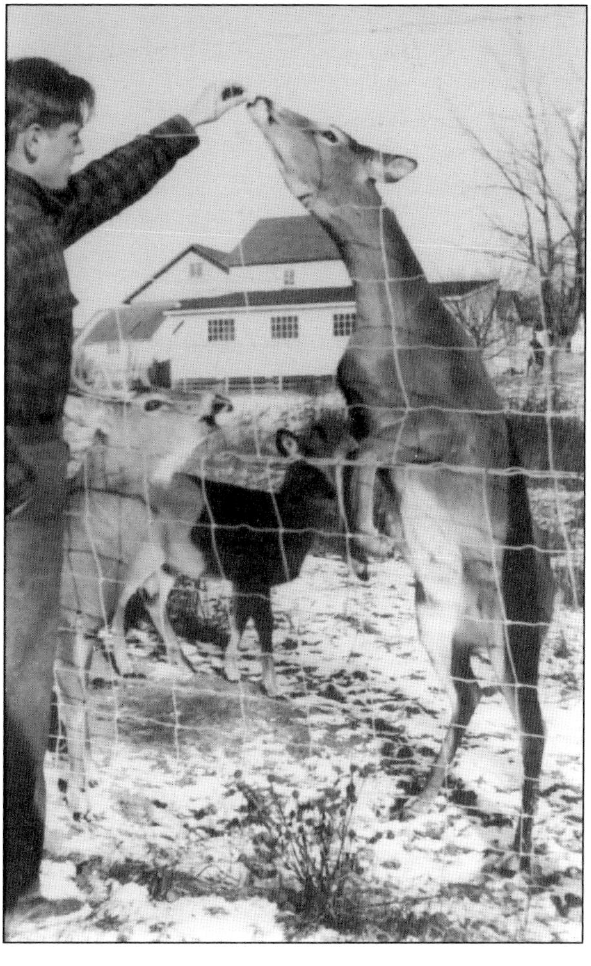

George Wilbur also had a state permit to keep deer on his property, in a fenced area between 92 and 102 Gay Street. He took in injured deer and they were kept as family pets. Here, young Bill Wilbur, George's son, feeds a deer around 1940. Bill recalls that this particular deer enjoyed eating cigarettes. How times have changed. (Courtesy of Bill Wilbur.)

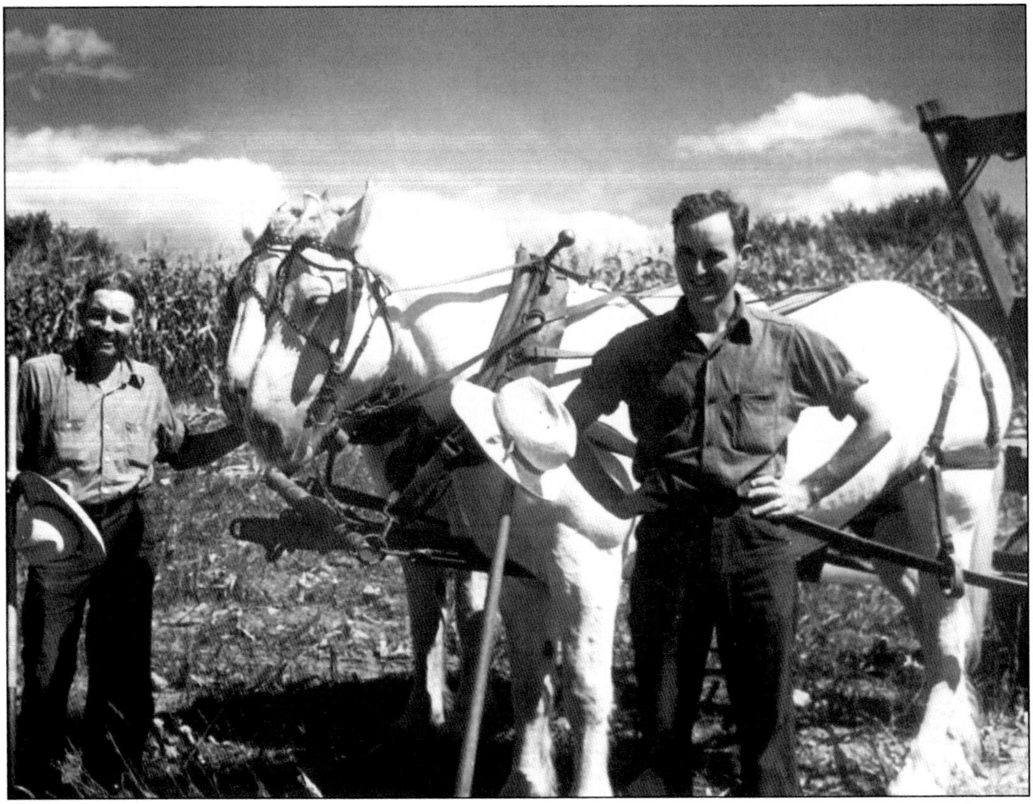

Brothers Eugene and Lewis Gobillot are shown in a field at their farm on Gay Street. The former Gobillot fields, running through to Low Road, are now owned by the Moore family and farmed by Nina Bennett. This dairy farm is one of two remaining in Sharon. In the mid-19th century, there were 65 dairy farms in Sharon. (Photograph by Fran Kelsey.)

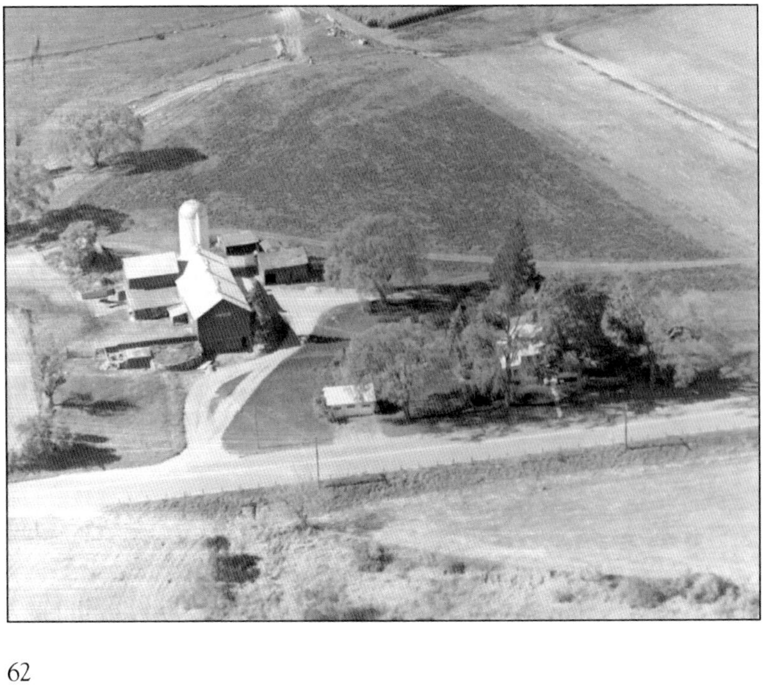

Seen here is Grandview Farm in 1965. Norm and Barbara Johnson owned and operated the farm, on Gay Street across from the reservoir. The gracious farmhouse sitting near the road is nearly invisible due to the surrounding elm trees, now gone due to the scourge of Dutch elm disease. The large barn is now a residence with horse stalls underneath. (Courtesy of Norm and Barbara Johnson.)

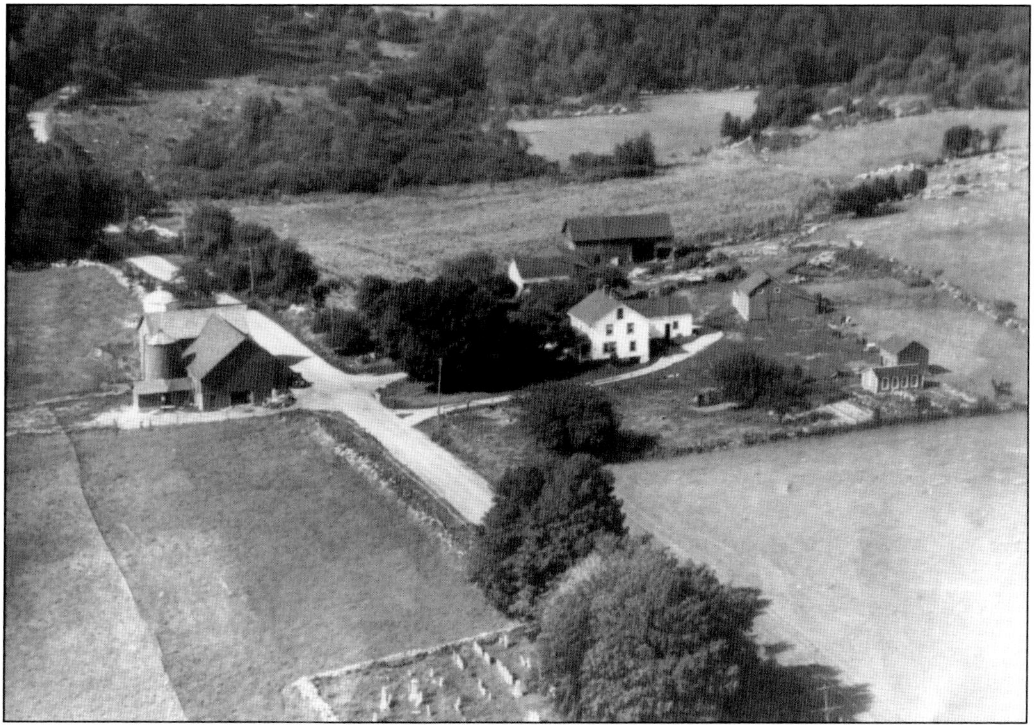

Sharon Mountain was dotted with farms and became a true farming enclave. This is an aerial view of the Euvrard farm, at 102 East Street. The large dairy barn on the left side of the road is no longer there. (Courtesy of Tom Euvrard.)

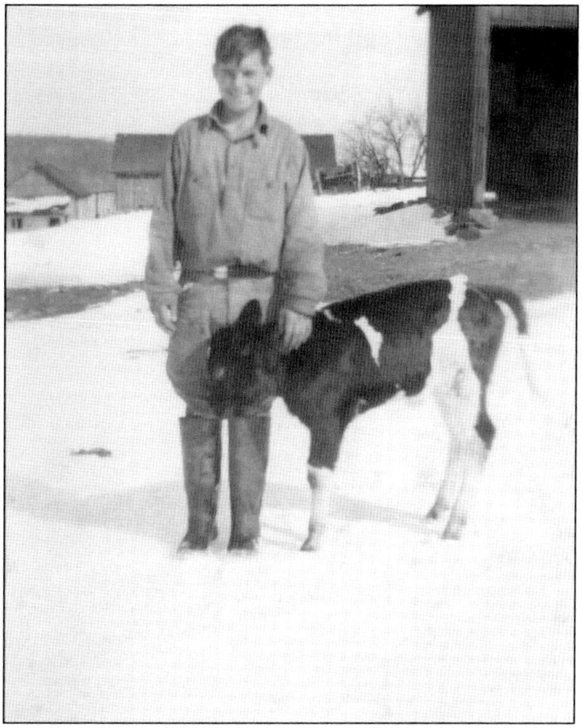

Due to the large number of farms and farm families in Sharon, 4-H was active in the area starting in the 1920s. Shown here is Hank Euvrard, the father of Tom Euvrard, at age 14 with his 4-H project in 1931. He kept a journal showing the amount of milk and grain fed to the calf and noted the calf's progress and costs, writing: "Value of calf: $30.00; Beginning cost 4.00; feed and care 19.41; Profit: $6.59." The goal of 4-H is to develop citizenship, leadership, responsibility, and life skills of youth through experiential learning programs and a positive youth development approach. Though typically thought of as an agriculturally focused organization as a result of its history, 4-H today focuses on citizenship, healthy living, science, engineering, and technology programs. It is still active in Sharon today. (Courtesy of Tom Euvrard.)

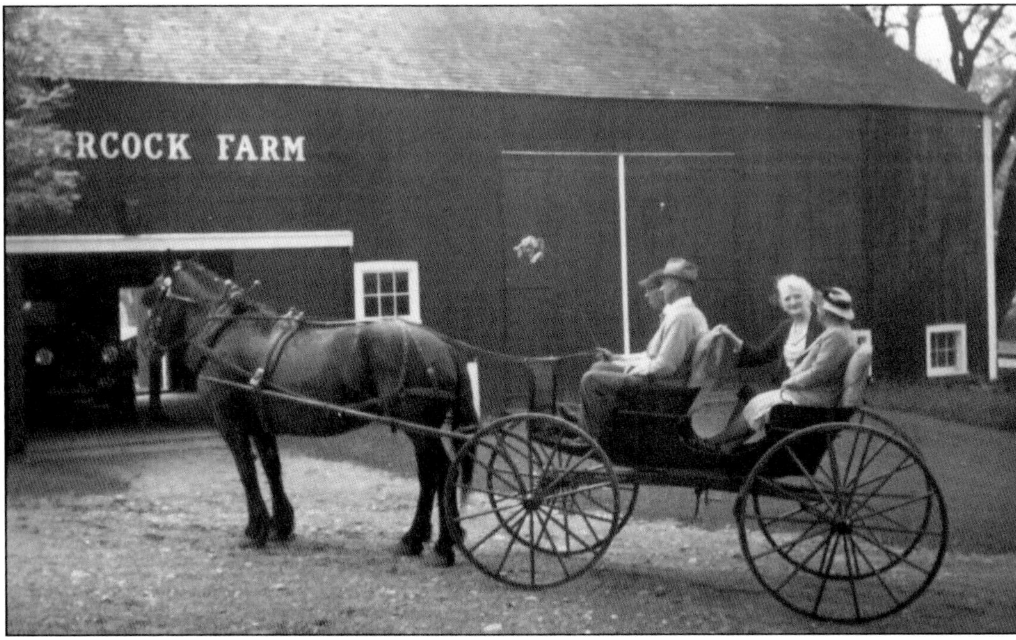

The barn at Weathercock Farm, in the Calkinstown section of Calkinstown Road, is shown here. The farm was owned by G. Louise Robinson and operated by the Roeske family. Pictured in this very smart gig from left to right are Ted Roeske Sr., Otto Roeske (driving), G. Louise Robinson, and Blanche Roeske. (Courtesy of Ted Roeske Jr.)

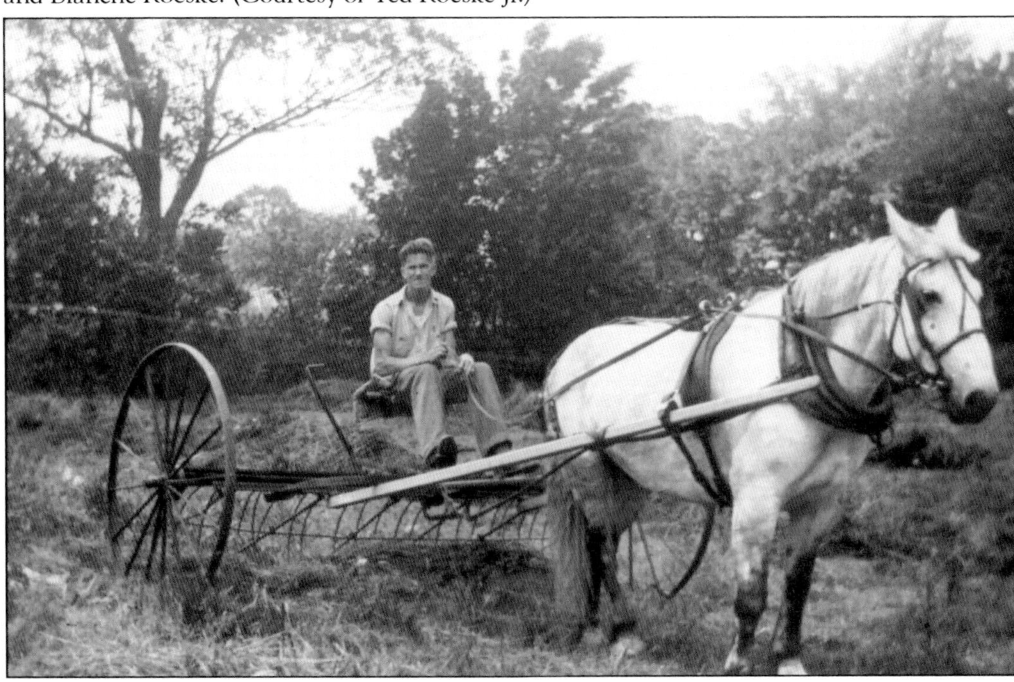

The old ways of farming lasted into the 20th century in town. Ted Roeske Sr. routinely used horses to plow well into the 1940s at Weathercock Farm. This photograph shows Roeske Sr. on a horse-drawn hay rake. William Grindrod, Phil Grindrod's father, used horses to plow for smaller jobs until the early 1990s. (Courtesy of Ted Roeske Jr.)

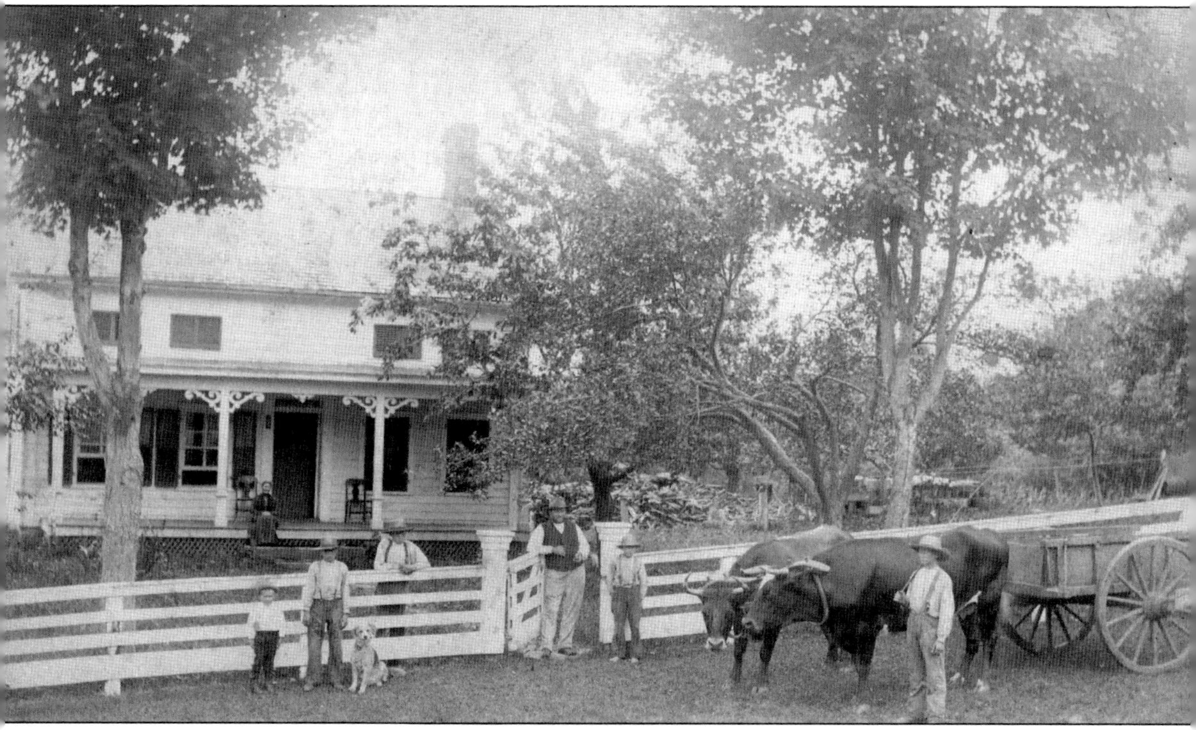

The Wike family homestead, at 38 White Hollow Road, was situated in the beautiful White Hollow Valley, with Red Mountain to the west and Mine Mountain to the east. In earlier days, the land was farmed by the senior Wikes, John E. and Mary Liner, who purchased the primary farm property from James L. Hayes on March 31, 1868. John and Mary raised five sons, all of whom grew up on the farm. The eldest was Frank W. (1872–1946), followed by John, Fred W. (1876–1910), Edward C. (1879–1969), and Benjamin Franklin (1885–1947). Two sons remained on the farm: John, who never married, and Ed, who married Alice R. Judd (1899–1980). Ed and Alice had two children, Edward Jr. (1920–1942) and Helen Wike Humeston, a retired Sharon tax assessor who still resides at the family's Wike Brothers Farm. From before World War I into the 1950s, the dairy farm was home to Holsteins, the big milk producers, with a scattering of Golden Guernsey stock to raise the butterfat percentage. The farm still operates today, raising and selling organic beef and produce. (Courtesy of Lynn Humeston.)

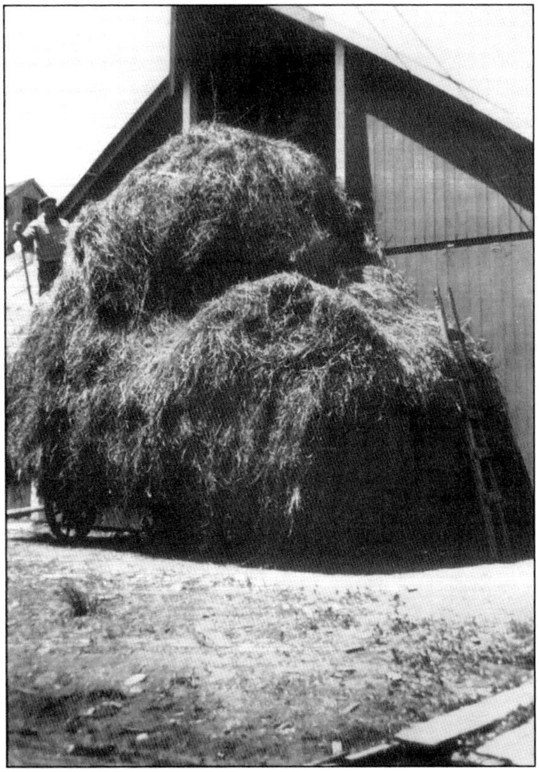

Richard "Dick" Carley was raised on a family farm on Sharon Mountain. In his book *Growing Up on the Farm*, he shares stories of how the farmers on the mountain would unload their hay with a hayfork: "In our main cowbarn, we used a straight fork which looked like an inverted U. Through pulleys and ropes—and a little help from a tractor or a team of horses—Dad was able to move the hay from the wagon to the haymow with very little effort." (Courtesy of Richard L. Carley.)

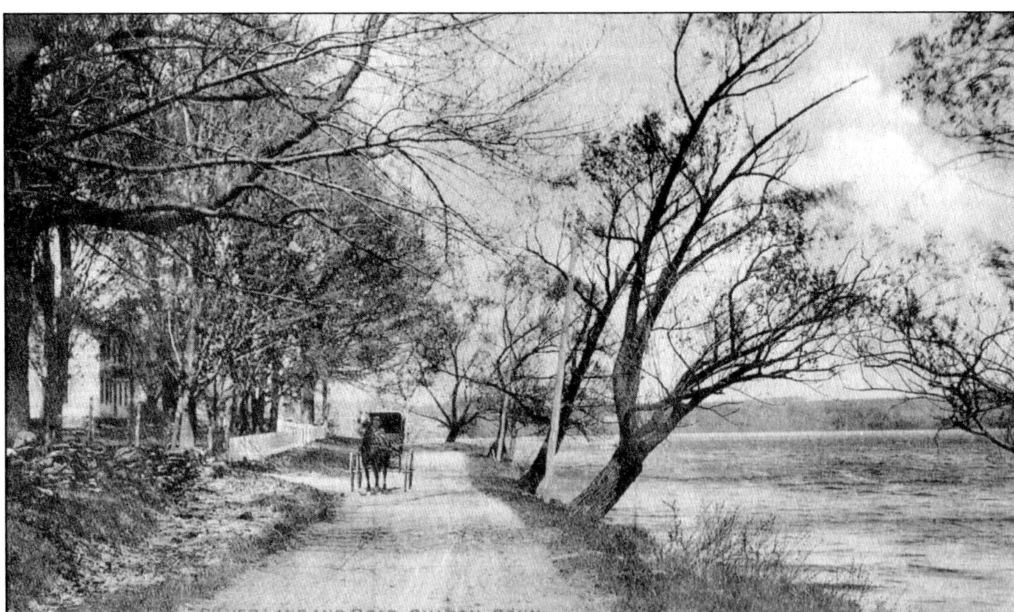

Sharon farms were not only located in Sharon Valley and up on Sharon Mountain, but also down on land bordering Mudge Pond. Here, a horse-drawn buggy is seen on the unpaved Mudge Pond Road (later renamed Silver Lake Road but still commonly known as Mudge Pond Road). The Hart farmhouse and fields, owned by Roswell Hart, are to the left. The house was later moved to sit at the top of the hill overlooking the pond.

Five

Building a Strong Community

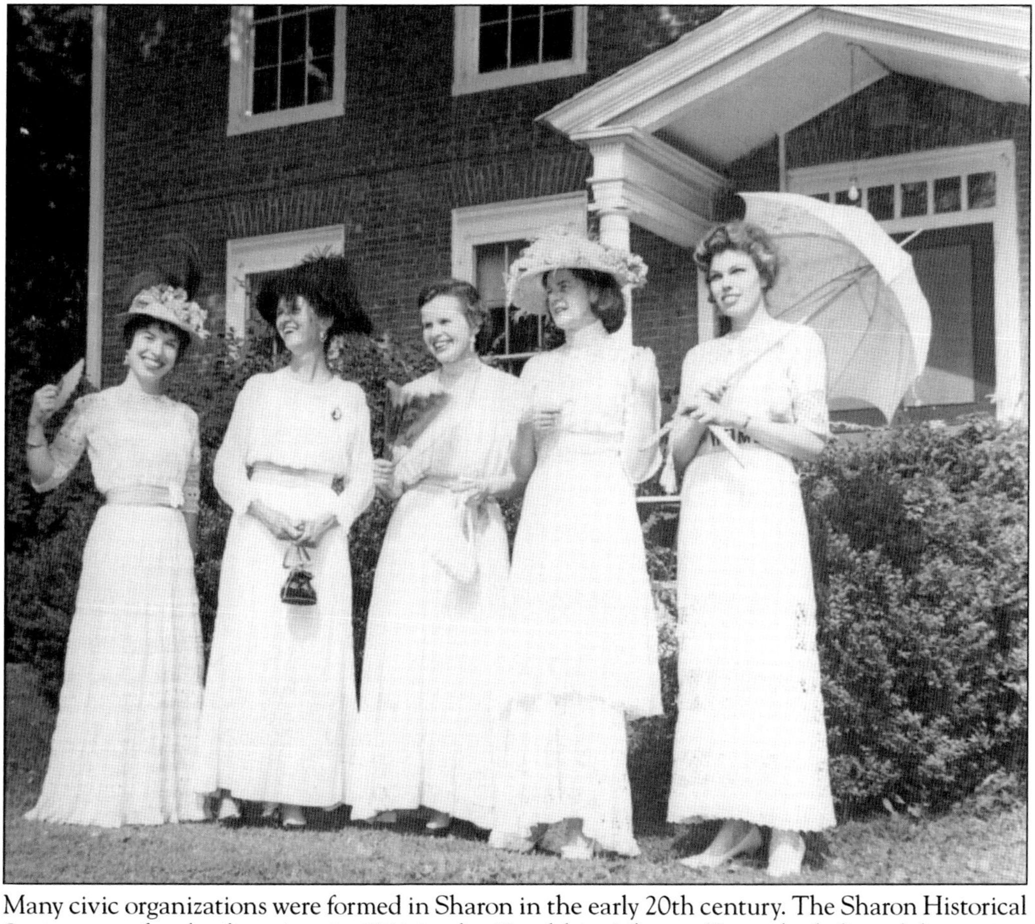

Many civic organizations were formed in Sharon in the early 20th century. The Sharon Historical Society met for the first time in 1911 in the Hotchkiss Library. Here, the ladies of the society dress in Edwardian fashion to celebrate the 50th anniversary of the organization in 1961. From left to right are Constance Gaylor, Josephine Gulnac, Adelaide Emory, Sally Hart, and Sarah Owens. (Photograph by Fran Kelsey.)

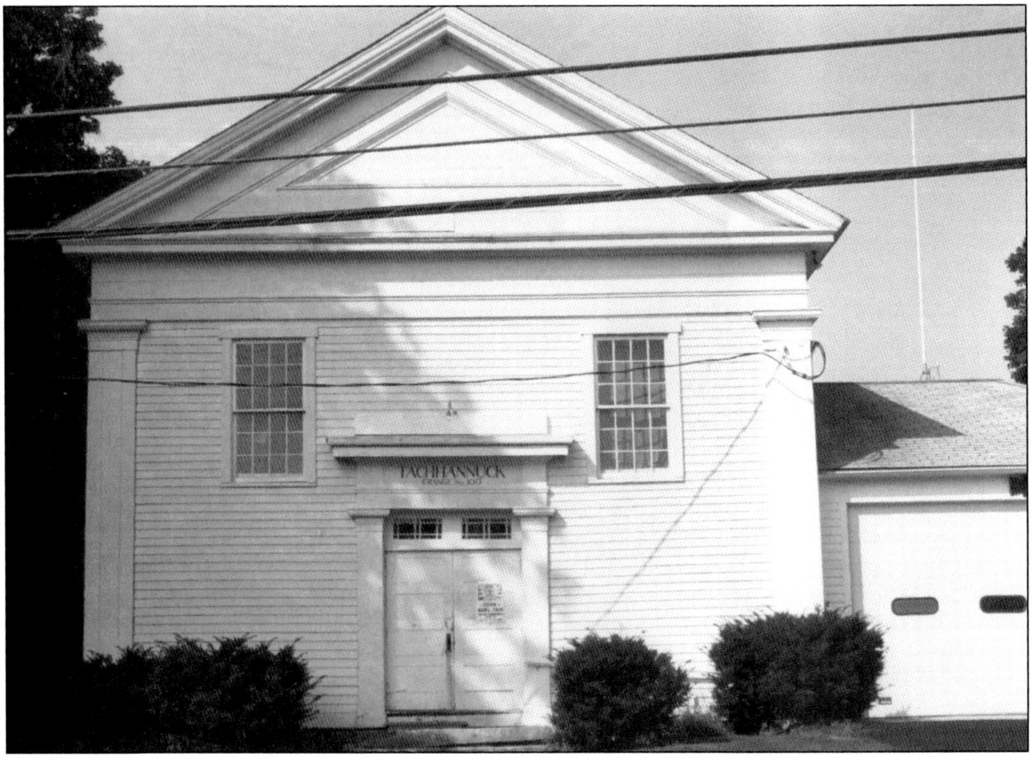

The Taghannuck Grange 100 was founded in 1889 and purchased its home in Ellsworth in 1928. The Grange, officially referred to as the National Grange of the Order of Patrons of Husbandry, is a fraternal organization that encourages families to band together to promote the economic and political well-being of the community and agriculture. The Grange, founded after the Civil War in 1867, is the oldest American agricultural advocacy group that has a national scope. Major accomplishments credited to Grange advocacy include passage of the Granger Laws and the establishment of free rural mail delivery.

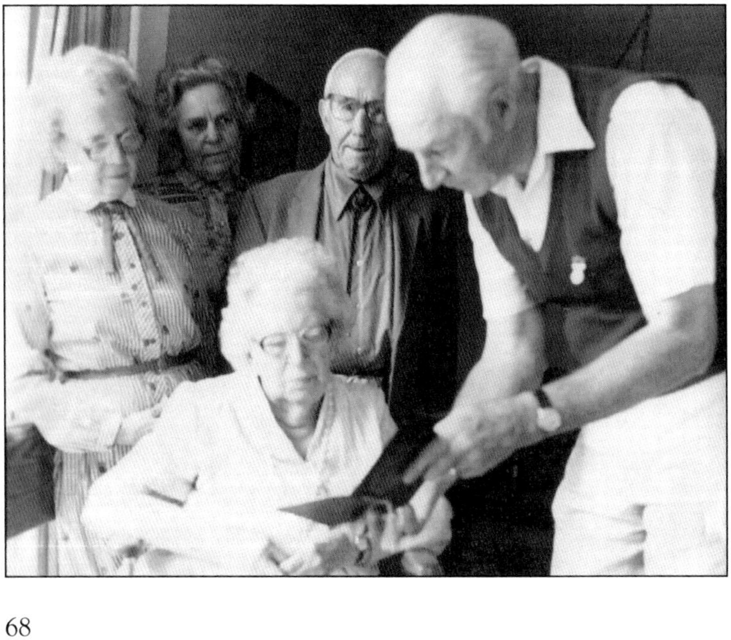

Art Lorch presents an award to Johanna Schlichting for 50 years of membership in the Grange. Standing from left to right are Jean Lundeen, Laura Hamlin, Eldred Hamlin, and Art Lorch. (Courtesy of Barbara and Brent Prindle.)

There is nothing like a spaghetti supper fundraiser. Here, Fred Amerighi is pictured with the tools of his trade outside the Sharon Town Hall. Amerighi willingly prepared gallons of spaghetti sauce for suppers benefiting the Lion's Club, the Sharon Fire Department, and St. Bernard Church, among others. His recipe appeared in *Yankee* magazine. (Courtesy of Linda Amerighi.)

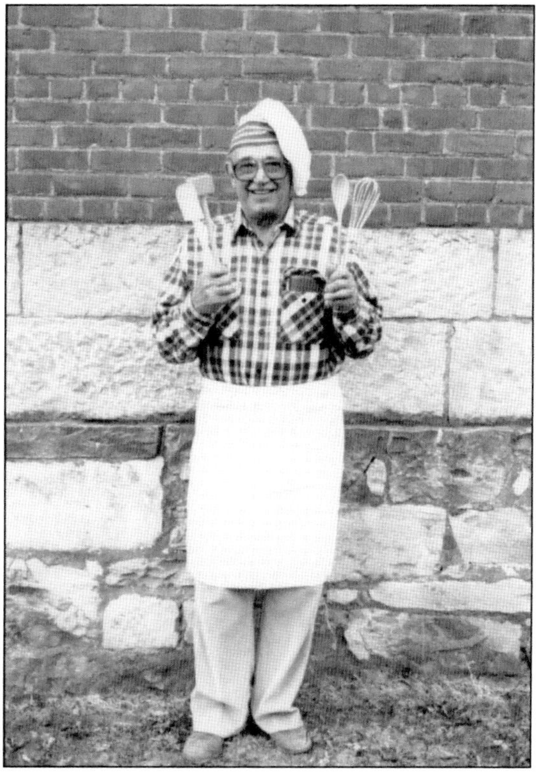

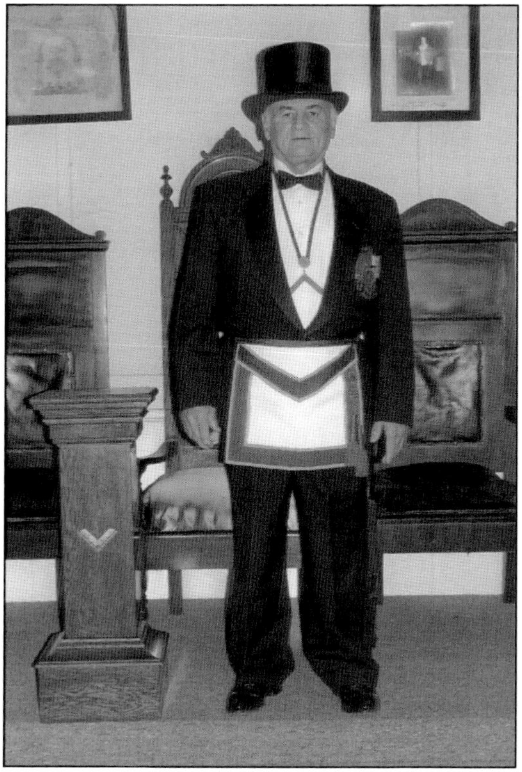

The Hamilton Lodge No. 54 of Sharon was chartered on May 15, 1815. It merged with the Montgomery Lodge in Lakeville in 1996. The most notable Mason from Sharon was Connecticut governor John Cotton Smith (1765–1845). The last master of the Sharon Lodge was Robert L. Thompson, posing here in the lodge building on Gay Street (now the Sharon Community Center, adjacent to Sharon Center School), which was dedicated in 1926. (Courtesy of Robert L. Thompson.)

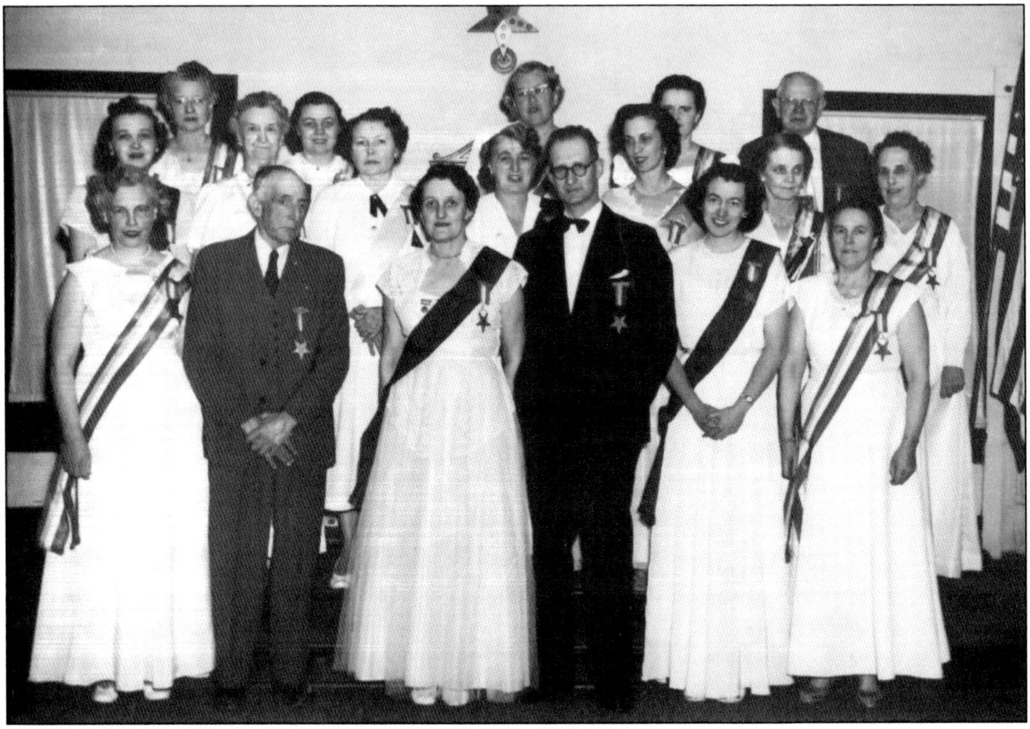

The members of Rose Chapter 114 Order of the Eastern Star are seen here in 1955. Pictured here from left to right are (first row) Dorothy Stenman, Maynard Bartram, Lilian Metcalf, Jack Metcalf, Barbara Bartram, and Laura Hamlin; (second row) Lily MacMillan, Grace Klebes, Edith Parsons, Violet Riley, Jackie Hotaling, Mable Hamlin, and Mamie Duffy; (third row) Hazel MacMillan, Ruth Nickerson, Clara Lamb, Flora Stoner, and Newton Klebes. The Order of the Eastern Star is a freemasonry-related fraternal organization open to both men and women. It was established in 1850 by Boston lawyer and educator Rob Morris, a former Freemason official. Members of the order are age 18 and older; men must be master Masons and women must have specific relationships with Masons. (Courtesy of Mary Lamb.)

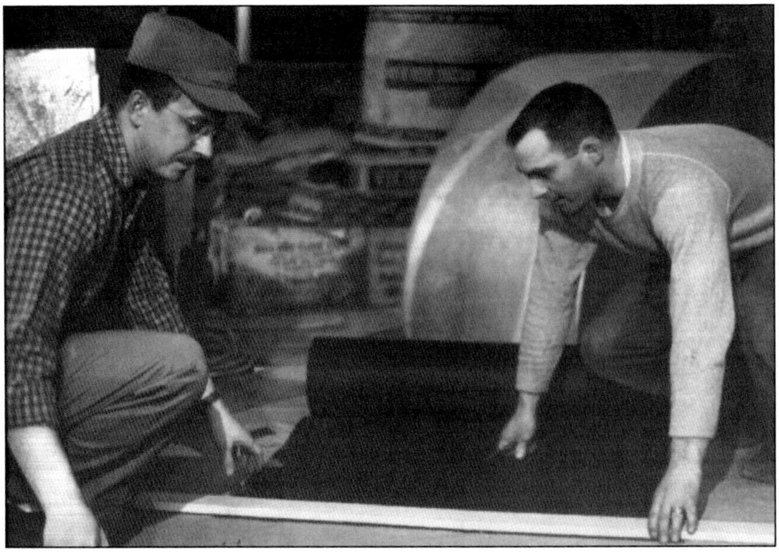

The American Legion was founded in 1919 by veterans returning from Europe after World War I. Here, American Legion Post 126 members Robert "Tuck" Cunningham and William Riley III work on finishing the interior of the new legion post on New Street in 1954–1955. (Courtesy of American Legion Post 126.)

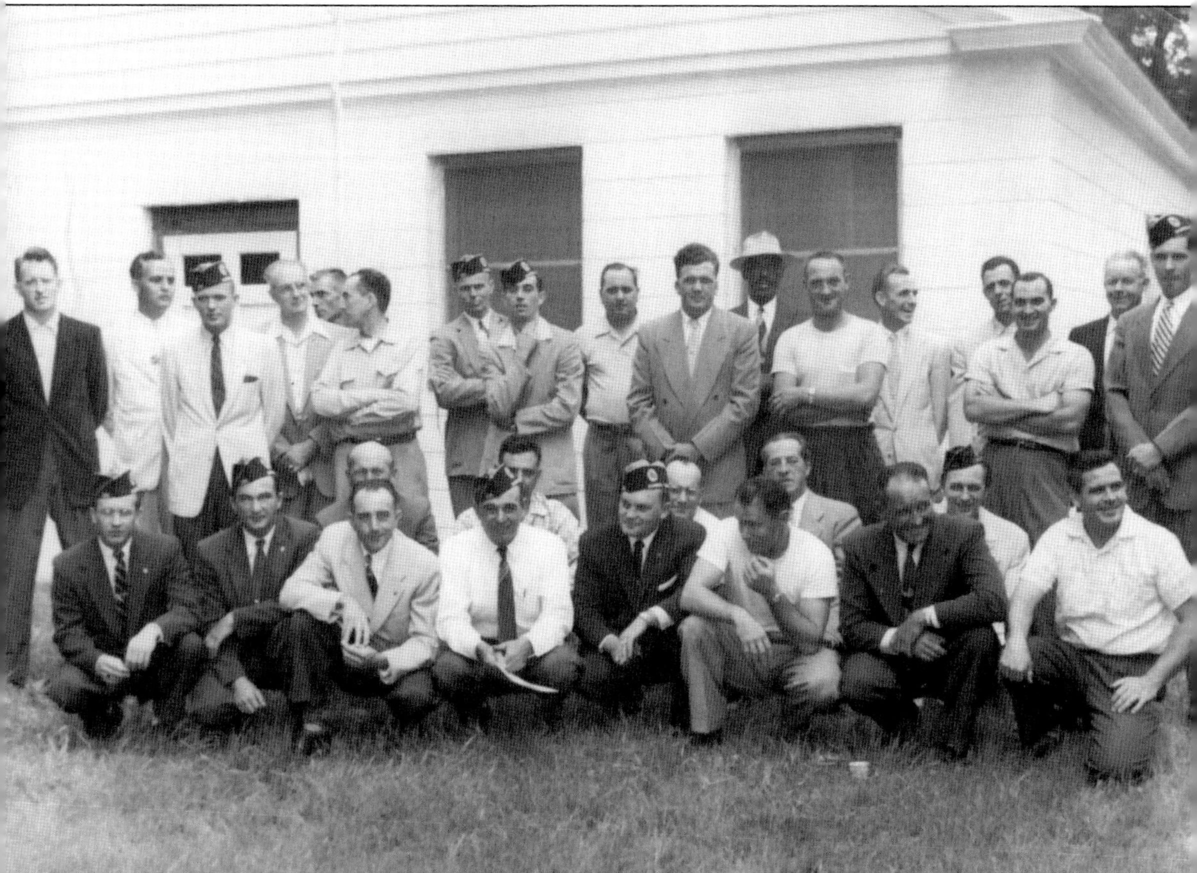

The dedication of the Herbert G. Klebes American Legion Post 126 in 1955 included, from left to right, (first row) Robert "Tuck" Cunningham, Bob Carberry, Bob Hansen, Fred Amerighi, Jake Shoifet, Jerry Pitcher, Leon Gobillot, and Don Carley; (second row) Dutch Lehnert, Morris Paley, Tom Flanagan, Bill Tomkins, and Nelson Larkin; (third row) Red Golden, Joe Pickering, Joe Madaras, Al Jenkins, Perry MacNeil, Dick Cook, Reidar Holst-Grubbe, Larry Riley, Ron Duffy, Walt Peterson, Wes Willis, Charles Wilbur, Danny Larkin, Fred Adams, William Riley III, Percy Conklin, and John McKee. (Courtesy of American Legion Post 126.)

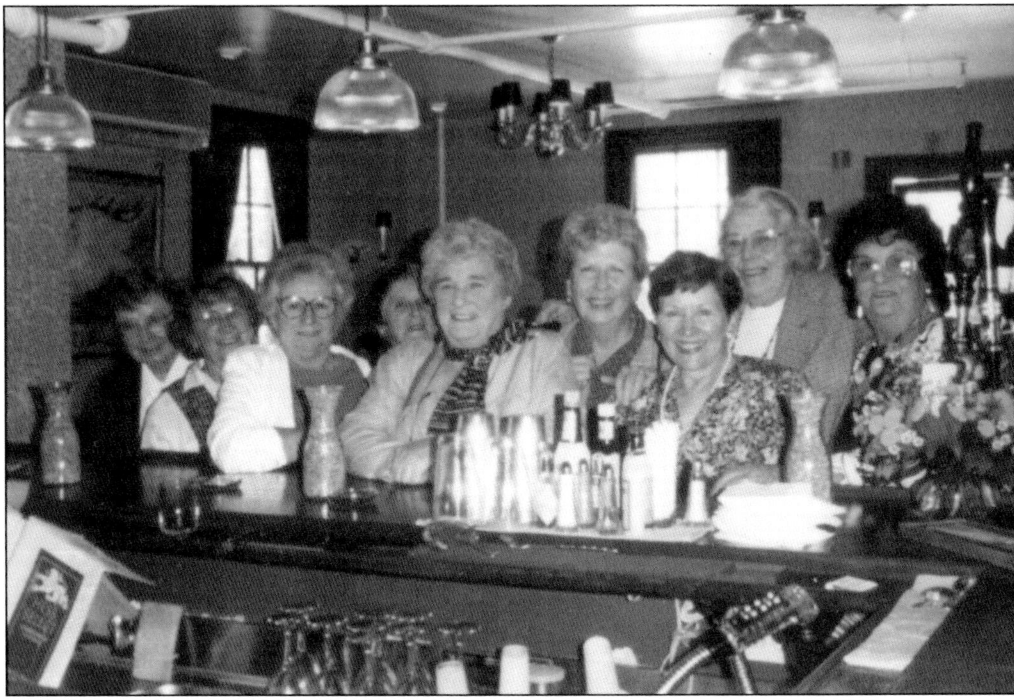

This picture was taken at a reunion of the V 16s. Anne Gudernatch, wife of Dr. Gaert Gudernatch, was an inveterate community organizer. During World War II, she organized young women of Sharon into the V 16s, a group of young women who met every Monday night at her home. The groups did yearly trips to New York City and ran events to raise money for the war effort and to support community organizations. One fundraiser provided startup money for the Sharon Woman's Club scholarship fund. At a later reunion are, from left to right, Emma "Dolly" Paley, Doris Carberry, Barbara Pitcher, Lois Middlebrook, Adele Middlebrook Casey, Roberta Donovan, Carol Donovan, Anne Gudernatch, and Esther McKee. (Courtesy of Doris Carberry.)

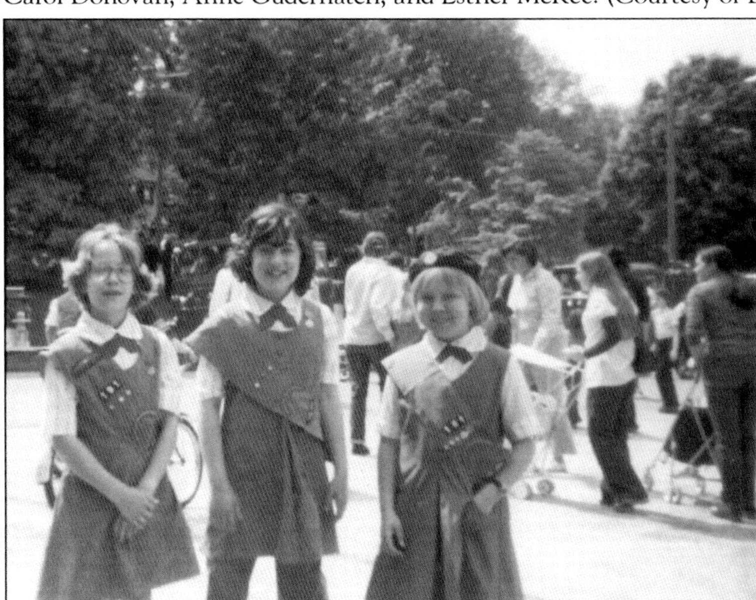

What would an American town be without a Girl Scout troop? This photograph of Junior Girl Scouts shows, from left to right, Sharon Waldow, Sarah Paley, and Colleen Pitcher. This image was probably taken at one of Sharon's famous Memorial Day parade celebrations, and dates from the late 1970s. (Courtesy of Emma Paley.)

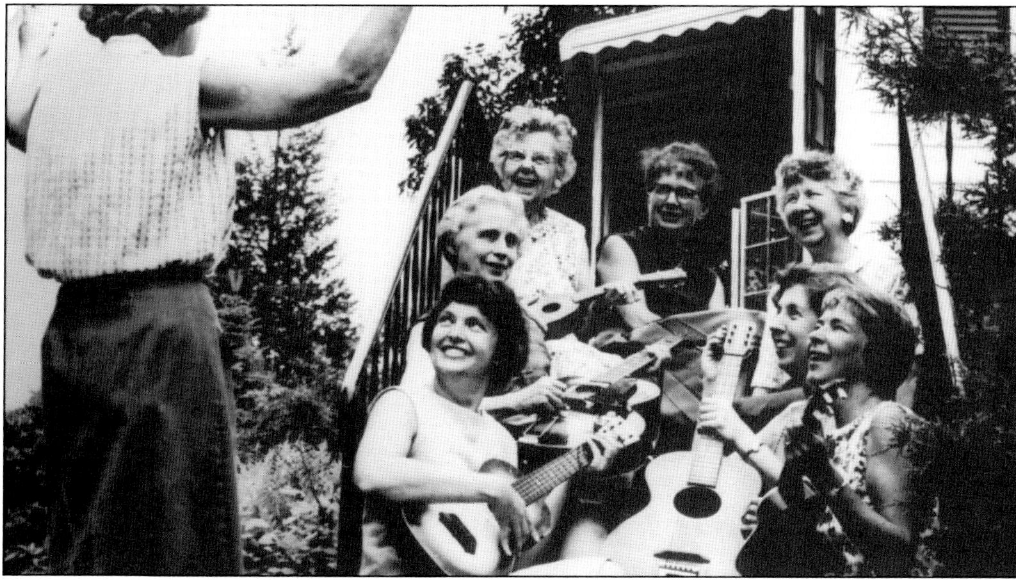

The Sharon Woman's Club was founded in 1911 and is a proud chapter of the General Federation of Women's Clubs. Always active in town beautification and in raising funds for a wide variety of projects, the club sponsored a musical play at Sharon Creative Arts Foundation (SCAF) to benefit the club's scholarship fund in 1968. Anne Gudernatch was chairwoman. From left to right are (first row) Kathryn Heacox and Ginny Palmer; (second row) Peggy Becker and Joan Blanchette; (third row) Mary Grindrod, Meta Holst, and Mary Bennett. (Courtesy of the Sharon Woman's Club.)

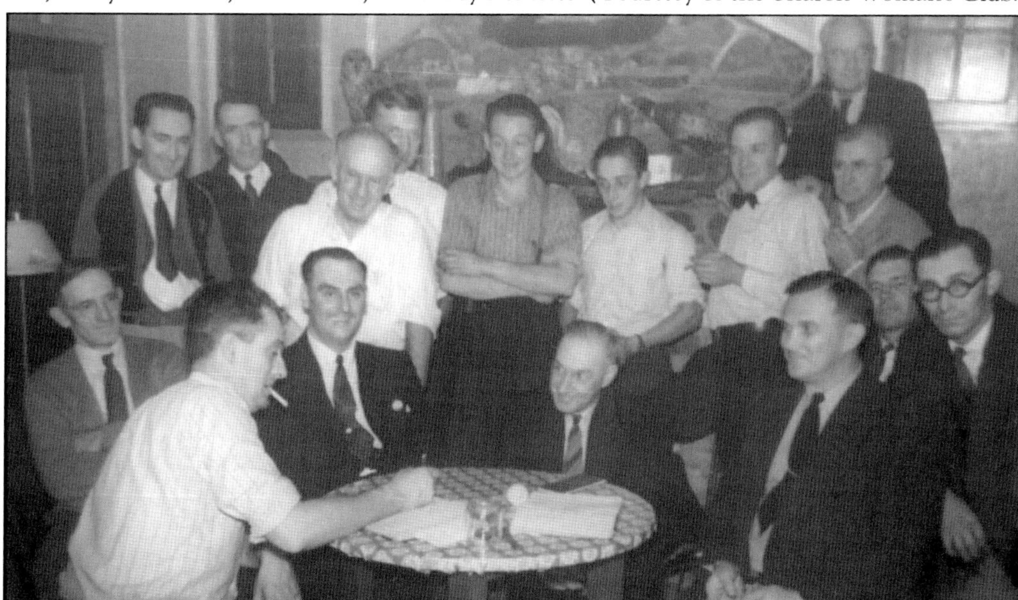

Sharon's Fish & Game Club still stocks the rivers and ponds in Sharon. This photograph was taken at the planning meeting for the first Fish & Game Club dinner, at Al Jenkins's retreat on Mudge Pond Road. From left to right are (seated) George Wilbur Sr., Al Jenkins, Bill Morehouse, Floyd Laird, Lance Middlebrook, George Drumm, and Dwight Bierce; (standing) Dick Cooke, Bernie Manning, John Humeston, unidentified, Elmer Aakjar, Bub Nodine, Elwood Tuthill, J.V. Carberry, and Everett Pitcher Sr. (Courtesy of Ray and Bonnie Aakjar.)

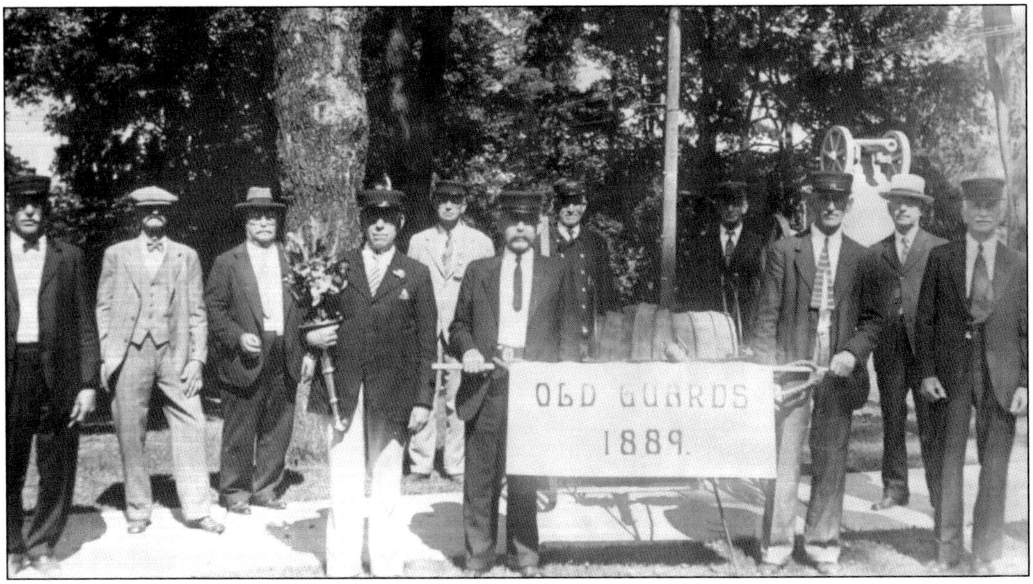

This photograph from 1889 features the founding members of the Sharon Fire Department. Included in the group are, in no particular order, N. Pitcher, F. Rhynus, E. Middlebrook, H. Hoag, F. Paul, C. Harris, W. Klebes, W. Baker, A. Walters, and C. Loucks. (Courtesy of Jack Murtagh.)

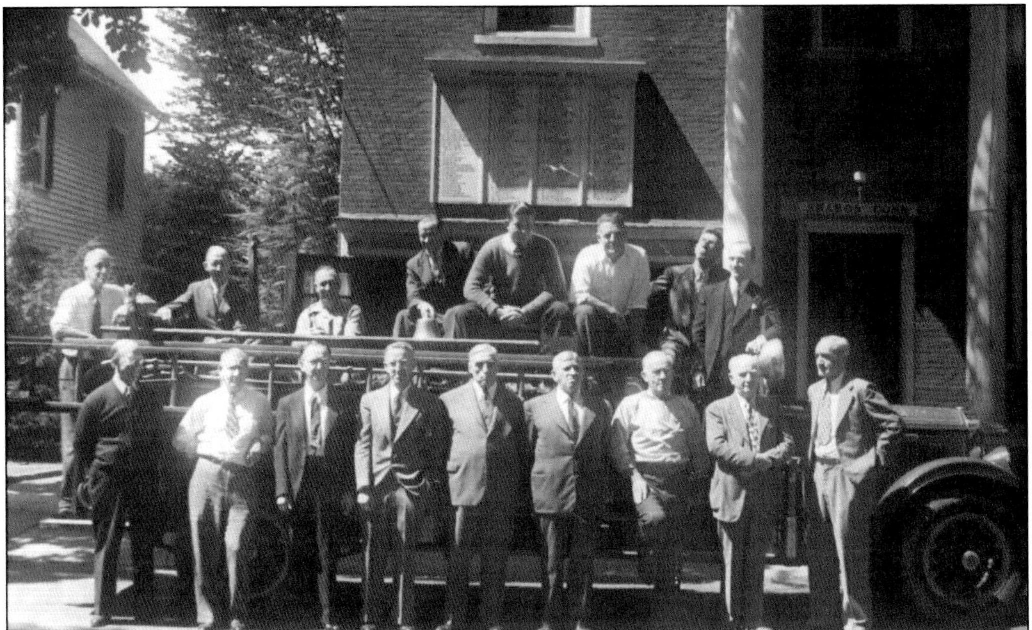

In 1924, the Sharon Fire Department took over the lower room of the tower and part of the lockup to house their new fire truck. To be a firefighter, a volunteer had to live within the sound of the fire bell, which rang from the Methodist church, in the north part of town, and the Congregational church, in the south. The fire district—the area served by the department—was a separate taxing authority. The district did not expand much farther than downtown and the areas immediately surrounding. The district was disbanded around 1980, but the fire department continues as a volunteer group to this day.

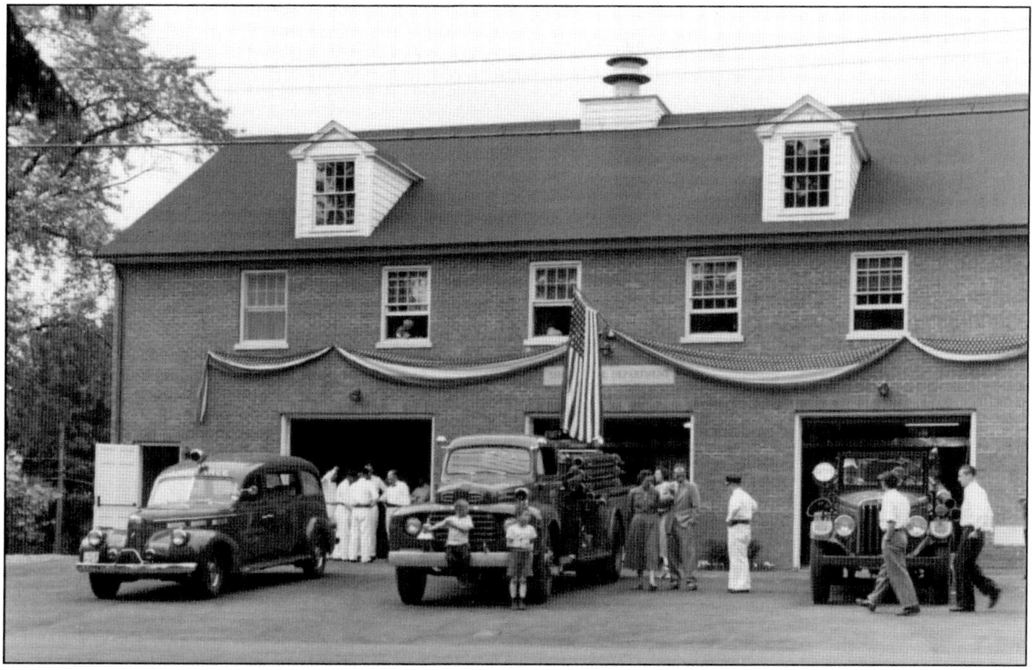

The new firehouse was decorated for its dedication in 1951. The LaSalle ambulance (left) was the first placed in service by the Taghannuck Grange in 1948. The two engines in the photograph are the Ford F8 and the 1932 Reo Engine 2. (Courtesy of Jack Murtagh.)

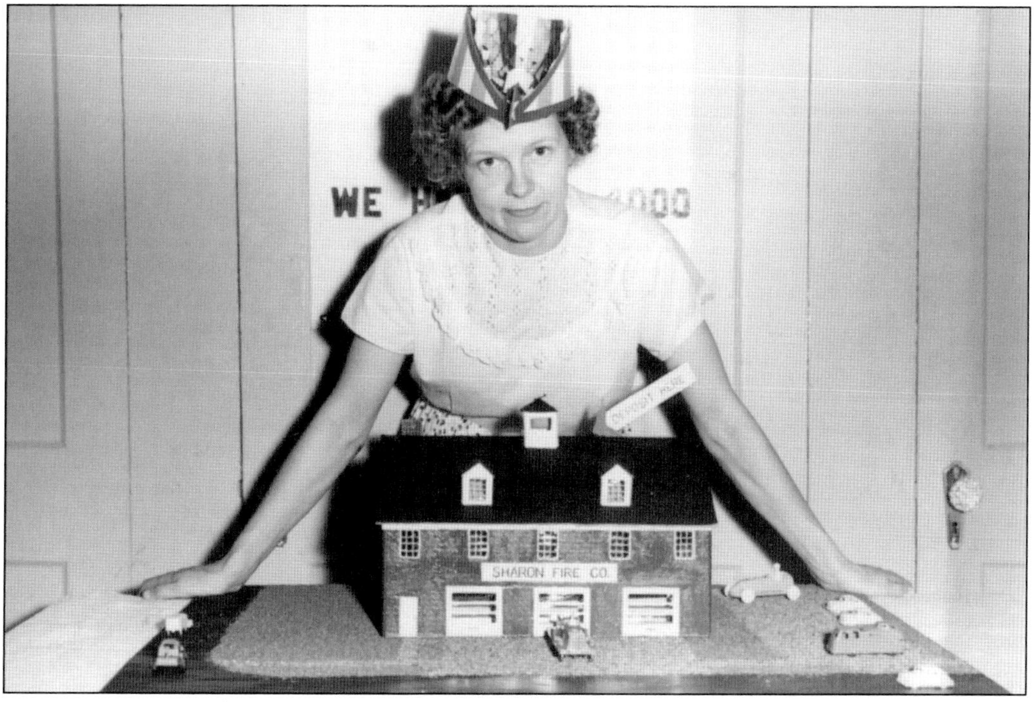

Marie Peterson, Mel Peterson's wife, constructed this replica of the Sharon Fire Department for the dedication in 1951. Members of the Peterson family still live in Sharon today. (Courtesy of Jayne Larsen.)

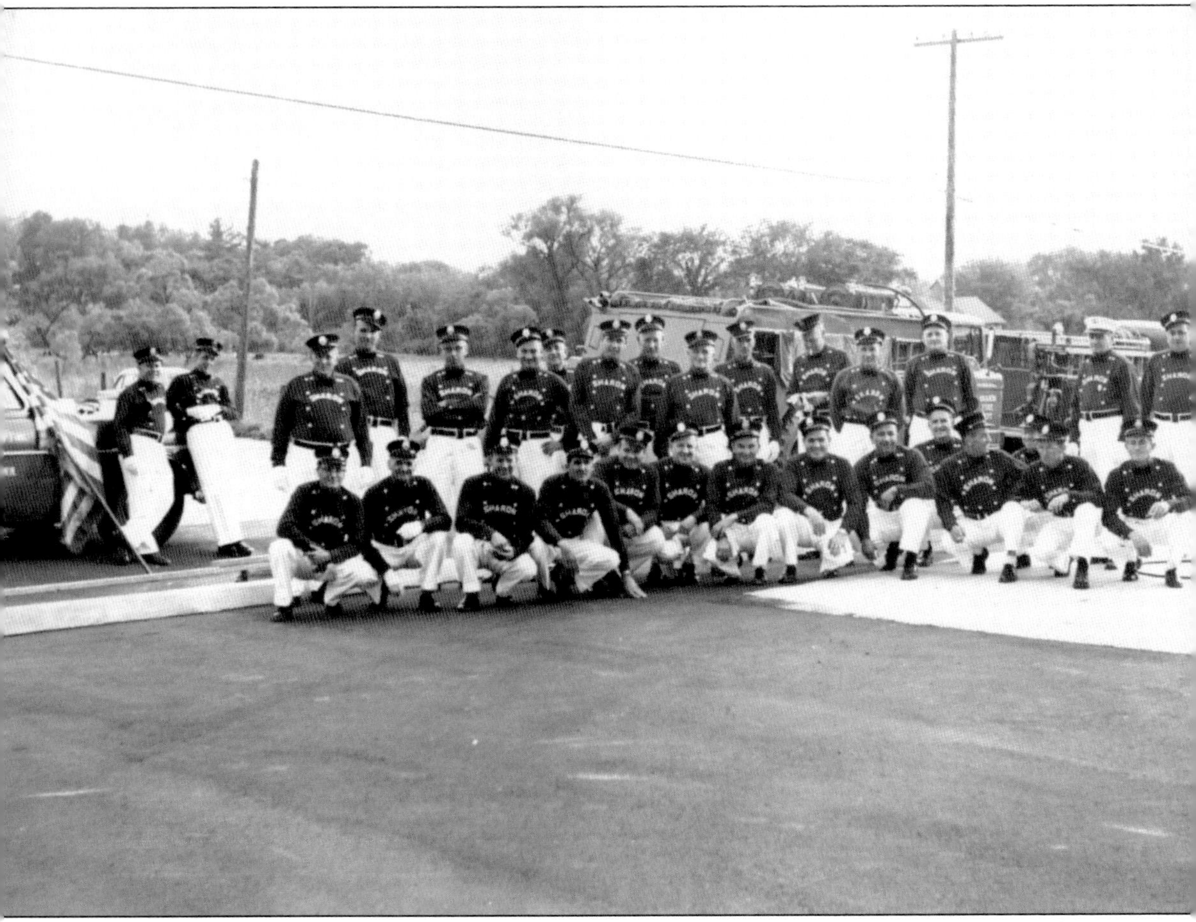

Sharon Fire Department members in uniform are shown here around 1950. From left to right are (first row) Buck Flanagan, Pete Selino, Kermit Kinsman, Tom McKee, Charles Duplessis, Reed Gillette, Robert Carberry, Don Carley, Bud Reed, Claude "Red" Golden, George Hosier, Morris McCann, Don Carberry, and William Tompkins; (second row), Jerry Pitcher, Fred Adams, Roswell Kinney, William Pitcher, George Albig, Charles Wilbur, Arthur Petit, John McKee, Peder Aakjar, Norm Ecklund, Perry McNeil, Newt Bristol, Paul Carberry, John Kaminsky, David Duffy, and Ronald Duffy.

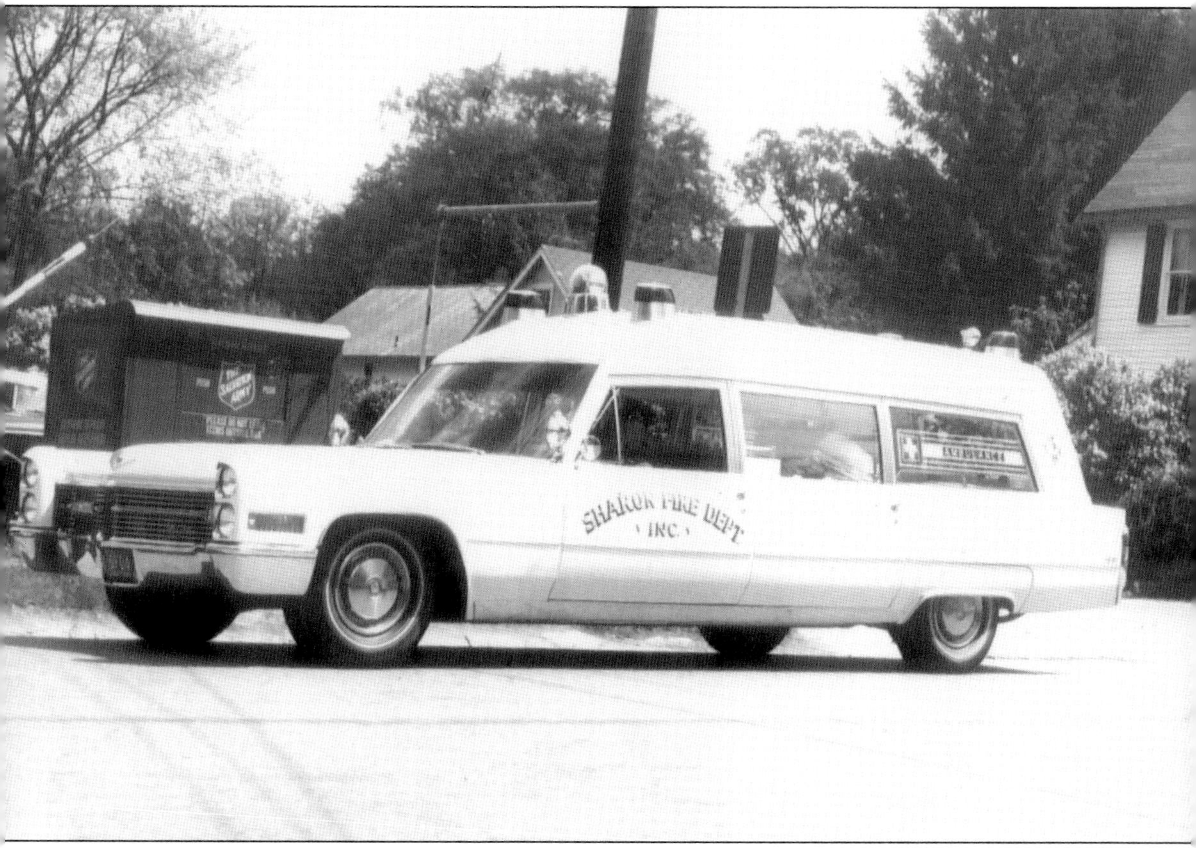

This top-of-the-line Cadillac ambulance was in service from 1966 to 1977. A Packard ambulance donated by Dr. George Fowler on August 4, 1952, followed the original 1948 LaSalle, which was donated by the Taghannuck Grange. It was not until 1968 that Dr. W. Peter Reyelt began a training program for ambulance personnel. For many years, the Sharon ambulance was the only one that served the region. (Courtesy of Barbara Bartram.)

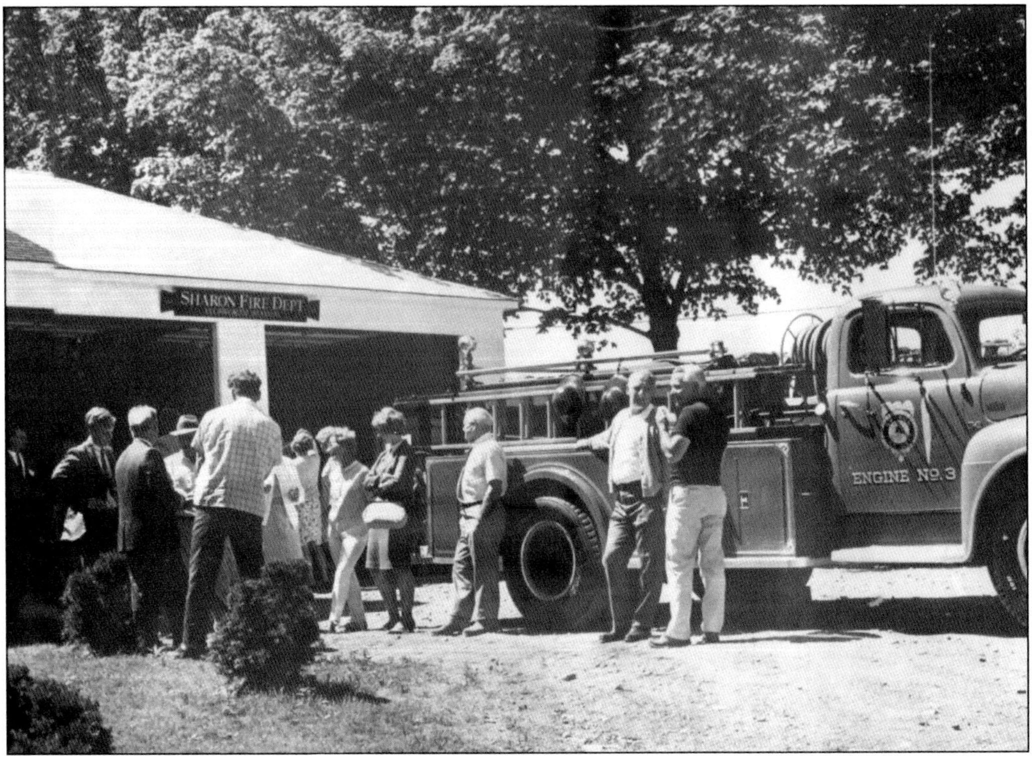

Even into the 1960s, Sharon's hilly terrain and winding roads had an effect on town logistics and service organizations. The location of the central fire station in downtown Sharon could make it difficult to respond to emergencies in the outlying neighborhoods. In 1967, a substation of the Sharon Fire Department was dedicated at the Taghannuck Grange in Ellsworth, on Route 4. Pictured near its new home is Engine No. 3, with Vince Johnson (left) and Tom Lovell (right) identified in the right foreground. (Courtesy of Barbara and Brent Prindle.)

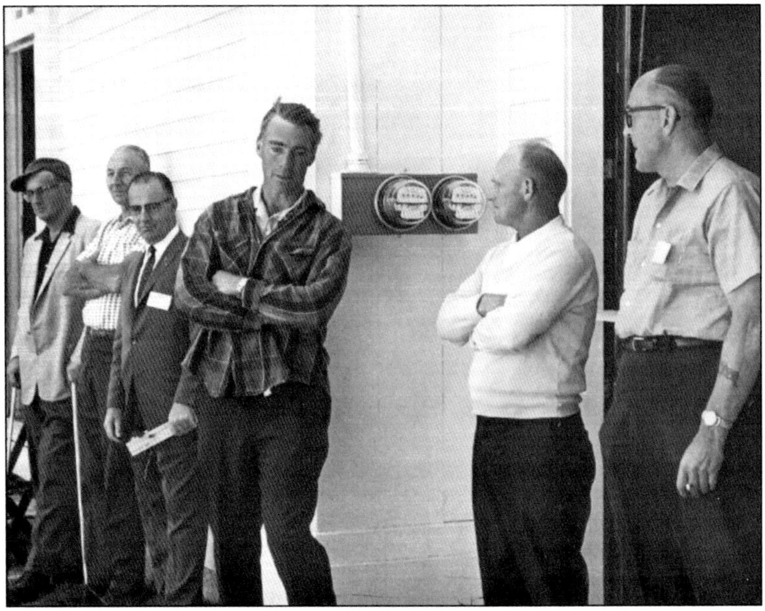

Members of the Sharon Fire Department wait outside the substation at the dedication in 1967. From left to right are Ernest Morgan, unidentified, an unidentified official, Burr Morgan, Art Drake, and George Lamb. (Courtesy of Barbara and Brent Prindle.)

Six

PLAY BALL!

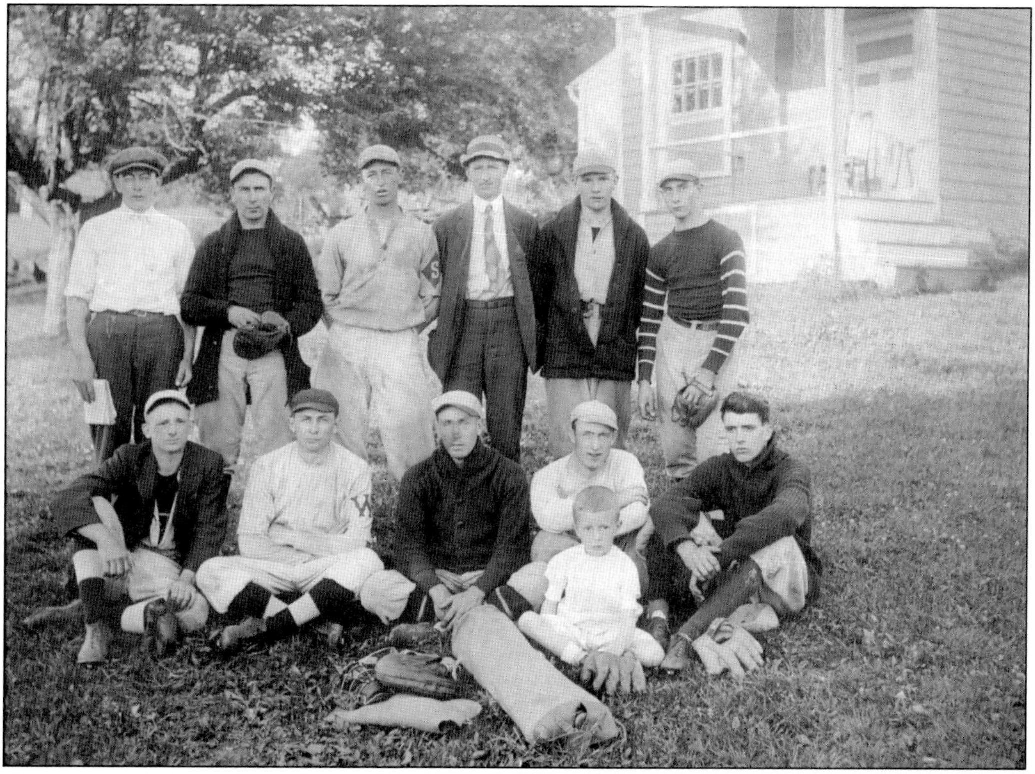

Sharon people have always been a hearty and athletic bunch. Baseball, basketball, softball, and more were popular sports, for players and spectators. This early photograph shows the Sharon town baseball team from the 1920s. From left to right are (first row) Del Middlebrook, ? O'Neil, Howard Pitcher, ? Goodwin, and Al Jenkins; (second row) Edward Kenny, Everett Pitcher, George MacDonald, Frank Byron, Herman Middlebrook, and Willie Pitcher. The young batboy in front is Robert Harris.

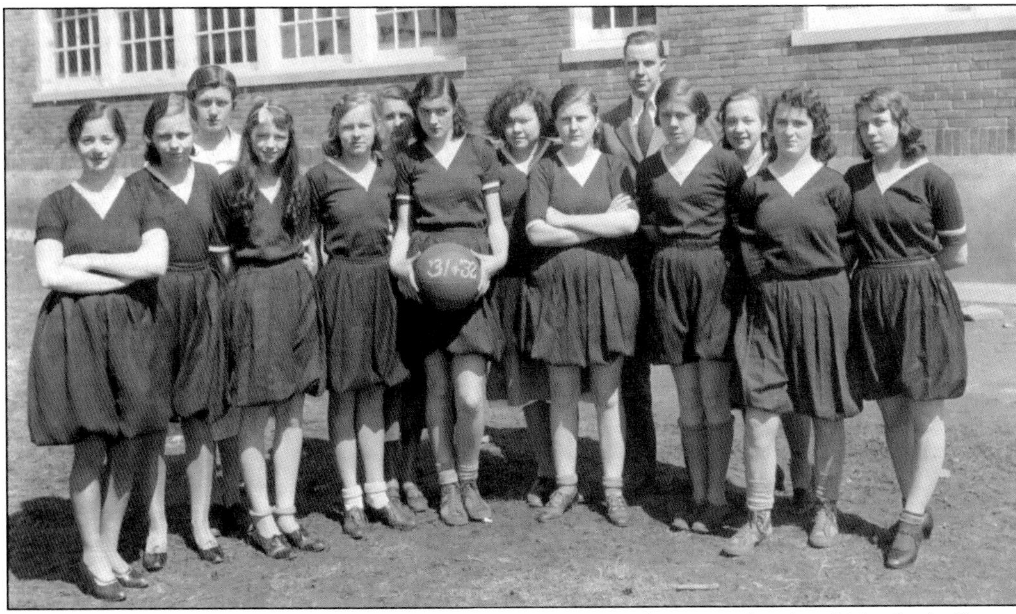

Team sports were not limited to the boys. The 1931–1932 Sharon School girls' basketball team donned sporty uniforms. Winning season or not, these girls look ready for action. Pictured from left to right are Mary Tompkins, Jeanne Platt, Hazel Lewis, Avis Wiley, Marie Aakjar, Josephine Moore, Grace Buckley, Delia Valyou, Margaret Pitcher, coach Zeke Jewell, Margaret Humeston, Mildred Osolin, Mildred Lovell, and Jean Drake. (Courtesy of Jayne Larsen.)

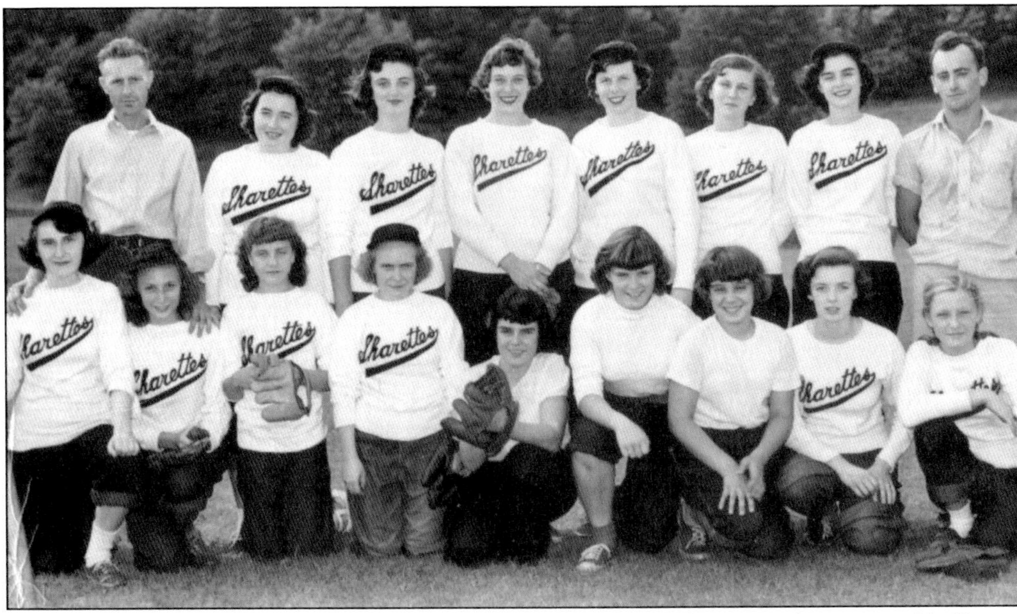

Sharon even fielded a girls' softball team after World War II. The 1949 Sharettes softball team was coached by Tom Flanagan and Myron Tuncy. From left to right are (first row) Mary Faith Pitcher, Elaine Seeley, Joan McKee, Jean Barratt, Mary Kenny, Sheila Lehnert, Jane Gottschalk, Jean Beeman, and Sarah Hansell; (second row) Coach Tuncy, Mary J. Juckett, Peggy Casteel, Joan Gottschalk, Sally Jenkins, Pattye L. Hansell, Sally Kenny, and Coach Flanagan. (Courtesy of Jean Hansell.)

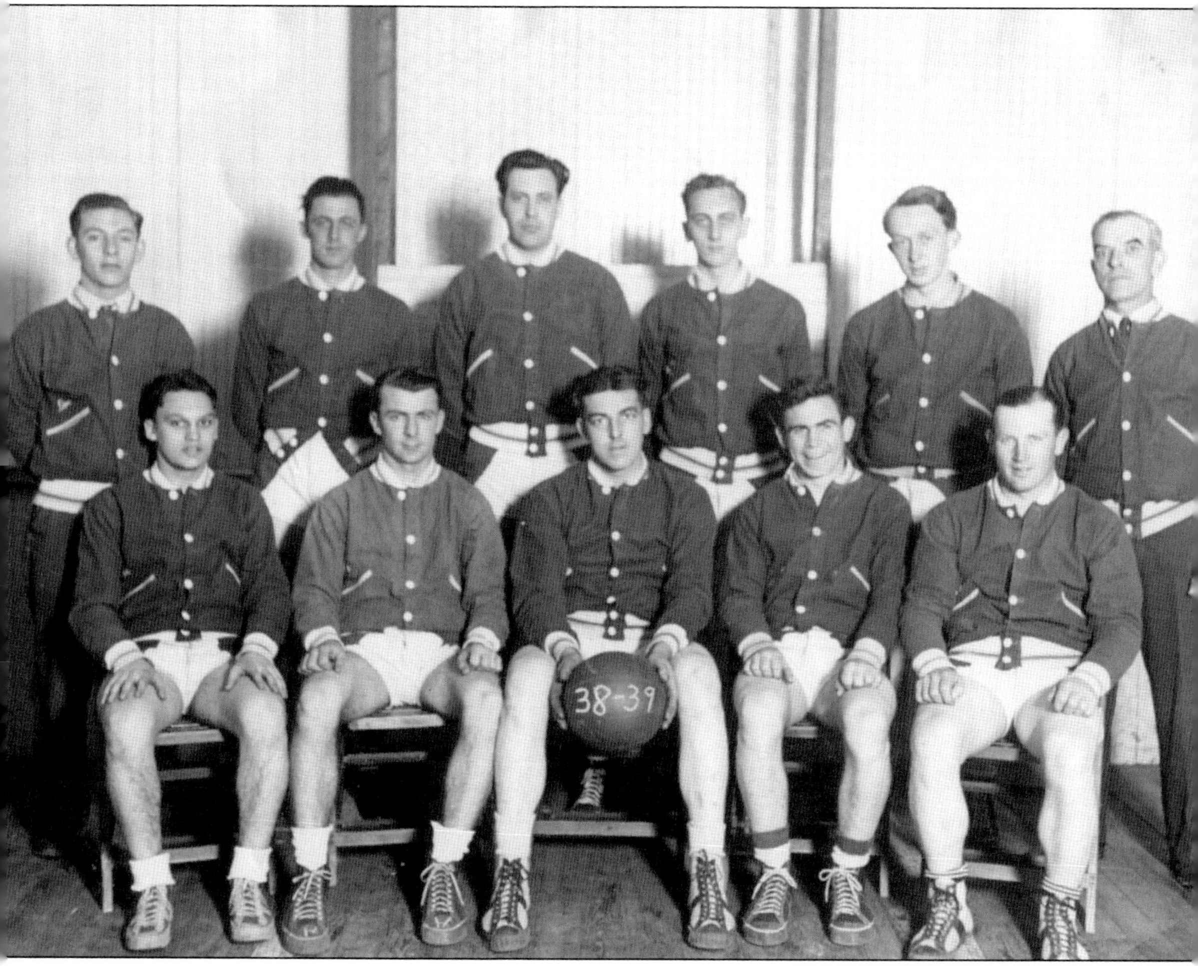

The 1938–1939 basketball team played its games on the court on the second floor of the Sharon Town Hall. From left to right are (first row) Jake Shoifet, Everett "Bub" Pitcher, George Lamb, Don Carley, and Kermit Kinsman; (second row) Gaylord Eggleston, Fred Adams, Ed Dorsett, Ron Duffy, Don Humeston, and coach Harold Lehnert. Ed Dorsett later became the vice principal of the high school. (Courtesy of Everett Pitcher.)

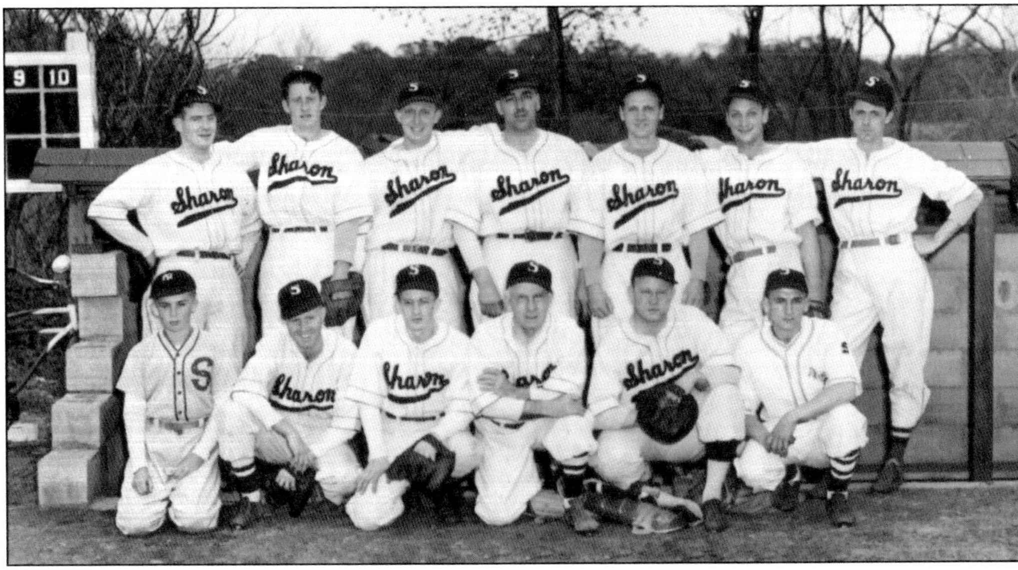

The 1948 town baseball team included, from left to right, (first row) Peter Lamb, Myron Tuncy, Robert "Tuck" Cunningham, manager John Humeston, B. Burdette, and Gilbert Hall; (second row) Larry Cunningham, Red Golden, Don Humeston, George Lamb, Bill Wilbur, Charles Wilbur, and Fred Adams. The team competed in the Interstate League, which operated from 1933 to 1969. Peter Lamb was an outstanding pitcher for Housatonic Valley Regional High School, the University of Connecticut, and the Interstate League. He did not graduate high school until 1955, but he was good enough to play with the men's team by 1948, as seen here. (Courtesy of Helen Humeston.)

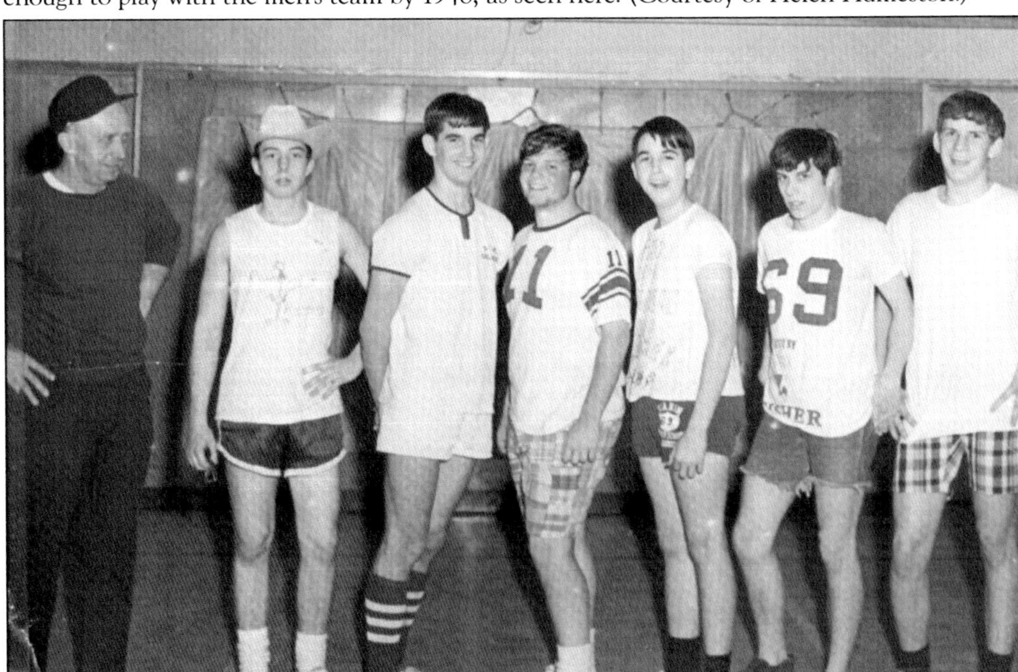

These are obviously the "cool" kids from the American Legion basketball team, around 1965. From left to right are coach Don Humeston, Gary Cunningham, Mark Miles, Pete Van Deusen, Marshall Miles, Jim Van Deusen, and John McKee. (Courtesy of American Legion Post 126.)

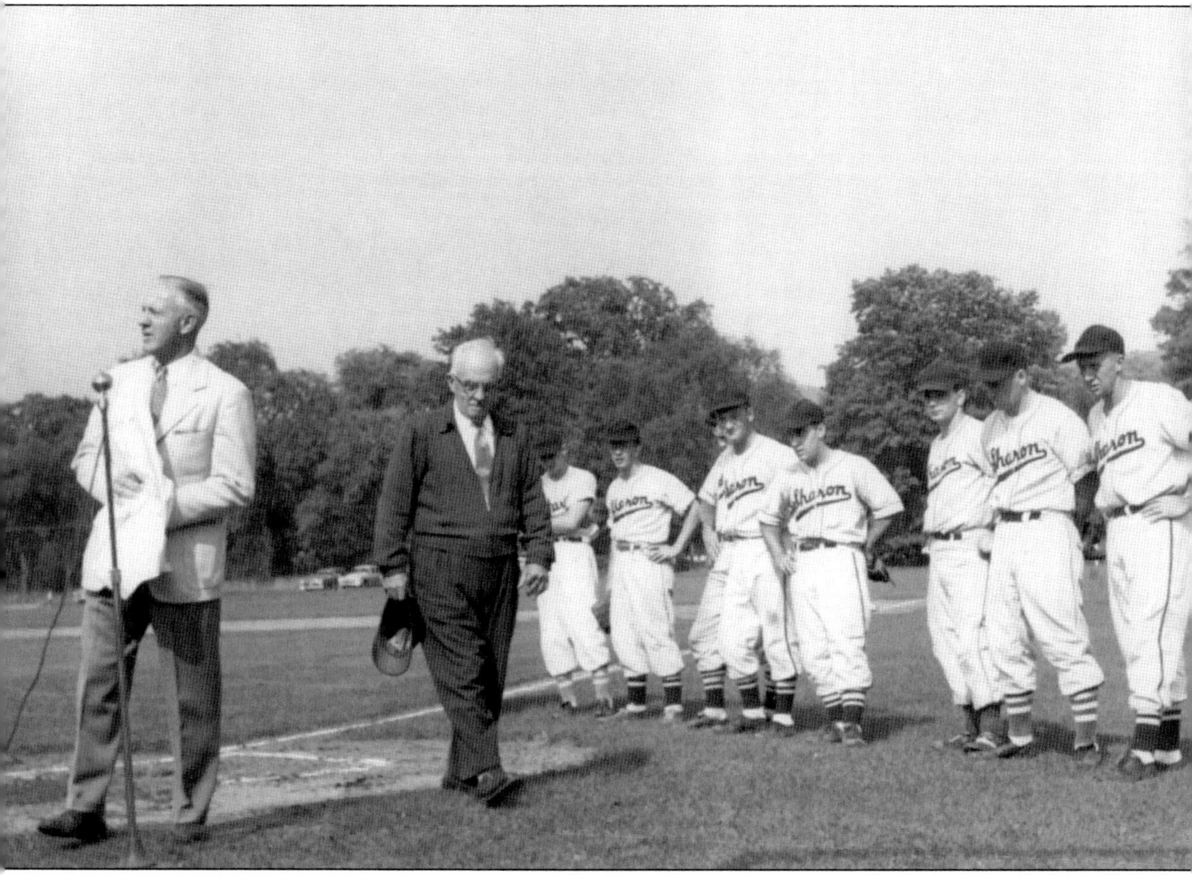

Veteran's Field in Sharon Valley was dedicated shortly after World War II. It replaced Adams Field, on Gay Street behind Odge's Egg Farm. Speaking at the dedication ceremony is Amenia's "Doc" Bartlett. The gentleman in the dark outfit is manager John Humeston. The players are, from left to right, Rusty Hansell, Robert "Tuck" Cunningham, unidentified, Charles Wilbur, Pete St. Martin, George Hosier, Bill Wilbur, and Don Humeston. The equipment building at the field was subsequently dedicated to John Humeston to acknowledge his efforts in the creation of Veteran's Field. (Courtesy of Diane Monroe.)

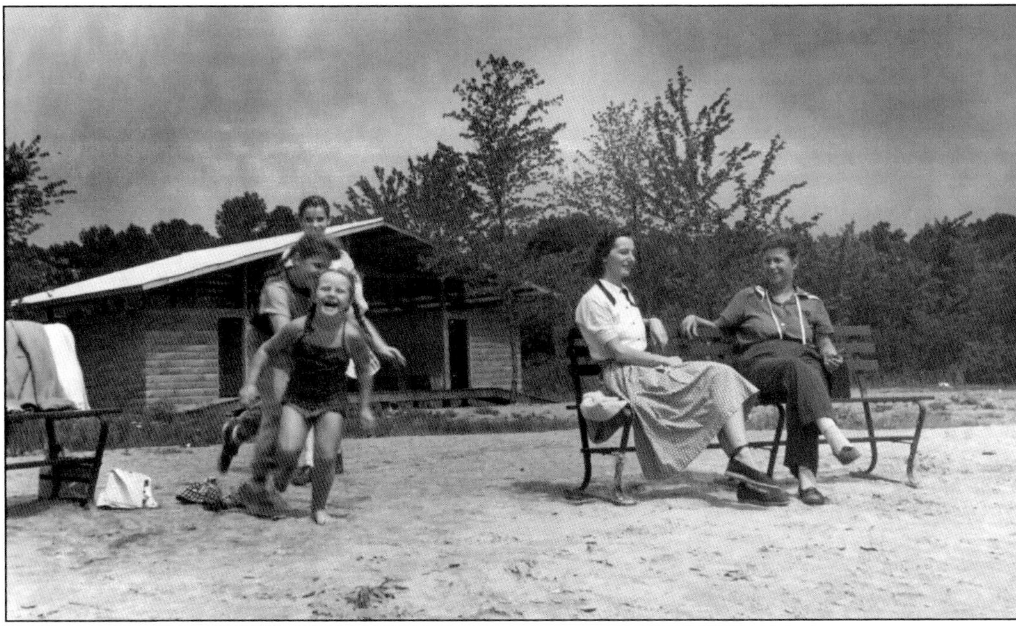

One of the longest lasting projects undertaken by the Sharon Woman's Club was fundraising for the town's beach project. The club raised funds for a bathhouse and landscaping. In 1955, the club won the State Federation Community Improvement Award in recognition of this project. Here, club member Betty Scribner (right) enjoys the sun while children race around in the sand.

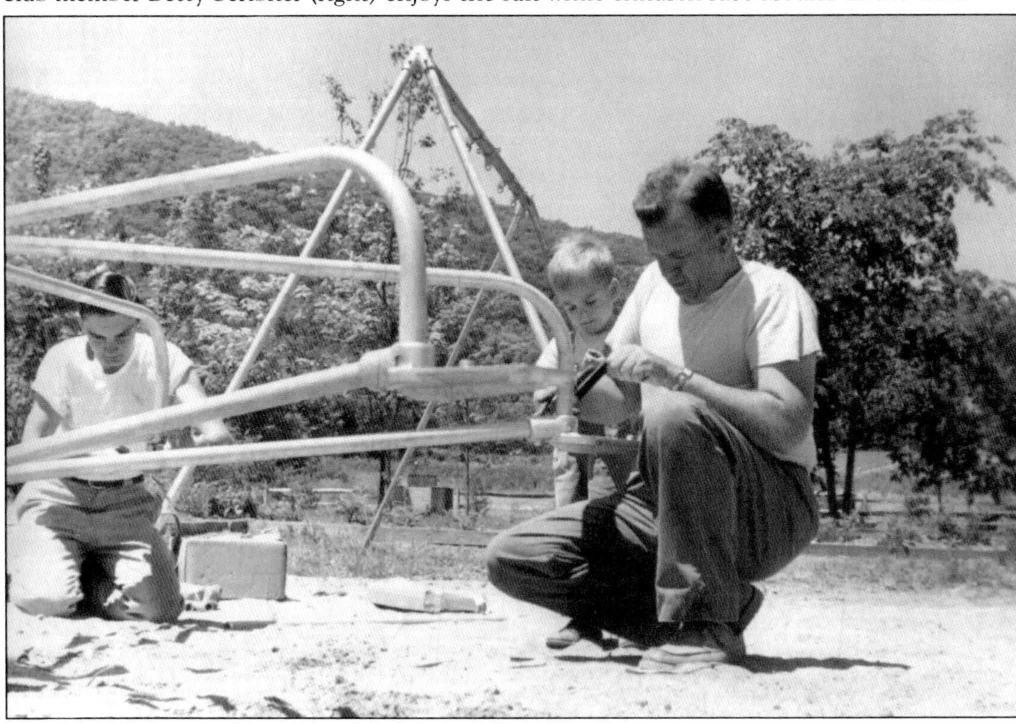

A very young Rick Hotaling helps his father, Bob, assemble a merry-go-round for the playground at the new Sharon Beach. Lance Pruyn (left) also assists on the project. Rick and his wife, Clare, own Rick's Wine & Spirits in the Sharon Shopping Center.

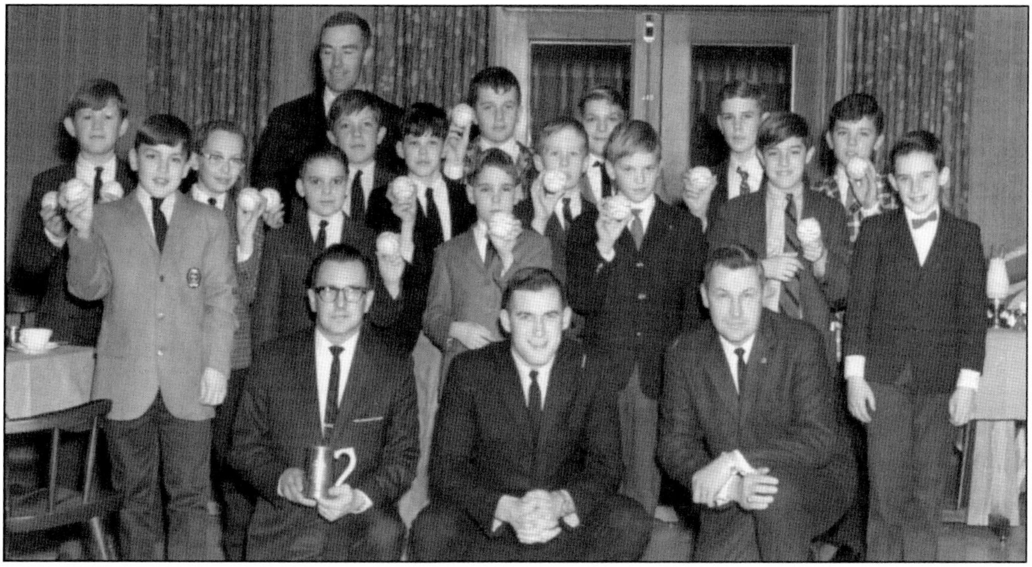

The champion Little League team of 1966 was sponsored by the Sharon Lion's Club and coached by Ed Kirby and Robert "Tuck" Cunningham. From left to right are (first row) Robert "Tuck" Cunningham; Steve Blass, a pitcher for the Pittsburgh Pirates and a Falls Village native; and Edward Heacox; (second row) Bruce Harford, Mike March, Frank Williams, Eddie Pitcher, Peter Buckley, Stephen Marston, Dave McMillen, Peter Anderson (back), Kevin Kirby, Kevin Tuttle, Brian Cahill, Barry Tuncy, Peter Warner, Mike Cahill, and Dave Hosier. Ed Kirby is in the back left. (Courtesy of Kathryn M. Heacox.)

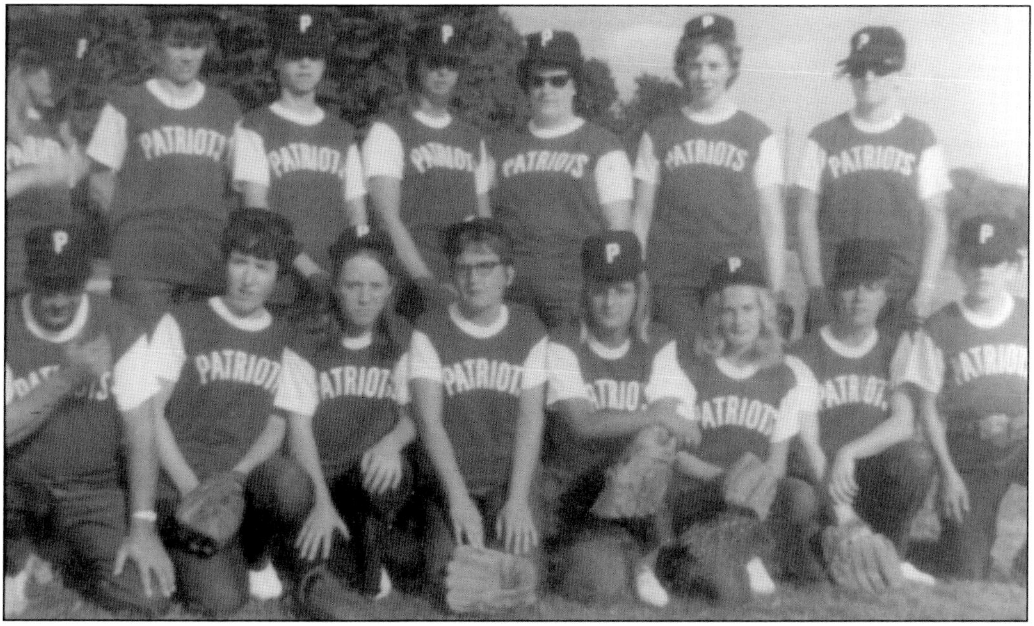

Sharon's 1972 Patriots softball team was a 13-woman wonder and part of a local women's softball league. From left to right are (first row) coach Jim Smith, Maureen Cahill, Pam Brazee, Lee Milton, Audrey Garay, Bev Brazee, Rosie Jones, and batboy Bobby Smith; (second row) Anita Dodge, Glenda Lynehan, Ginny Golden, Helen Cahill, Renee Smith, Eleanor Cahill, and Ida VonRichtofen. The scorekeeper was Avis Morehouse (not pictured). (Courtesy of Maureen Cahill.)

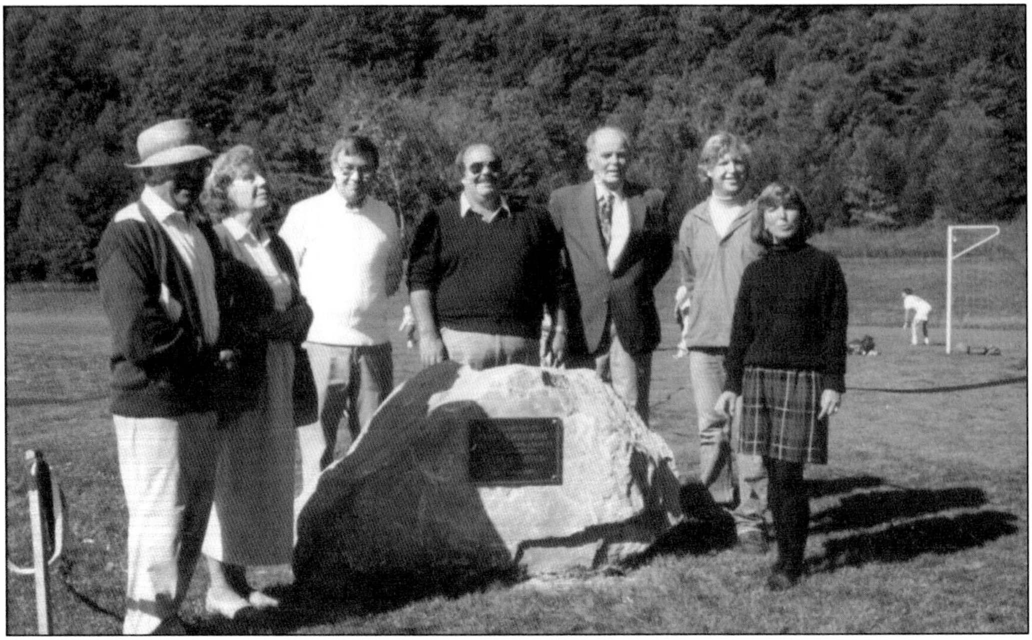

In 1993, the soccer field at Veteran's Field was dedicated to Fred Amerighi, who coached the American Legion team that advanced to the state championship finals in the 1960s. One famous game played in Middletown lasted until 3:00 a.m., when it was put on hold until the next day. Pictured at the field are, from left to right, Fred and Rose Amerighi, Bob Moeller, Gary Smith, Reidar Holst-Grubbe, John Mathews, and Rosellen Schnurr. (Courtesy of Linda Amerighi.)

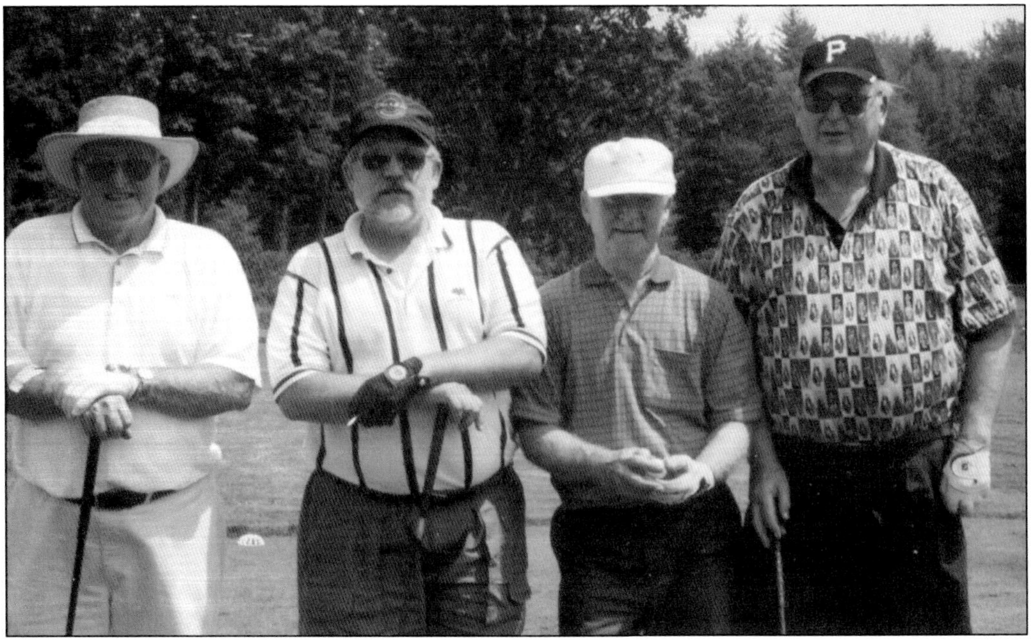

The Sharon Country Club invites Sharon residents to play on the club's course on town league evenings, known as the Five O'Clock League. Here, an infamous golf foursome from town league night is shown. They are, from left to right, Red Golden, Elliot Robertson, Everett "Bub" Pitcher, and Pete Lamb. All four men were outstanding golfers. (Courtesy of Mary Lamb.)

Seven

They Came From New York

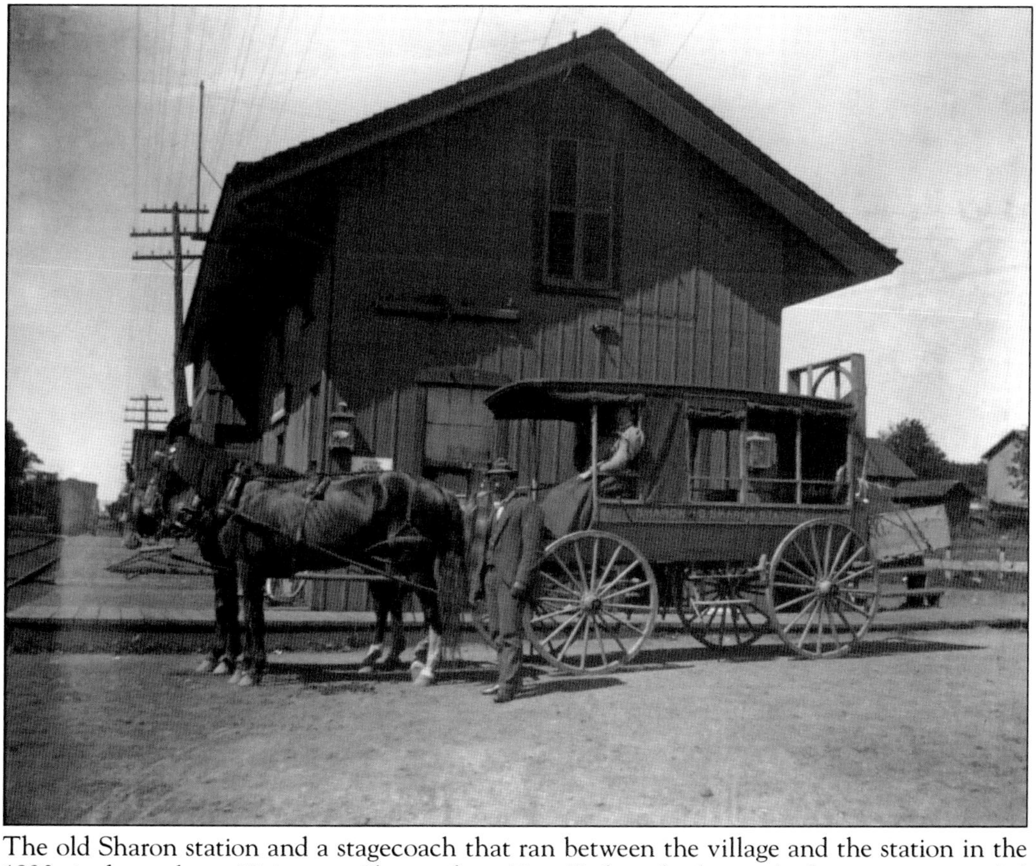

The old Sharon station and a stagecoach that ran between the village and the station in the 1890s is shown here. Visitors to Sharon from New York and other embarkation points ended their train journey here and traveled by horse and cart to the local inns. The sign on the coach says "Sharon to Sharon Station." Partially visible behind the rear of the coach is the large metal ring mounted in a frame. Such a ring was typically used by fire departments—it was struck with a mallet and the sound carried for miles to announce a fire.

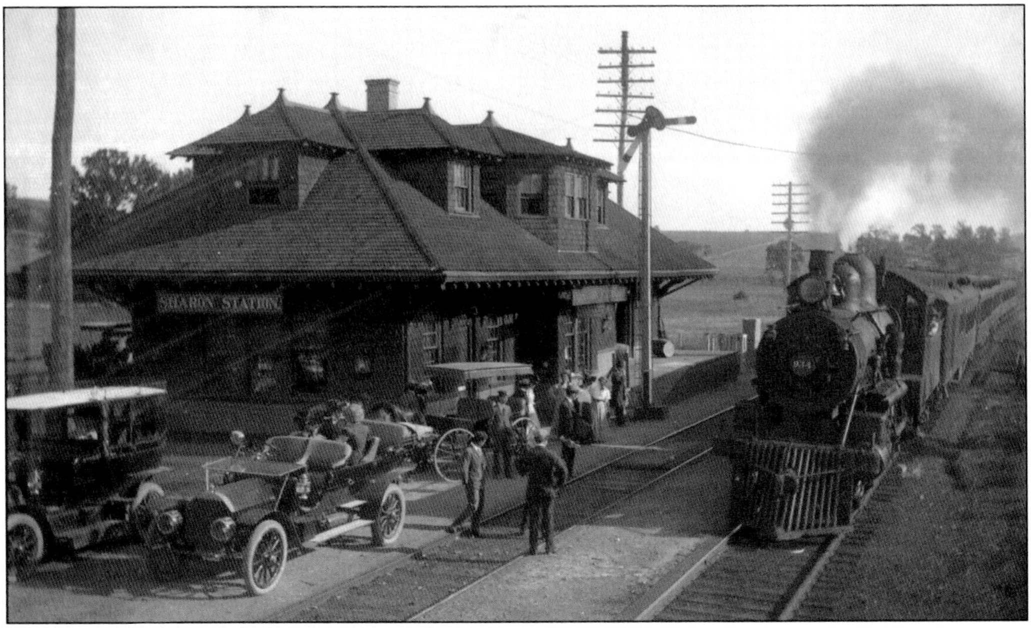

The new Sharon station, which is now a private home, is seen here. In the early 1920s, there was a fire in Pawling, New York, and the Sharon Fire Department put a truck on a train flatbed and sent it to Pawling to fight the fire. The truck was requested because it was the only motorized fire truck around. For those who do not know, the Sharon station is actually located in Sharon Station, New York. (Photograph by George M. Marckres.)

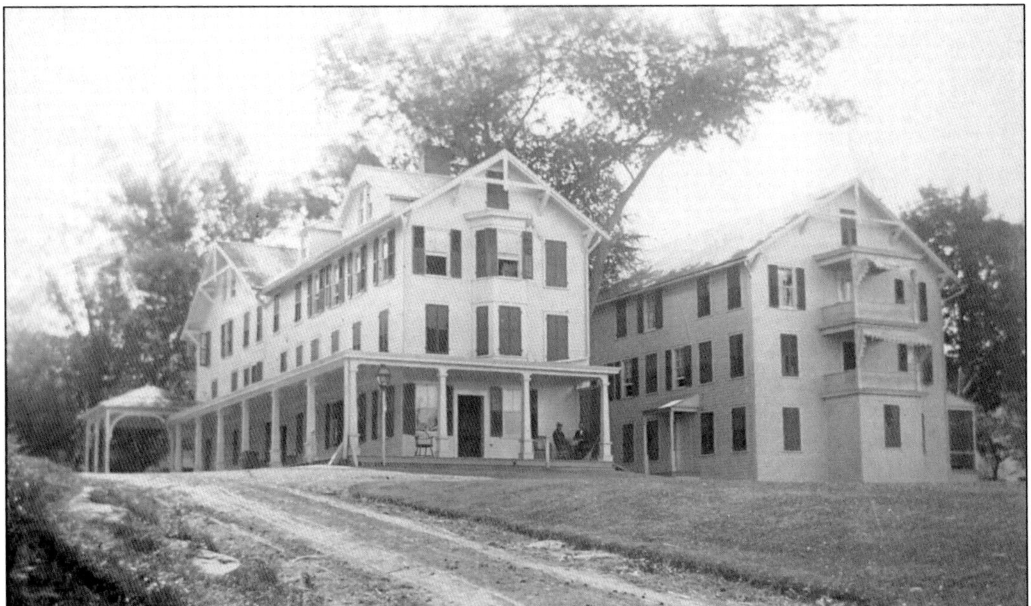

The Sharon Inn was the center of community life until it was torn down in 1954. It was located in what is now known as Memorial Park, on the southwest corner of the intersection of Main Street (Route 41) and Amenia Road (Route 343.) This photograph was taken after dormers were put on the rear addition but before the tearoom was added in 1920. Amenia Road, on the left, is unpaved.

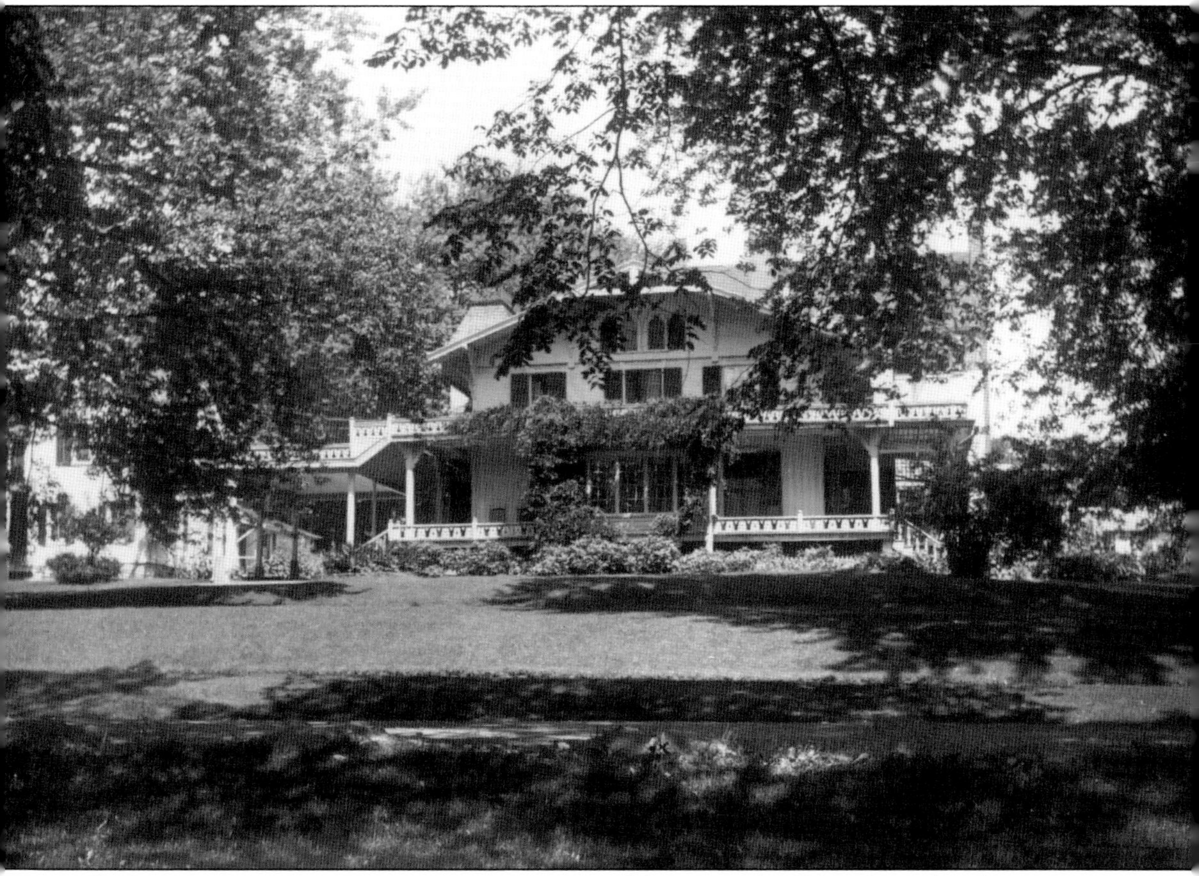

The Bartram Inn, at 79 Upper Main Street, was a well-known and well-loved travelers' destination. When Isaac Newton and Helen Bartram bought the place in 1879, it had already changed hands 14 times. Local lore suggests that when the Bartrams purchased the property, they had the house moved away from the road to its present position. As I.N. Bartram was a builder of notable ability, this story bears weight. By 1910, the house, by then named the Bartram Inn, was defined as a large dwelling or boardinghouse. It was known for its lovely gardens. This photograph was taken in 1918. (Photograph by George M. Marckres.)

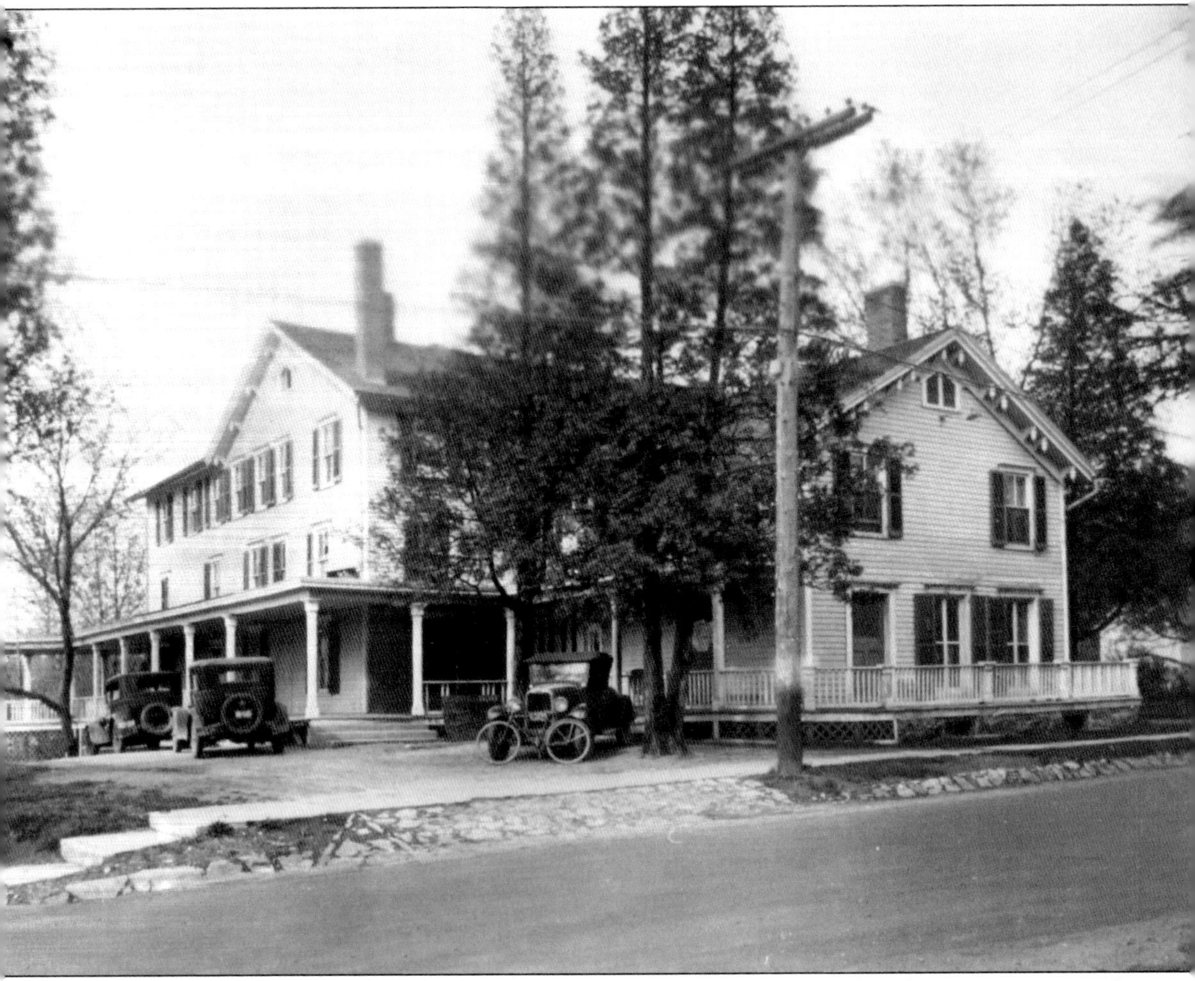

This lovely, sprawling building on West Main Street has been operated under many names and has had many owners. Before it was the Taghkanic Inn, it was originally a small tavern known as the Pleasant View House. Renovated in 1845, it was later expanded as the Kirby House and operated by Georgia Kirby, the niece of Solomon Kirby, proprietor of the Sharon Inn. After the Casino fire in 1925, the building was remodeled with a theater, the Sharon Playhouse, on the ground floor and apartments above. The theater was also used as a basketball court. The building was demolished in 1935 and is now the site of the Sharon Fire Department.

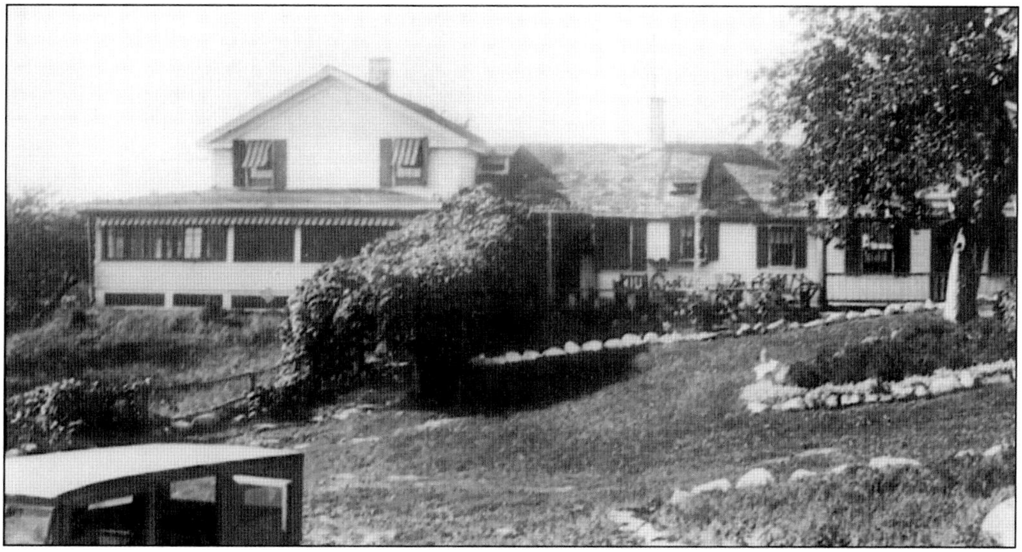

As the number of summer visitors to town increased, some Sharon residents vacated their Main Street homes and moved to nominally "finished" garages and carriage houses in their rear yards in order to rent their family residences to summer people. The sheer number of travelers to Sharon grew so that guest homes and inns were not only confined to the area surrounding the Green. Hilltop Lodge, also known as Weber's Rest, pictured here, was located off of Weber Road in Amenia Union.

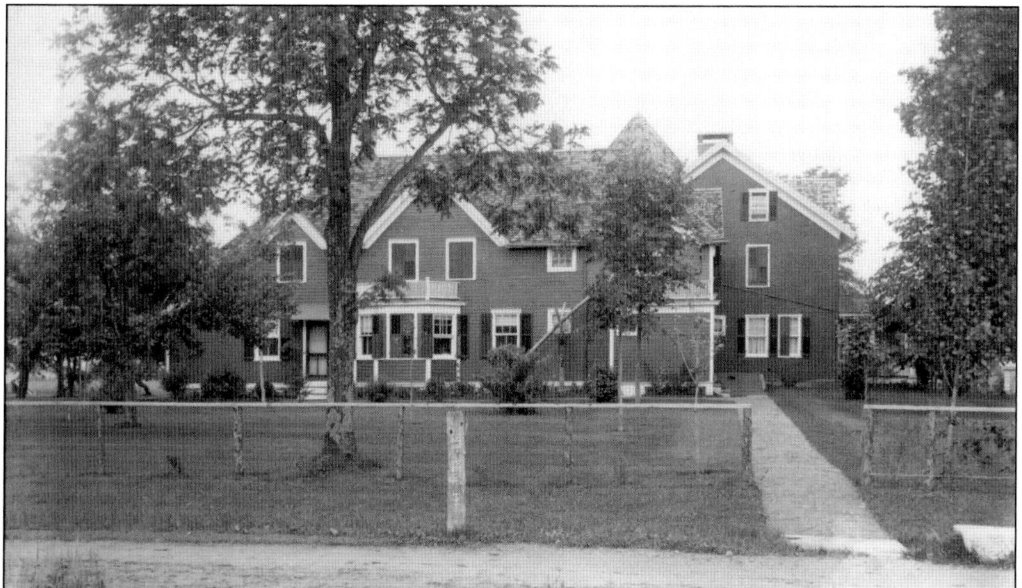

Operated around the turn of the 20th century as the Latches, yet another guesthouse, at 3 West Woods Road No. 1, is historically known as the Appollos Smith House. Located at the southwestern corner of Amenia Union Road and West Woods Road No. 1, the house commands a view of South Main Street stretching north, as well as panoramic views of the Dutchess County hills. This photograph was probably taken after the extensive renovations done by the Schleys, who bought it in 1927. This view is from West Woods Road No. 1; the main house, which still stands today, is to the right.

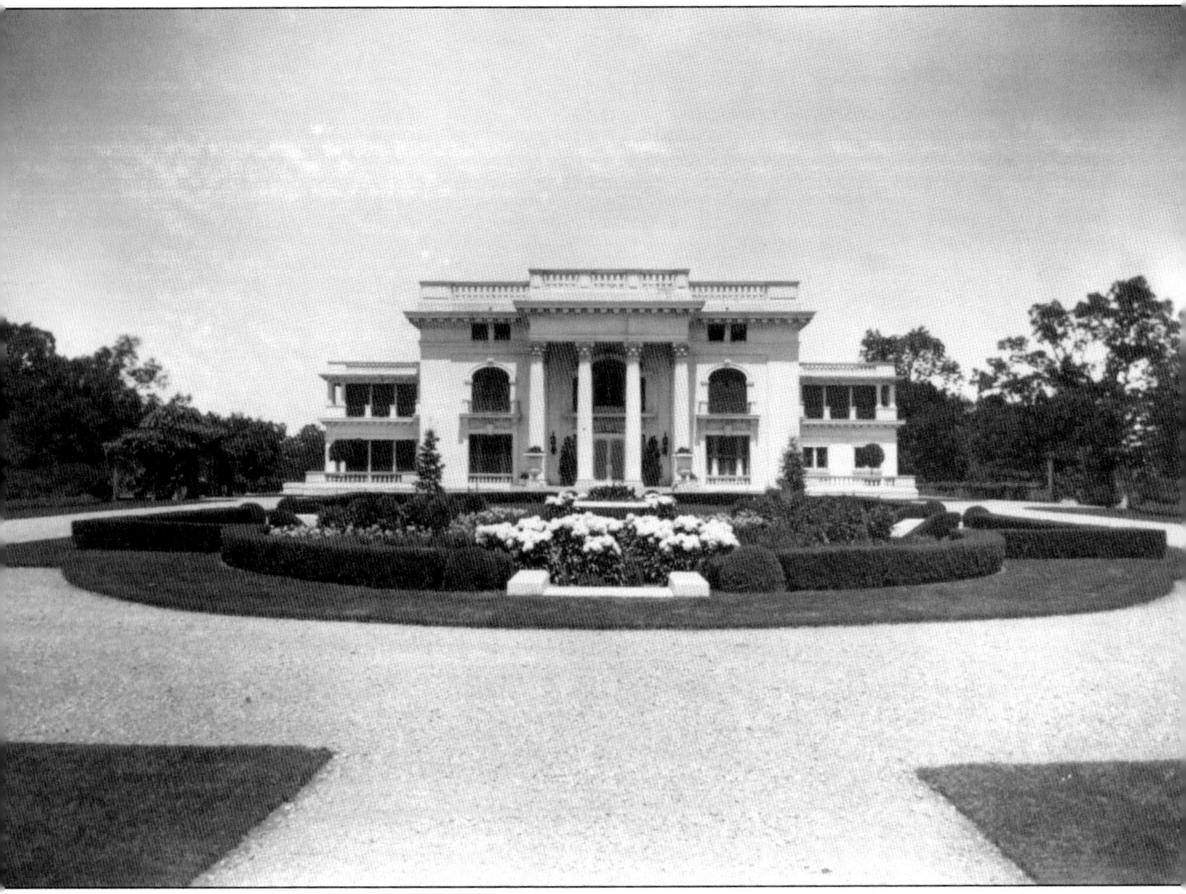

Filston is an old Sharon estate, also known as the Colgate Mansion and, more recently, Music Mansion. It was built by Romulus Riggs "R.R." Colgate, the grandson of William Colgate, founder of the soap and perfume empire, between 1903 and 1906. The mansion is an excellent example of neoclassical architecture and is a sister to the Hiddenhurst Mansion, just across the state line. Filston's gardens included formal, symmetrical plantings as well as naturalized landscapes. (Photograph by George M. Marckres.)

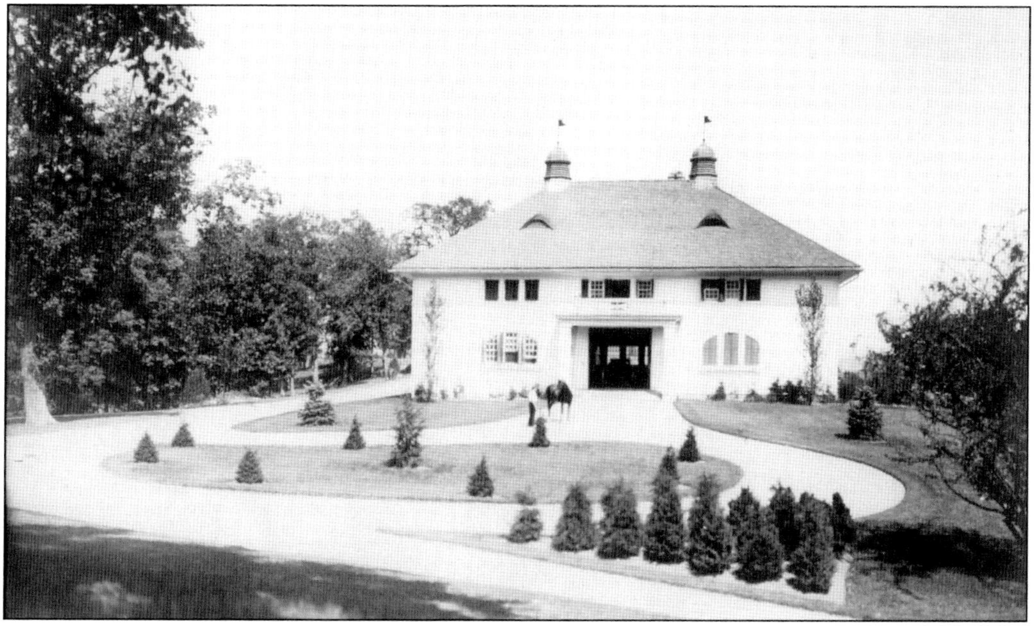

This is the carriage house for the Filston Estate. Outside the mansion, the grounds contained forestland, a hemlock grove, 34 acres of manicured lawn, several servant homes, and this three-story carriage house with four stalls, two box stalls, a tack room, a large carriage space, and six bedrooms on the second floor.

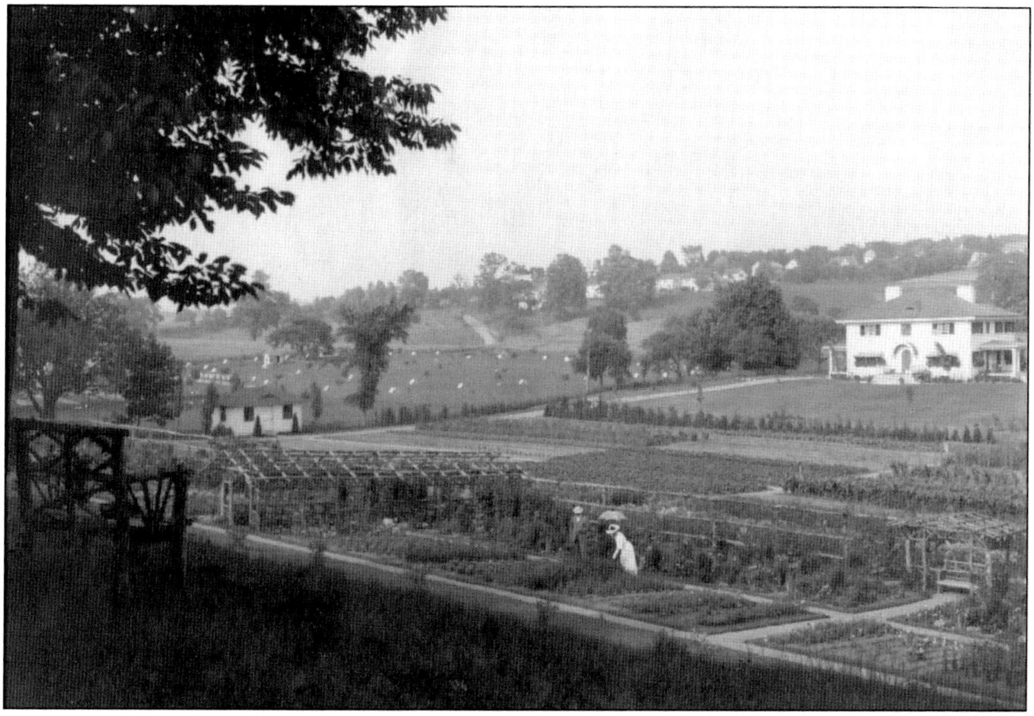

The house in the background of this photograph was home to R.R. Colgate's chauffeur. It is now a private dwelling at 130 Amenia Road. This view looks to the west and shows the Colgates in their extensive parterres. The house was later owned by Judge Thomas Murphy.

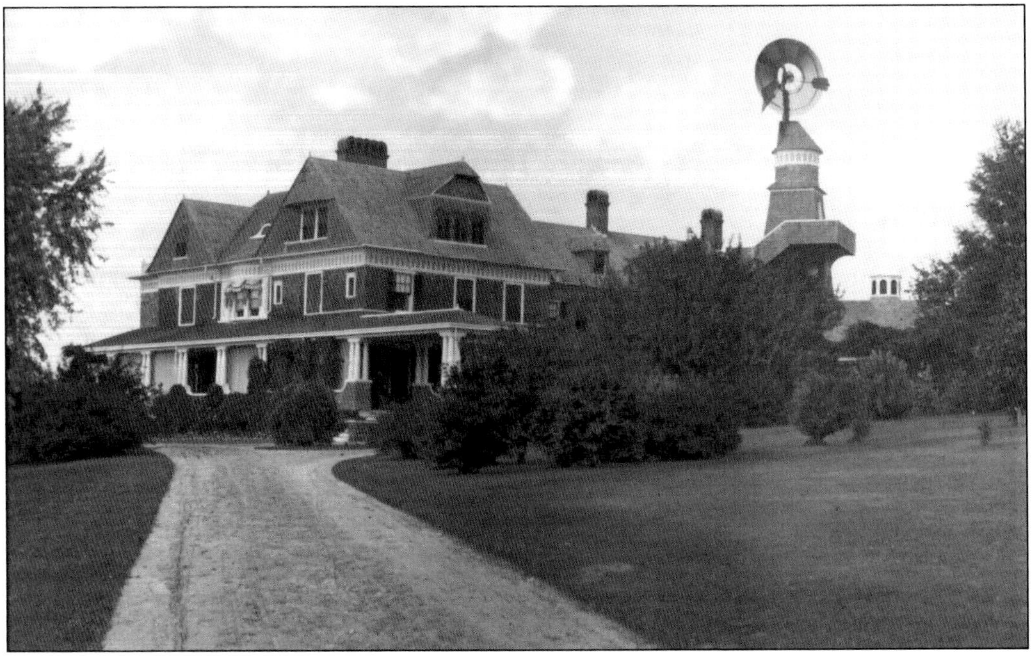

This extensive gentleman's farmhouse on Low Road was built by Edwin Cornell Jameson, one of the country's leading insurance men and a principal in the senatorial investigation of the 1928 political activities of Bishop James Cannon Jr. His estate was inherited by his son Edwin "Ted" C. Jameson Jr., a World War II pilot and an avid collector of antique automobiles and, most especially, antique fire engines. Jameson and his family supported and continue to play an active role in many town improvement projects. The large windmill was used to pump water for the property. The estate was sold to renowned artist Jasper Johns in 1994.

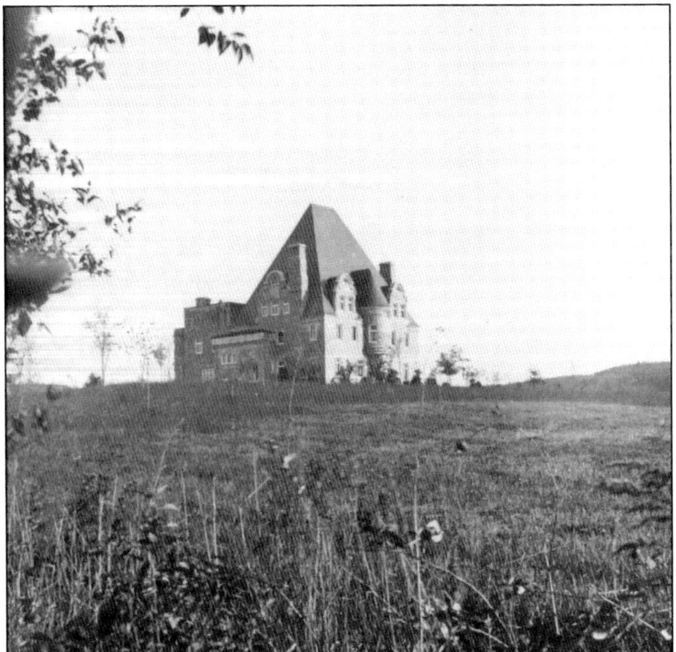

Located at the end of Lilac Lane, Perkins Castle, also known as Perkins Folly, was built by Albert Perkins shortly after 1861. Local gossip said that Perkins made his money smuggling during the Civil War. He was going to build a French chateau, but he ran out of money, and it was never finished. The building was torn down in 1920 when the property was purchased by Harold Hatch. Some of the stone was used to build the dam for Hatch Pond.

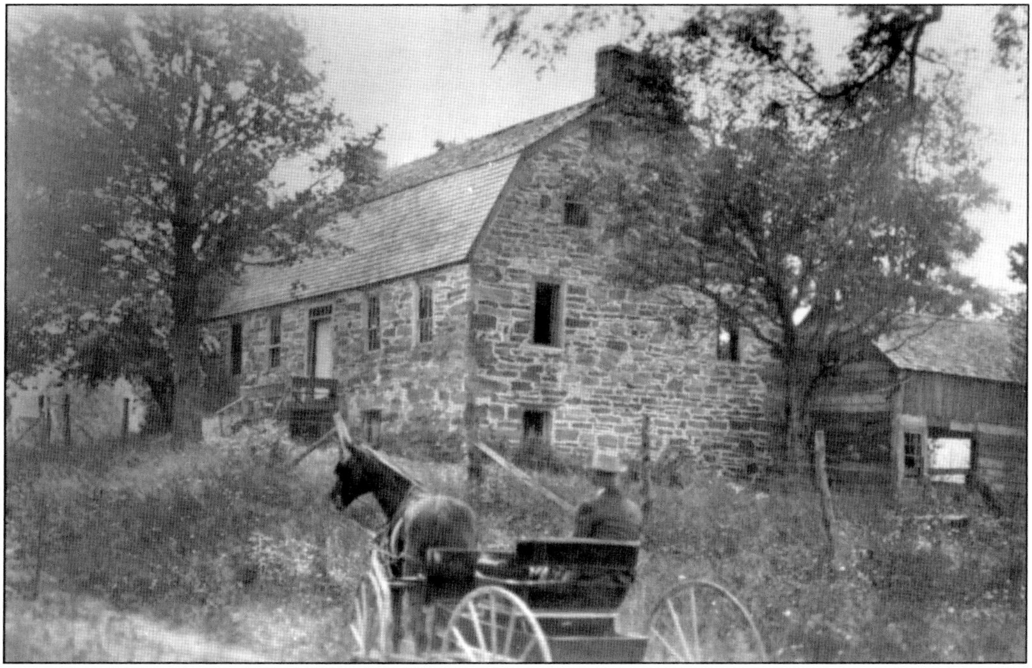

This charming photograph shows what is known as the Stone House, located at 15 Stone House Road, on the north border of Sharon and Salisbury, just off of Route 41. The derelict-looking home was probably built by John Gay Jr. around 1796. However, a set of initials, "M.C." or "M.G.," and a date, "1765," carved in the west gable call all written records into question. The house was owned by Leonard Twinem, a local historian and collector, after 1928. Perhaps one day, new records will be unearthed and this mystery will be solved. (Photograph by George M. Marckres.)

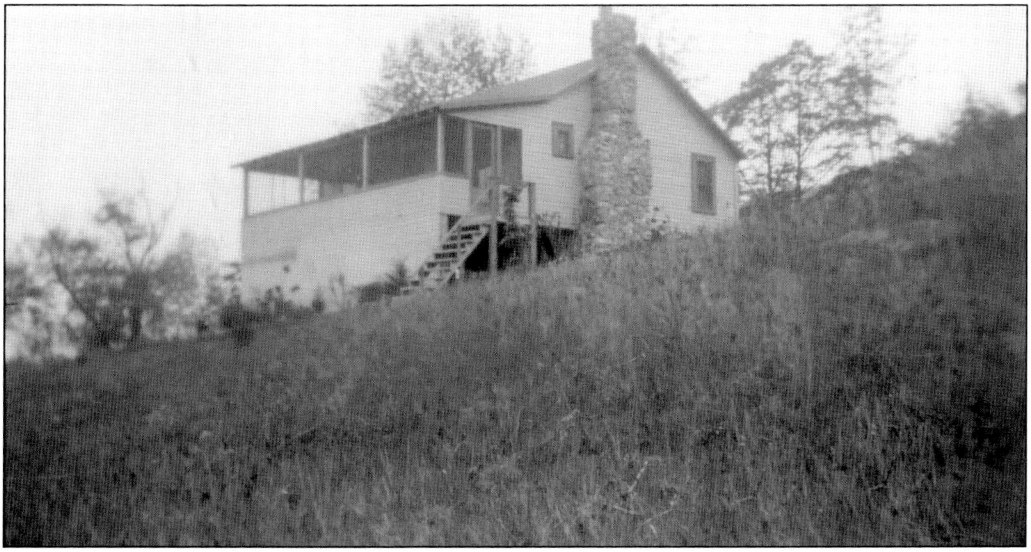

One of the lesser-known facts about Sharon is that some full-time Sharon residents had summer retreats outside of town, especially along Mudge Pond. Al Jenkins's second home, on Minneluta Trail, at the top of the hill overlooking Mudge Pond, was built by one of the Tuncy brothers. Next door was the summer home of Adolph Anderson, the caretaker for the Herrick estate. (Courtesy of Sally Jenkins.)

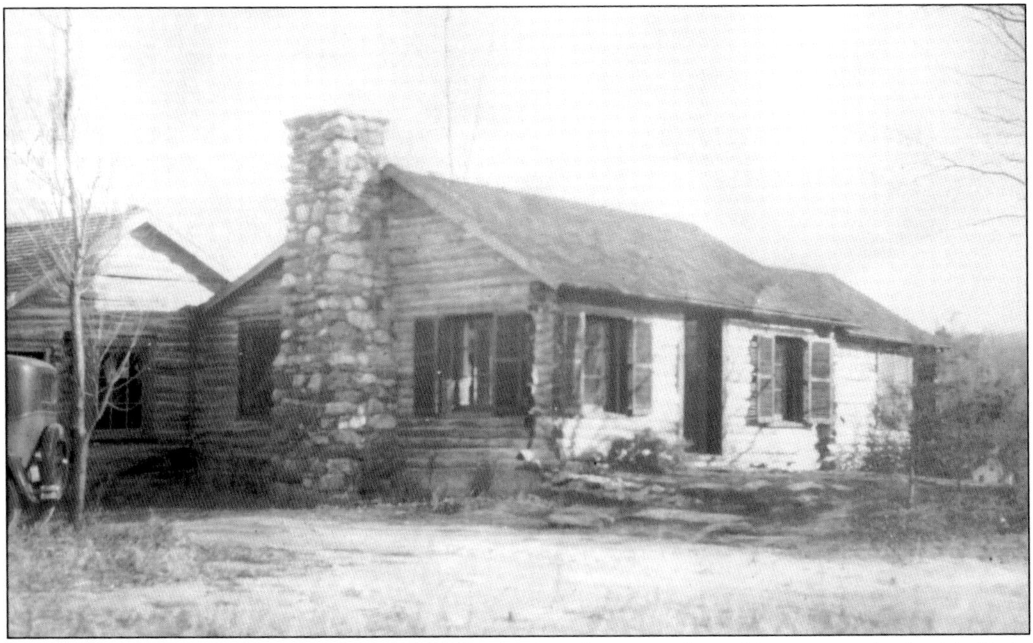

Dr. William Herrick, along with Adolph Anderson, the caretaker of his estate, built this little cabin retreat several hundred yards behind the main house on Herrick Road. (Courtesy of William Trowbridge.)

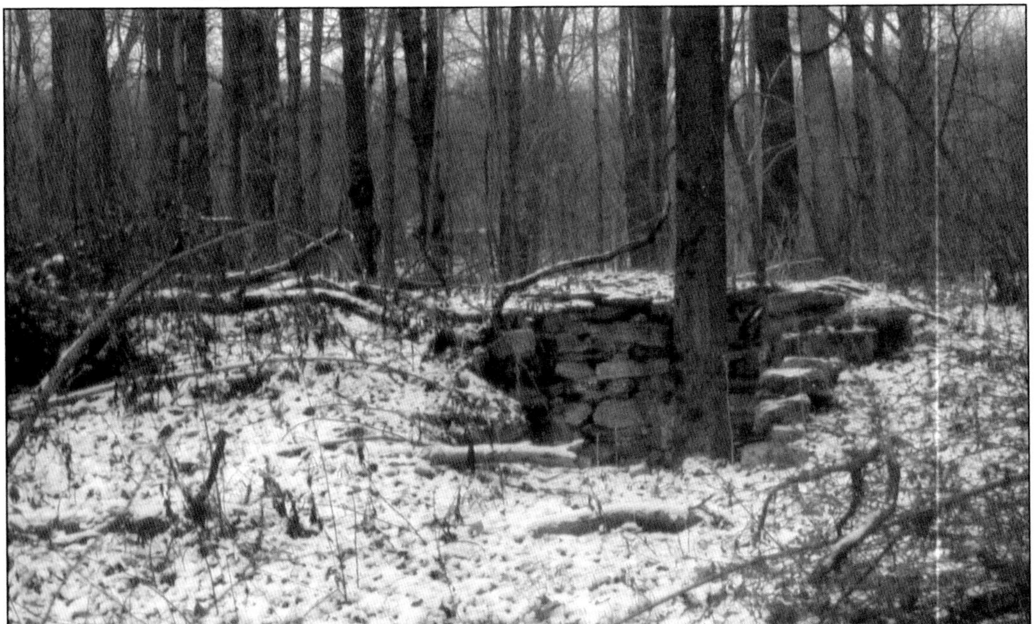

Even bad guys need a place to escape from the trials and tribulations of everyday life, and gangster Jim "Legs" Diamond was no exception. Prohibition made a folk hero of the New York City gangster, who made Sharon his secret hideaway when the city grew too hot. Sharon old-timers recount tales of the dapper Diamond, who took the train to Cornwall Bridge, bagged some food at Charlie Breen's store, and "legged" it to a hideout off of Old Sharon Road 4. This is the foundation of the chimney ruin of Diamond's hideout. (Courtesy of Harvey Hayden.)

Eight

Coming Together in Peace and in War

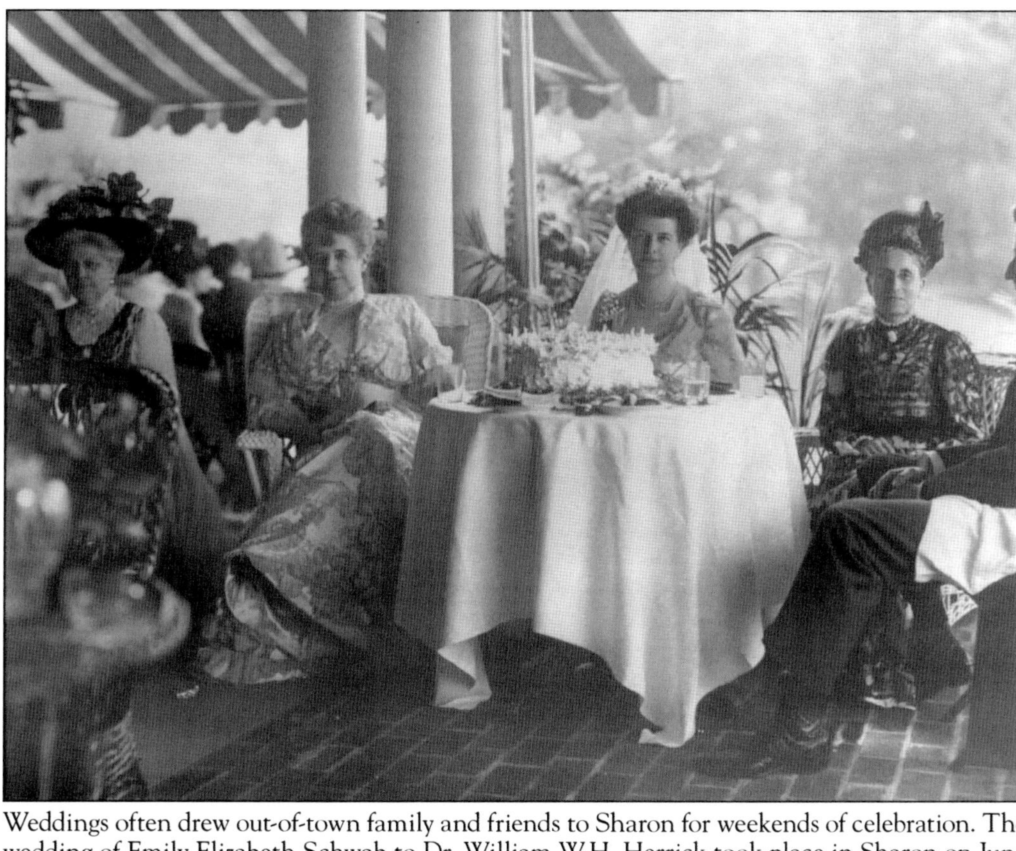

Weddings often drew out-of-town family and friends to Sharon for weekends of celebration. The wedding of Emily Elizabeth Schwab to Dr. William W.H. Herrick took place in Sharon on June 15, 1910. From left to right are an unidentified woman, Caroline Wheeler Schwab (the bride's mother), Emily Schwab, Pamela Goodrich Herrick (the groom's mother), and Dr. William Herrick. (Courtesy of Nancy Trowbridge.)

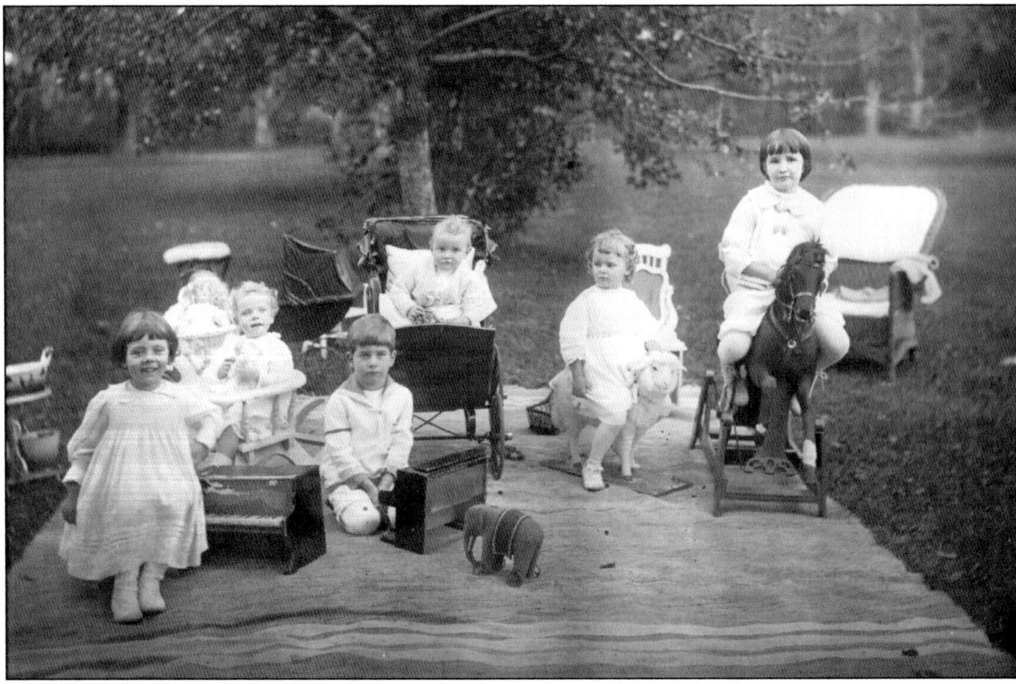

A more delightful child's birthday party can hardly be imagined than this one held in 1915 at Boscobel, the Herrick estate on Herrick Road. From left to right are Grace Mullins, Charlotte Mullins, Billy Herrick, Gustav Schwab, Caroline Schwab, and Helen Coley. (Courtesy of William Trowbridge.)

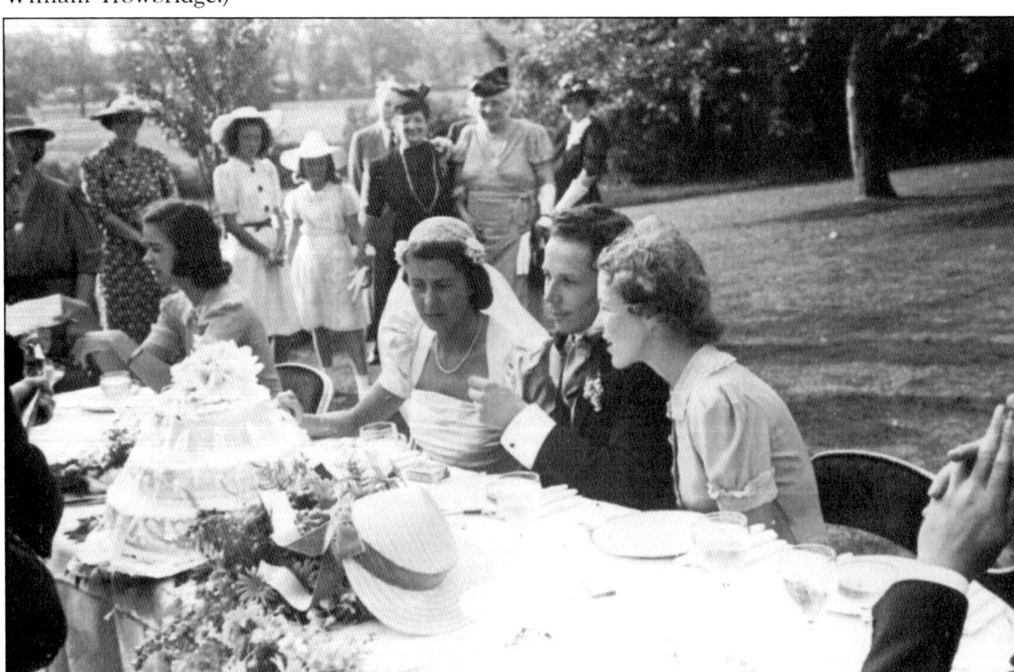

Another joyful celebration at Boscobel was the 1938 wedding of Eunice Herrick and Thomas Trowbridge. (Courtesy of Nancy Trowbridge.)

In the middle of the 20th century, Sharon was a very social place. Weekly parties and get-togethers were popular events, bringing together many members of the community. In this c. 1935 photograph, Meredith Gillette and William Riley Jr. are seen as Popeye and Olive Oyl. (Courtesy of Tom Riley.)

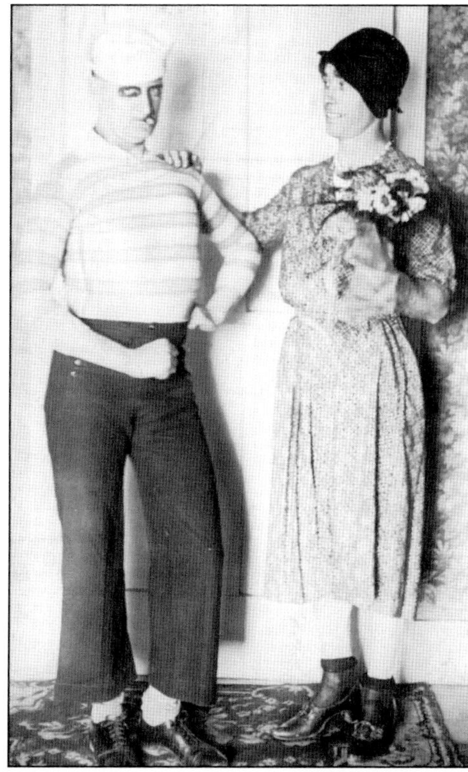

Al Jenkins's store was draped in bunting in 1939 to celebrate Sharon's 200th birthday, an occasion marked by town residents with concerts, parades, and a pageant. The Jenkins Store was previously known as E.F. Gillette & Son, until the Klebes Store relocated to the site from Sharon Valley in 1918. Al Jenkins married the boss's daughter, Bea, and they continued the business as the Jenkins Store. (Courtesy of Sally Jenkins.)

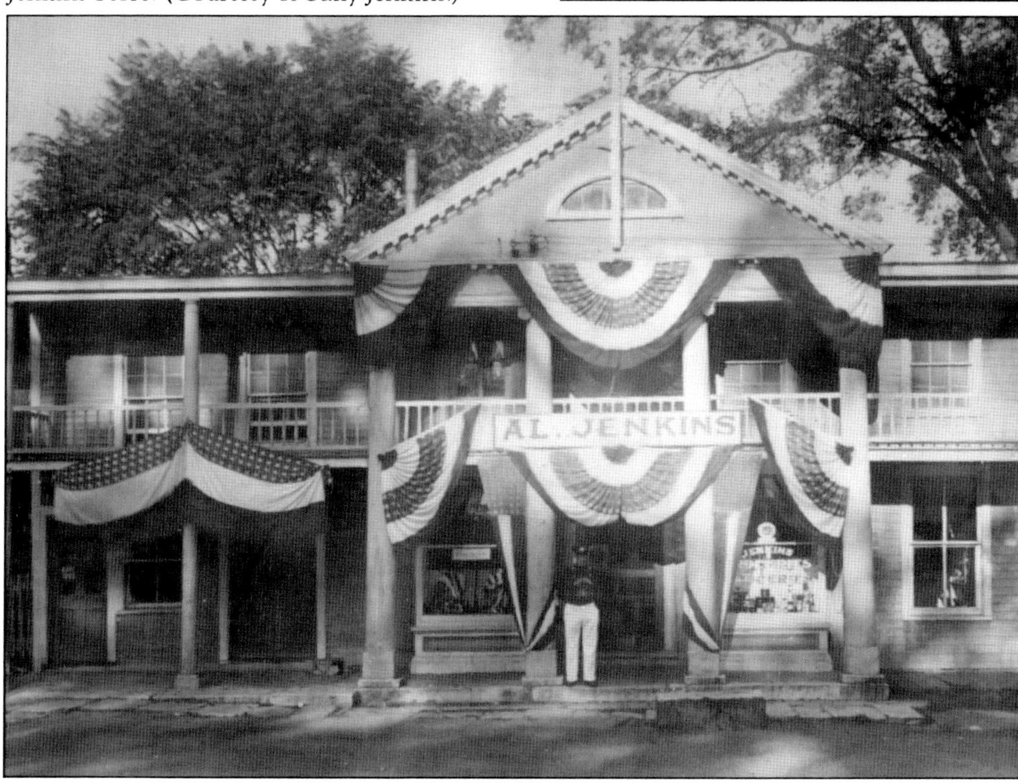

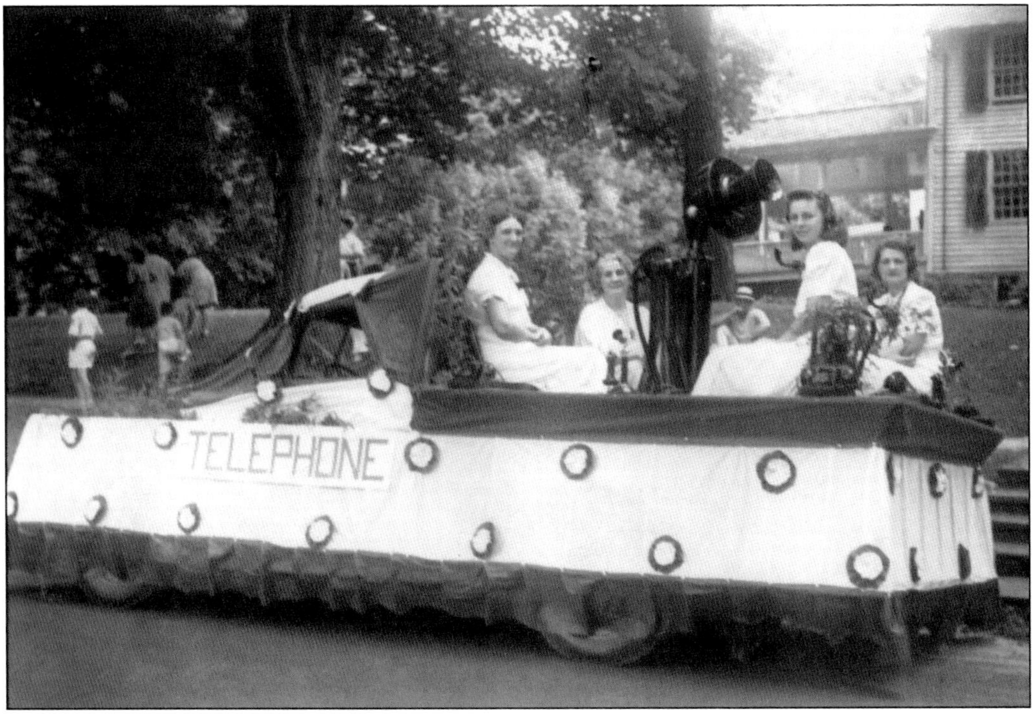

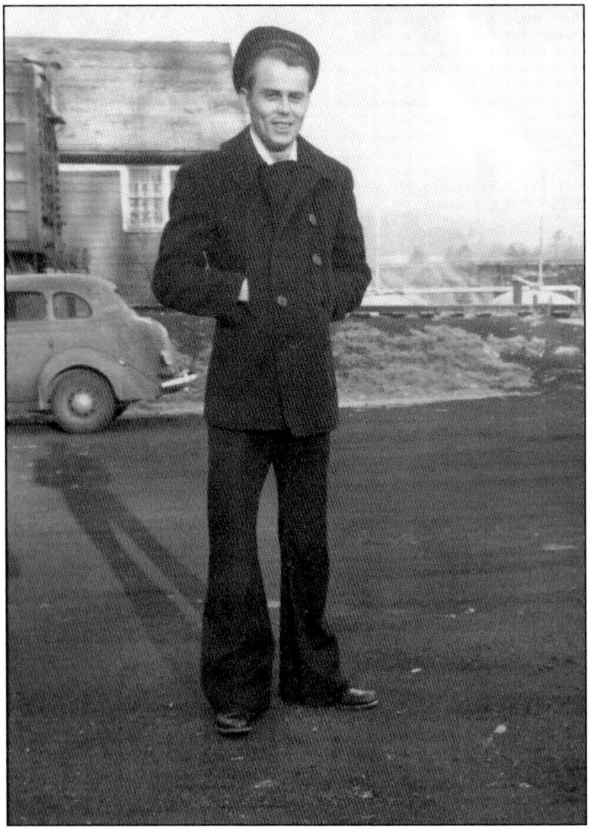

This Sharon Telephone Company float is lined up on Upper Main Street, waiting to parade down Main Street at the celebration of Sharon's 200th birthday in 1939. From left to right are Grace Klebes, Mabel Hotaling, Ruth Carley, and an unidentified woman. (Courtesy of Barbara Bartram.)

Reidar Holst-Grubbe, shown here in his naval uniform, piloted a Landing Ship Tank (LST) on D-Day. The LST is the military designation for naval vessels created during World War II to support amphibious operations by carrying significant quantities of vehicles, cargo, and landing troops directly onto an unimproved shore. Sharon was indeed fortunate to welcome Holst-Grubbe home after the war's end. (Courtesy of American Legion Post 126.)

Sharon did its proud duty during World War II, sending 247 men and welcoming 242 home. Pictured here on March 22, 1944, are, from left to right, Peder Aakjar, Welsey White (Sharon Center School principal), Pete St. Martin (Sharon barber), unidentified, and Melvin Peterson. Sharon residents who were killed during service included Lester Handelvich, Thomas C. Hart Jr., Joseph Kaminski, Robert B. Liner, and Donald A. Riley. (Courtesy of Jayne Larsen.)

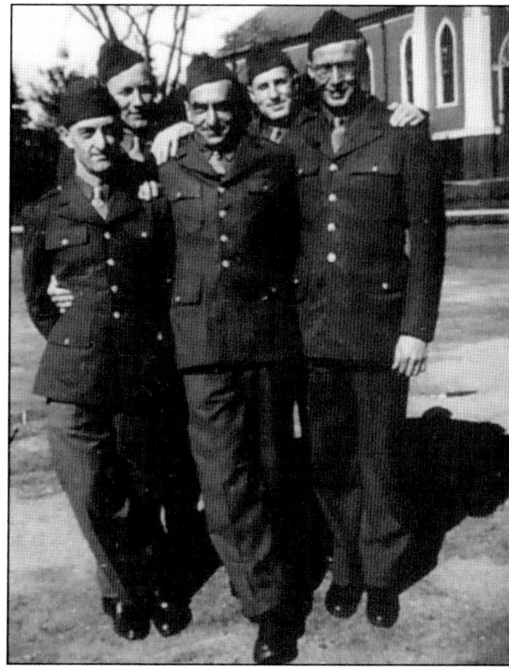

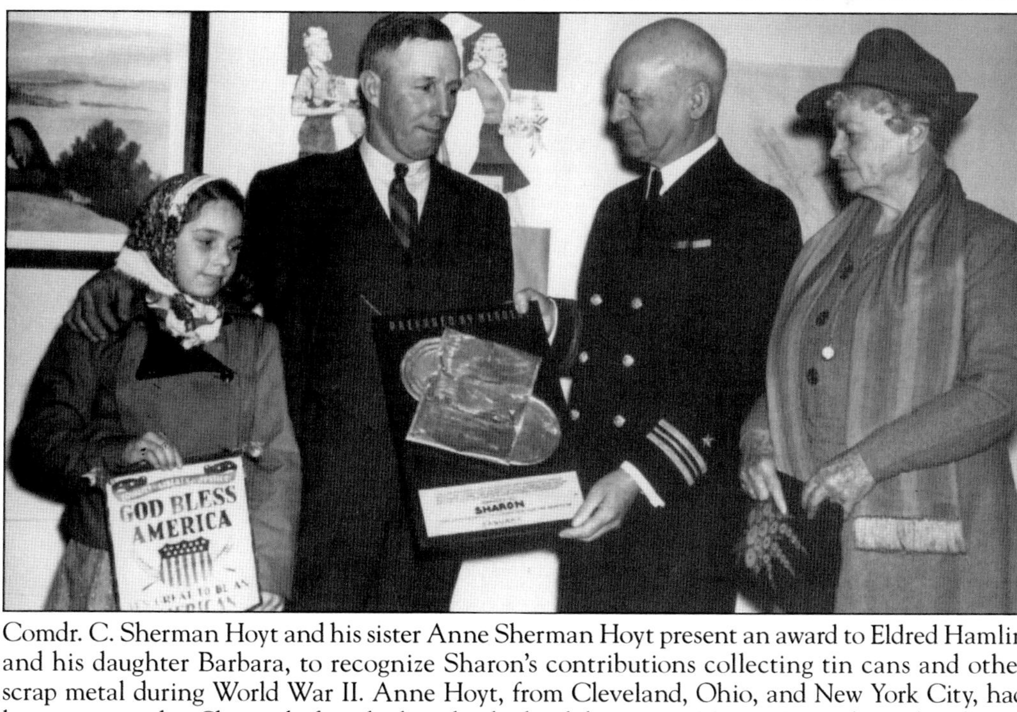

Comdr. C. Sherman Hoyt and his sister Anne Sherman Hoyt present an award to Eldred Hamlin and his daughter Barbara, to recognize Sharon's contributions collecting tin cans and other scrap metal during World War II. Anne Hoyt, from Cleveland, Ohio, and New York City, had long summered in Sharon before she bought the brick house at 18 Main Street (now the Sharon Historical Society). Though not a native, her ancestors were from Connecticut, and she felt at home here, entering into many phases of civic life in Sharon as a devoted and respected citizen. She served as president of the Sharon Historical Society from 1939 to 1948. She also served with the American Red Cross during World War I at several American bases overseas. Commander Hoyt was an ardent sailor who competed multiple times in the America's Cup.

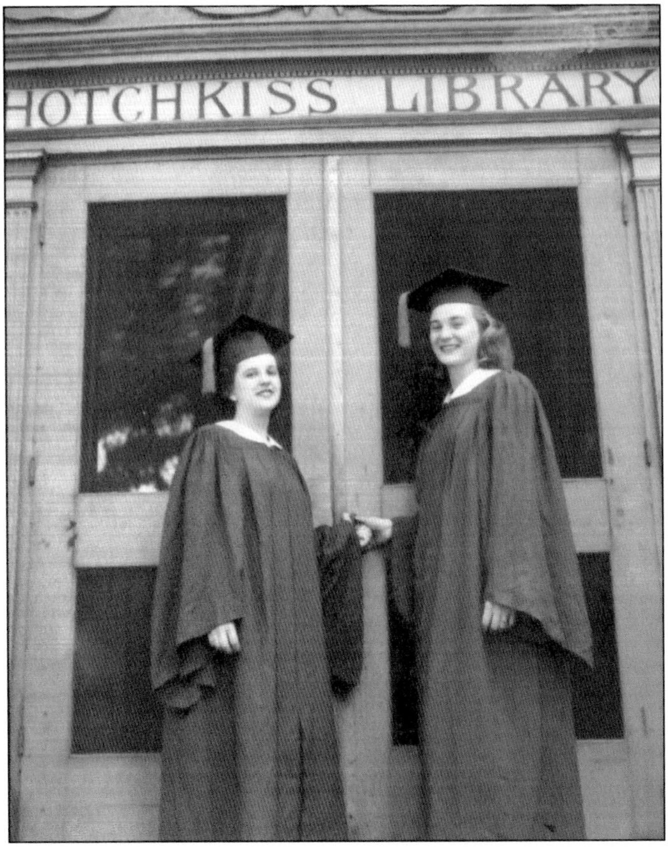

Two 1946 Housatonic Valley Regional High School graduates pose on the steps of the Hotchkiss Library. Lois "Sugar" Middlebrook Kain is on the left, while Adele Middlebrook Casey is on the right. (Courtesy of Thomas Casey.)

Guests arrive at the Congregational church for a celebration to honor 50-year members of the congregation, about 1970. Morris Paley, a farmer by vocation and a collector of vintage autos by avocation, plays chauffeur. Evelyn Hamlin sits in the car. Standing from left to right are Dorothy Hotaling, Nina Bartram, Clara Lamb, and Rev. Alan Johnson. (Photograph by Key Prindle; courtesy of Mary Lamb.)

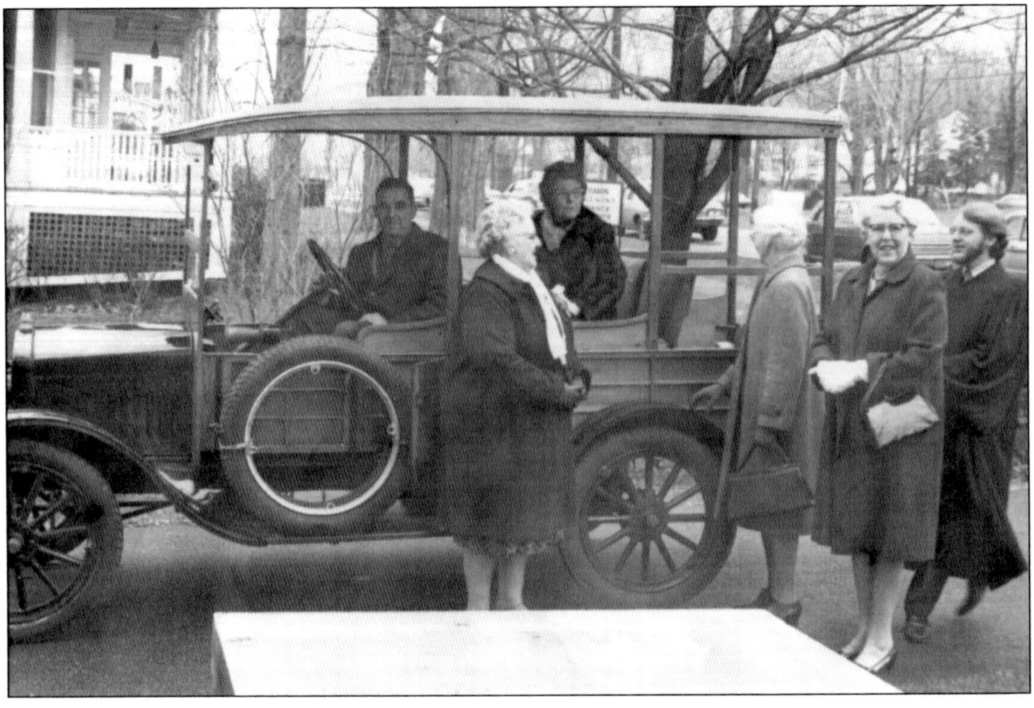

This wedding portrait of Margaret and Kenneth Bartram was taken in June 1946. Margaret emigrated from Country Roscommon, Ireland, in 1939 and was employed in the Jameson household. Kenneth's family had been in Sharon for generations, and he worked in the estate's greenhouse. They met when Kenneth followed Margaret home after mass at St. Bernard's, all the way up Cemetery Hill, to introduce himself. (Courtesy of Tom Bartram.)

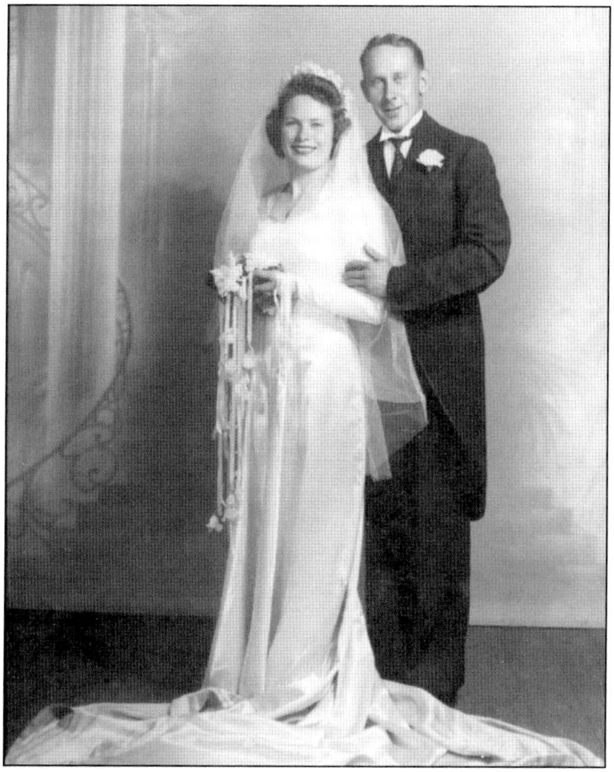

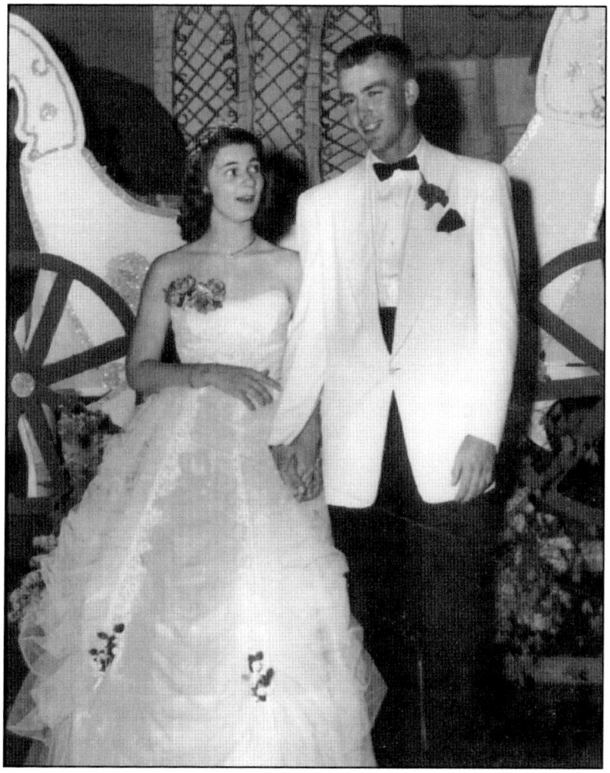

There are few Americans who cannot conjure up a memory or image from their prom night. Shown here are Mary Pitcher, junior prom queen, and Pete Lamb, a star athlete, in 1955. (Courtesy of Mary Lamb.)

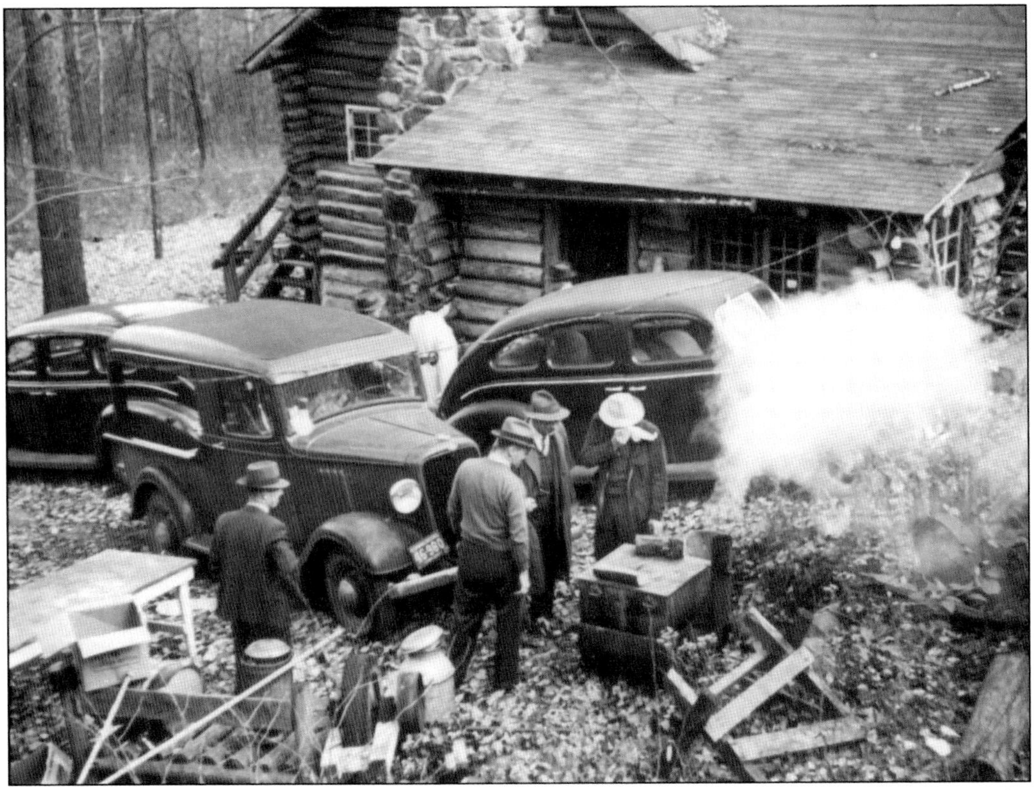

The most frequent guess as to the subject of this image is that moonshine is being cooked in the Sharon backwoods. Actually, the subject is far more benign. Folks are gathered for a clambake put on yearly by Del Middlebrook on West Woods Road. Pictured from left to right are Eldred Hamlin, Dan O'Connell, Abe Martin, and Del Middlebrook. (Courtesy of Del Prindle.)

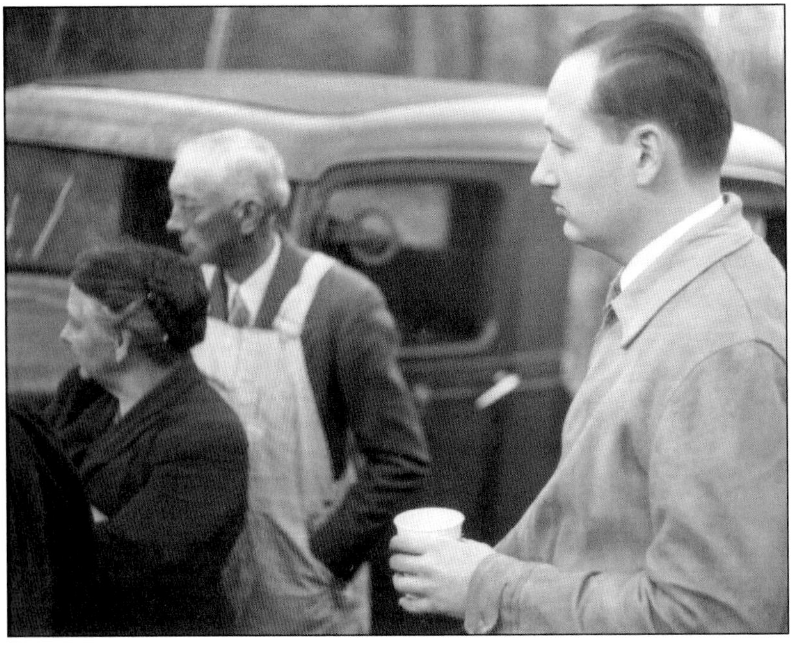

Attendants at the clambake included residents from all facets of life in Sharon. From left to right are Agnes Cherniske, a past president of the Sharon Historical Society; Lance Middlebrook, a storekeeper; and Gaert Gudernatch, a physician. (Courtesy of Del Prindle.)

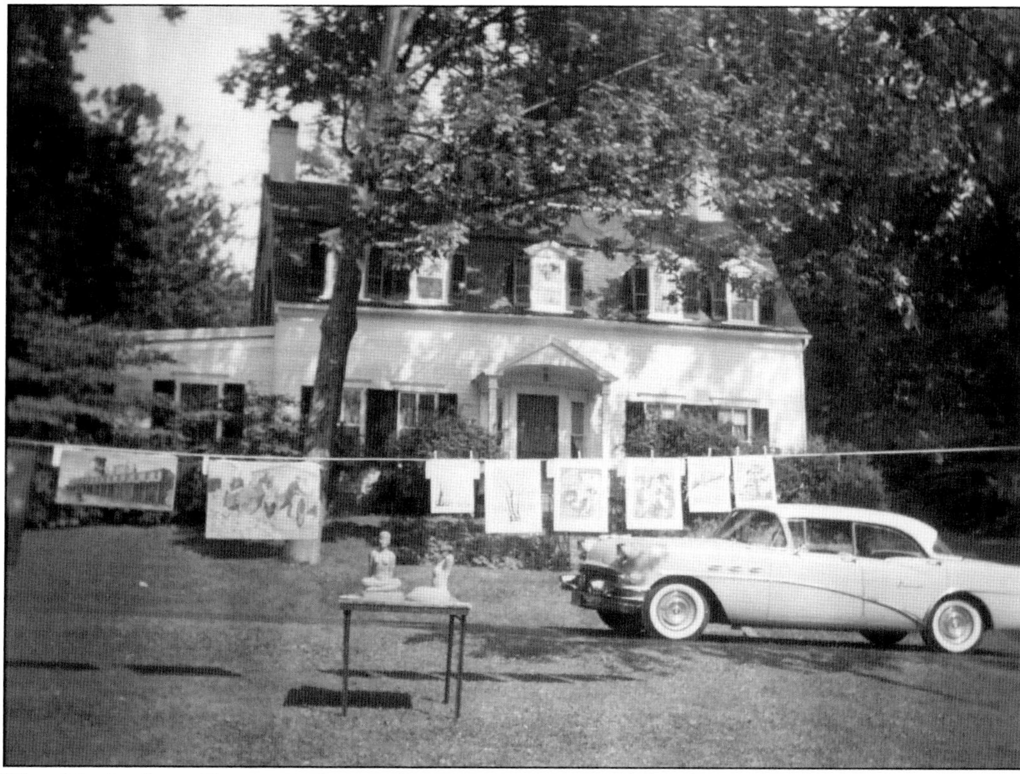

The Clothesline Show on Sharon Green was an annual fundraiser for the Sharon Creative Arts Foundation (SCAF). Artists were invited to come and literally hang their art for sale on a clothesline that circled the Green. This image, taken on the Green in front of 62 Upper Main Street in the early 1950s, gives a good sense of the show's logistics. This series of annual events was so ingrained in the memory of the community that the current arts and crafts show held on the Green in August is still referred to as the Clothesline Show.

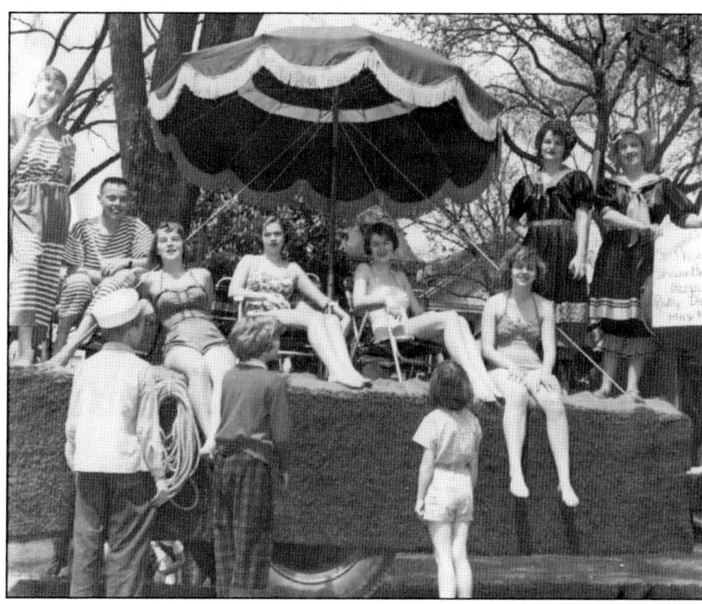

It is always more fun to raise money with a parade, and when a parade float is dotted with women in bathing suits, that is a sure winner. This picture was taken on Rally Day for the Sharon Beach project, around 1952–1953. The Sharon Woman's Club was one of the organizers of this event. From left to right are Dan O'Connell, Jimmy Gobillot, two unidentified women, Mary Beth Lamb, unidentified, Betty Mehmel, and Maria Reep. The younger children in front are unidentified.

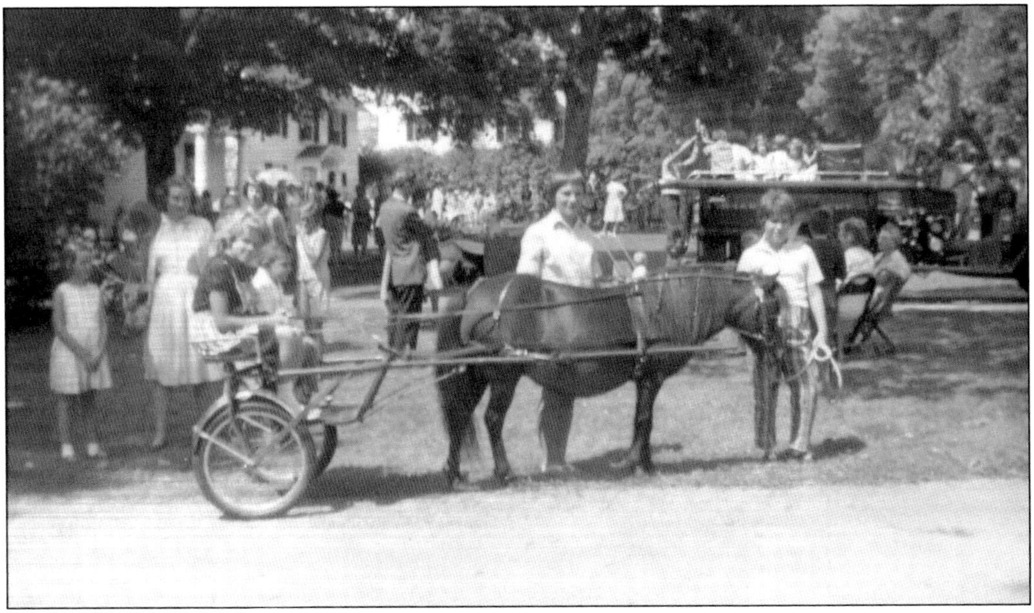

The community's churches had their fair share of celebrations and festivals. This photograph of Susan Pruyn (behind the pony) and Mimi Morgan (with the halter) leading the pony cart was taken at the Christ Church Episcopal Festival held in August 1961.

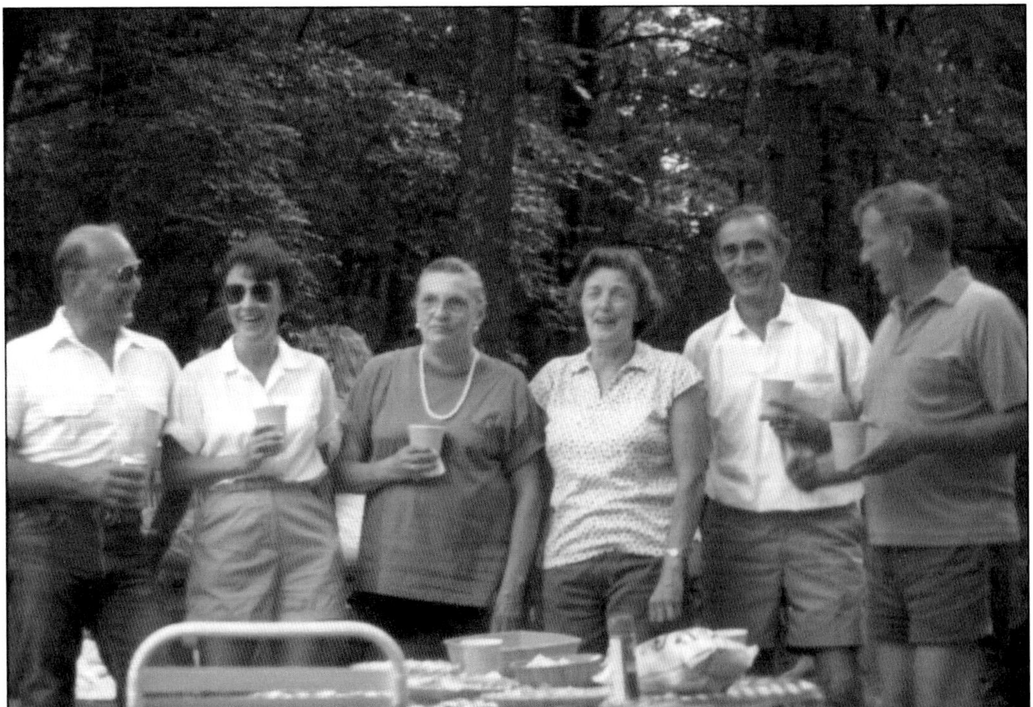

Images of public and private celebrations show that people in Sharon knew how to have fun. Pictured from left to right at this picnic at the Hansell home, at 26 Amenia Union Road, are Ed Wilbur, Joan Wilbur, Helen Riley, Jean Hansell, Larry Riley, and Rusty Hansell. (Courtesy of Jean Hansell.)

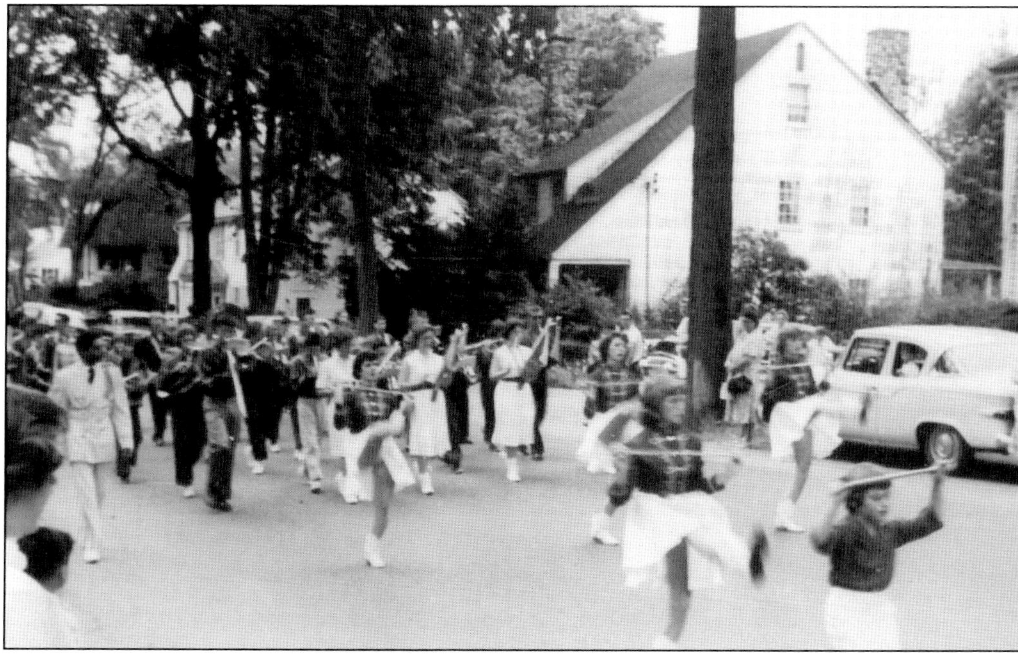

The Sharon Center School marching band has marched and played in Sharon's parades for many decades and is still alive and well. Here, the band is in full regalia marching at a firemen's parade in the late 1960s. Phil Garavoy, the music teacher at the school, is on the left in the white suit. (Courtesy of Kit Garavoy.)

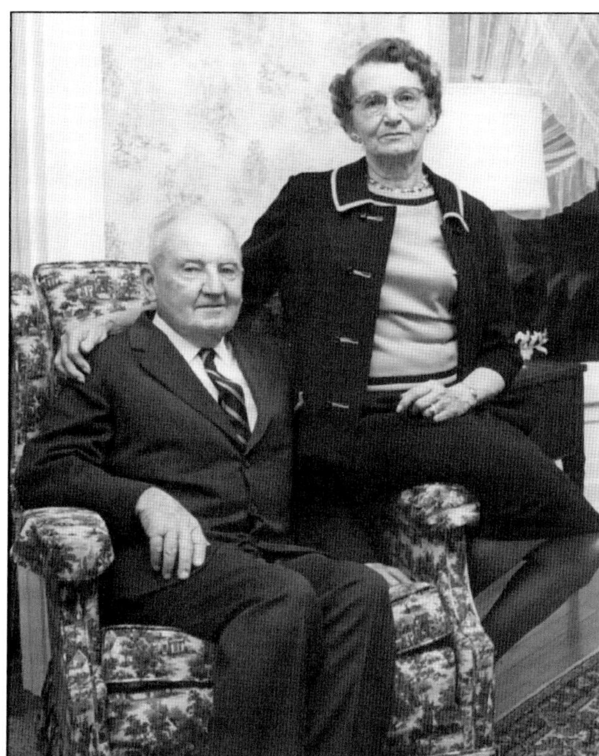

Many families in town were kin to the Carberry family. The Carberrys held many important jobs in town, including the care of the Green's elm trees. In 1965, Joseph Vincent Carberry and Elena Clum Carberry posed for this formal portrait to mark their 50th anniversary. They had 13 children. (Courtesy of Emma Paley.)

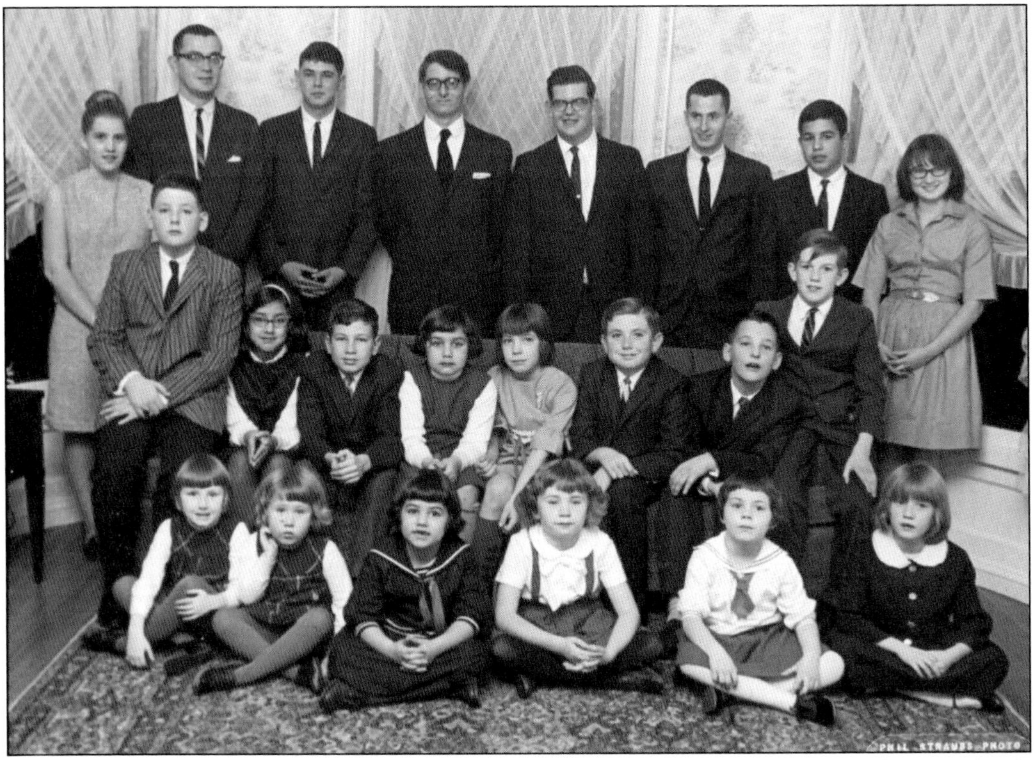

Having 13 children means a whole lot of grandchildren. Many of the men, women, boys, and girls in this photograph continue to live and work in the area, as do their children. This image of the Carberry grandchildren was taken at Joseph and Elena's 50th anniversary party in 1965. From left to right are (first row) Mary Catherine Maillet, Theresa Carberry, Susan Paley Kent, two young Carberry cousins from Poughkeepsie, and Virginia Carberry Casey; (second row) Richard Carberry, Elizabeth Paley Tong, Bob Carberry, Roberta Paley Scott, Debbie Carberry, Ron Carberry, Jimmy Carberry, and Peter Carberry; (third row) Pat Carberry, Tom Kendell, George Paley, Buddy Kline, Michael Carberry, Joe Frazier, Billy Paley, and Donna Carberry DiMartino. (Courtesy of Emma Paley.)

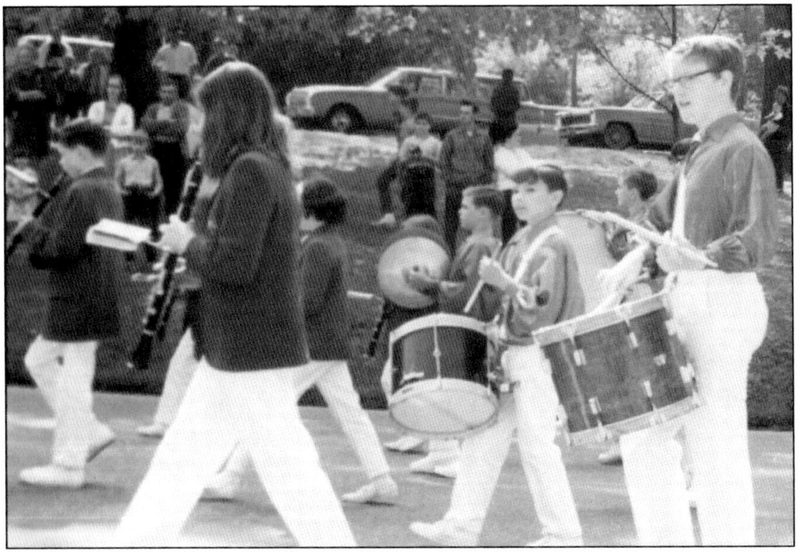

Future selectman Tom Bartram plays the drum in the right foreground of this image of Sharon's Memorial Day parade in 1968. (Courtesy of Barbara Bartram.)

Morris Paley never met a brush pile he did not want to burn. When Paley went to land use administrator Jamie Casey for a burn permit, Casey would always alert the fire department. Here, Paley and his grandson Sam Kent gather brush. (Courtesy of Emma Paley.)

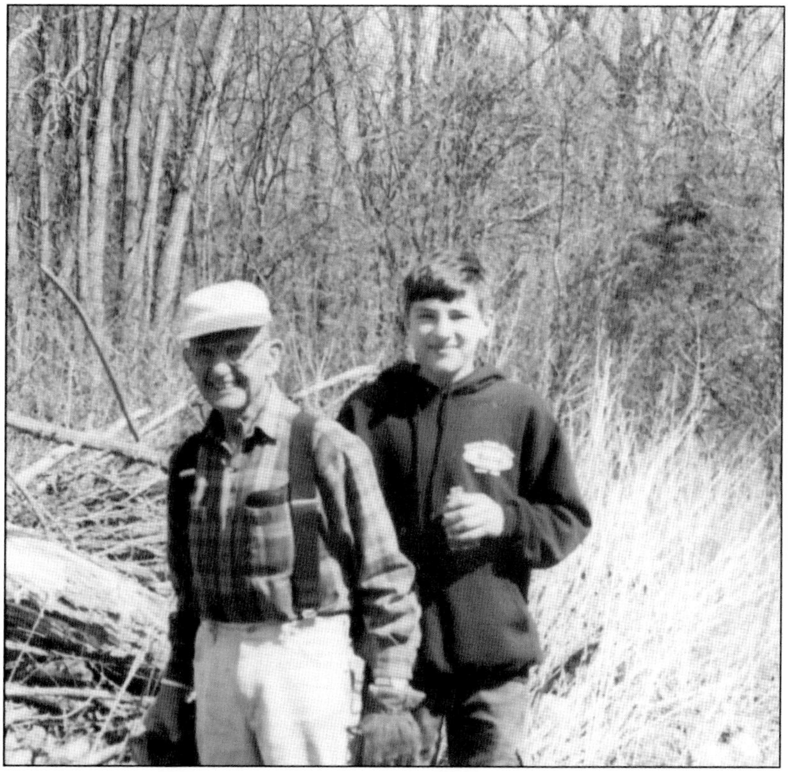

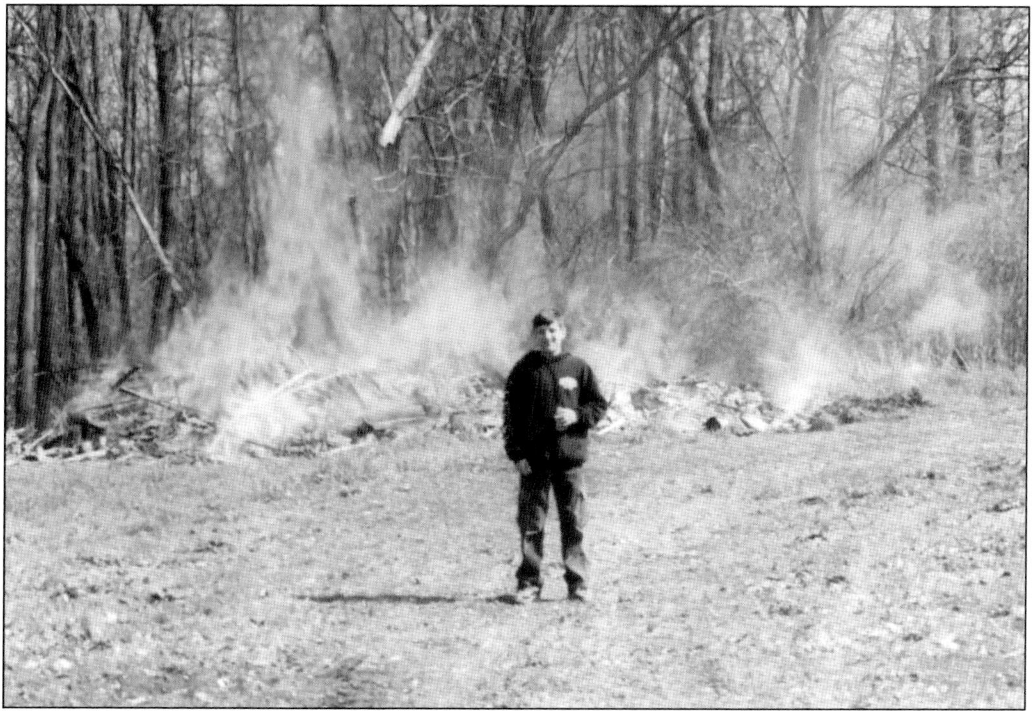

Sam Kent, Morris Paley's grandson, smiles in front of a smoldering pile of brush. Does the apple fall far from the tree? (Courtesy of Emma Paley.)

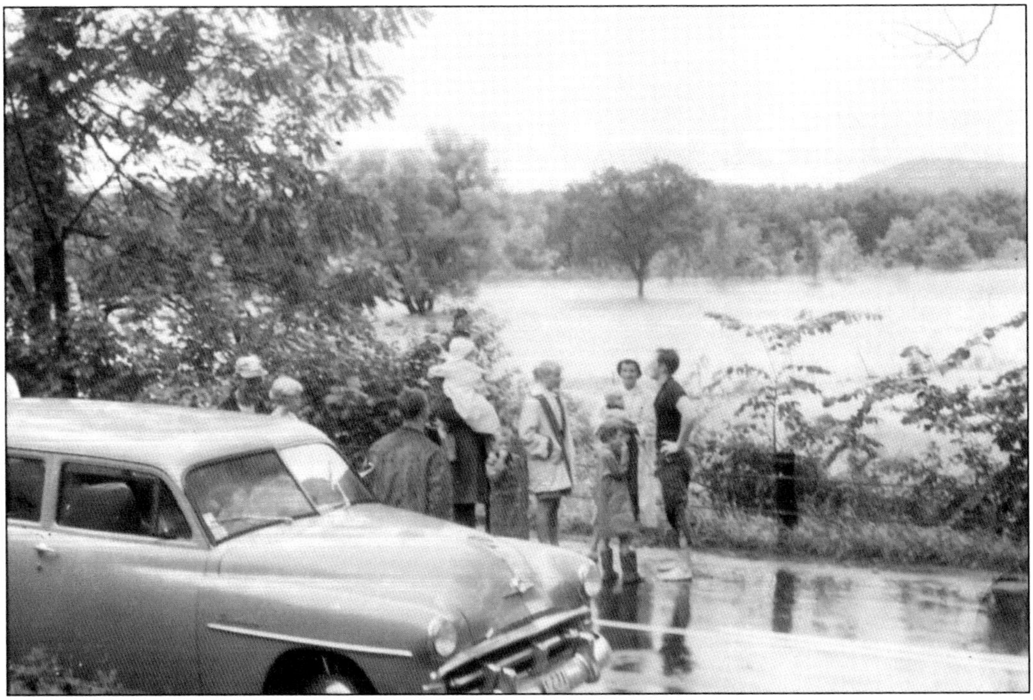

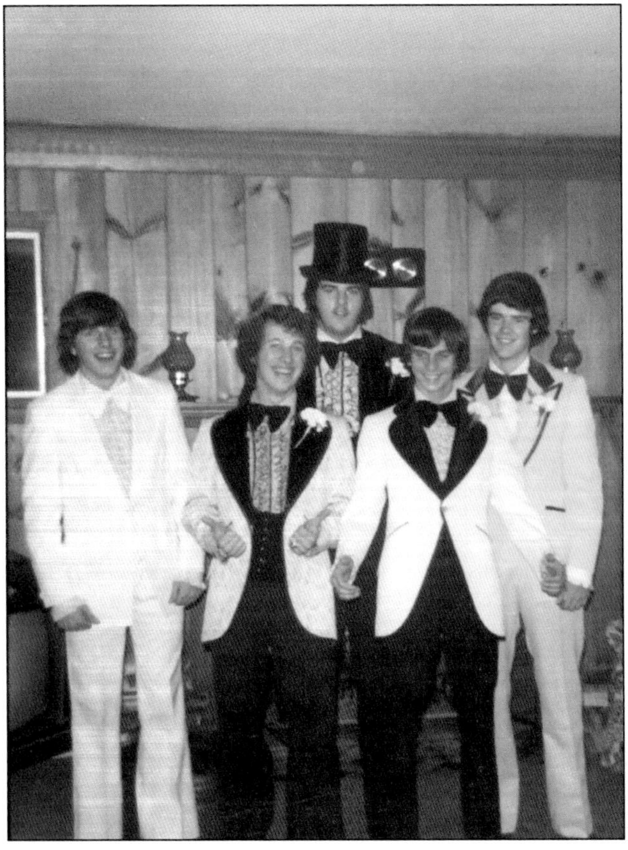

In August 1955, two back-to-back hurricanes saturated the land and several river valleys in the state, causing severe flooding that washed away bridges and buildings all along the Housatonic and Naugatuck Rivers. This photograph was taken on Millerton Road during the 1955 flood. The field beyond the road is submerged, and the bridge just beyond the car was washed away. (Courtesy of Barbara Bartram.)

Boys just want to have fun! These boys are celebrating prom night at Housatonic Valley Regional High School in 1976. They are, from left to right, K.C. Baird; Brian Carlson, sporting a thumbs-up sign like the famous "Fonz"; Don Lamb, sporting the family Masonic top hat; Rick Carley; and Brian Kenny. Don Lamb is the son of Sharon prom queen Mary (Pitcher) Lamb and Pete Lamb, pictured earlier. (Courtesy of Mary Lamb.)

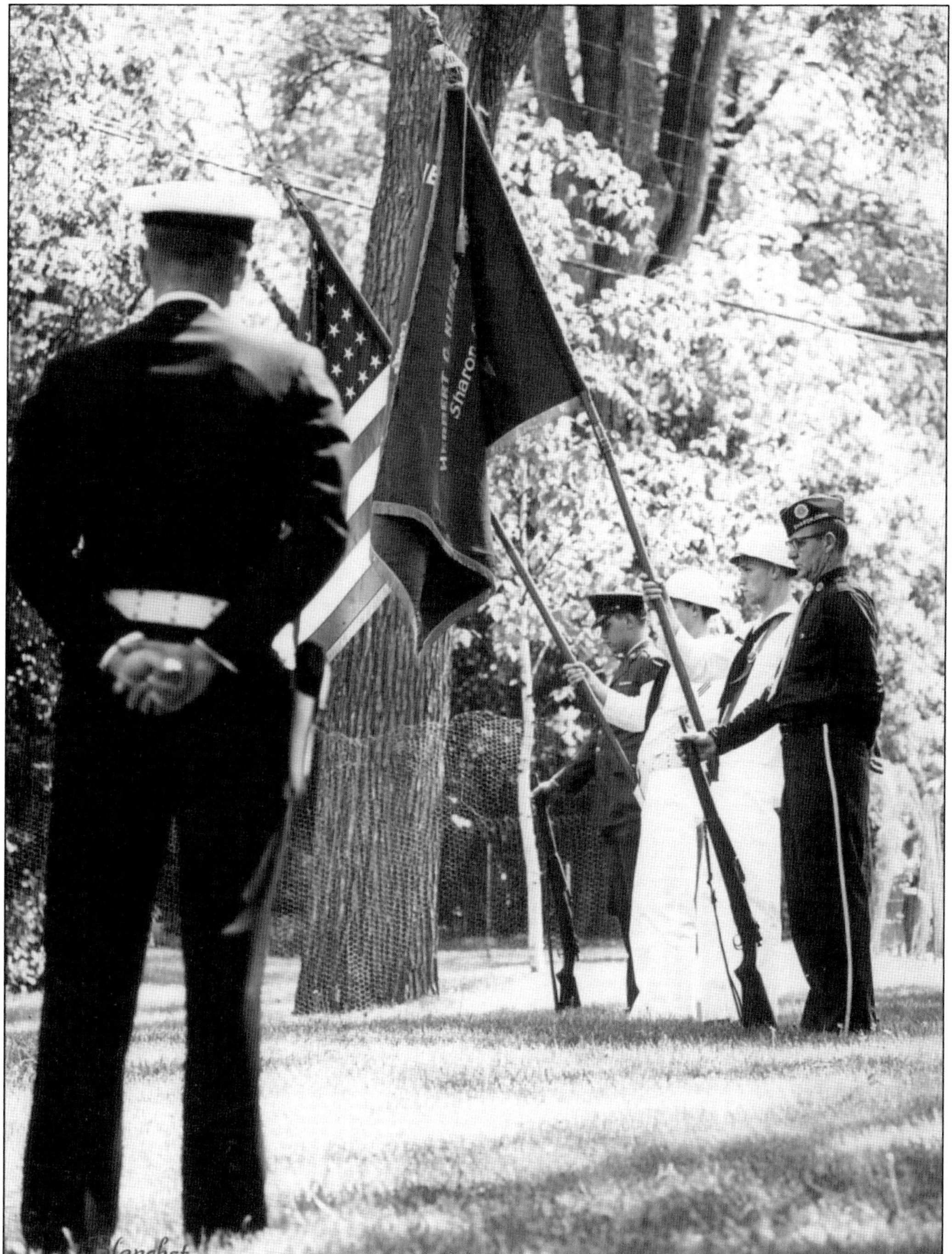

This yearly moment of both solemnity and celebration for town residents was held at the Memorial Day dedication ceremony at Veteran's Memorial Park in the 1980s. (Courtesy of American Legion Post 126.)

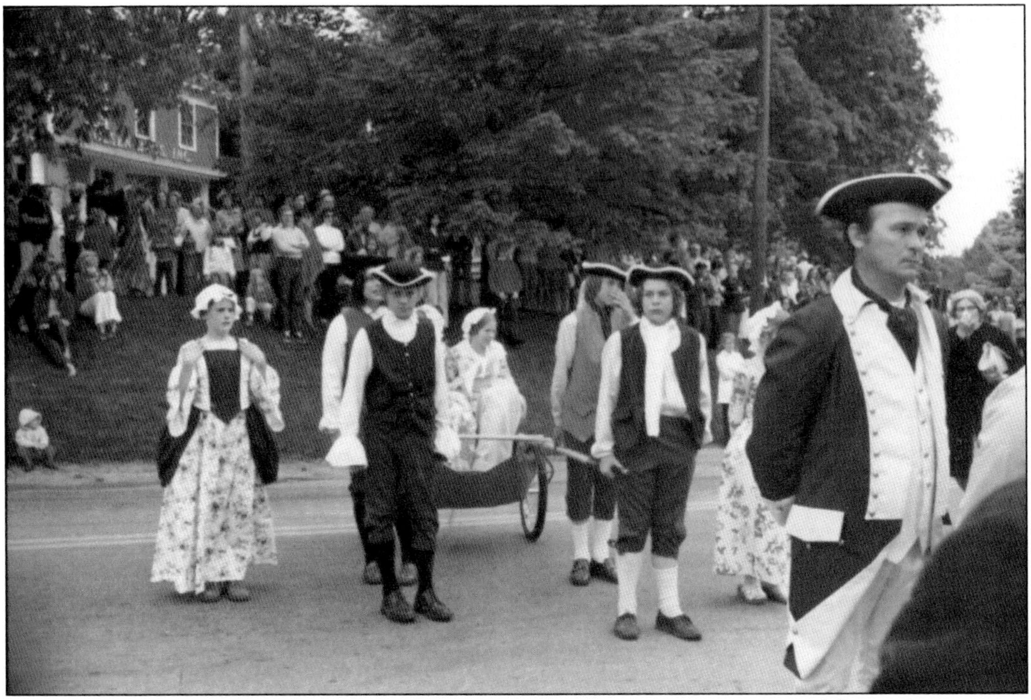

Townspeople gather in costume in front of the Sharon Soldier's Monument to celebrate the country's bicentennial in 1976. Fritz Cahill is in the right foreground. (Courtesy of Maureen Cahill.)

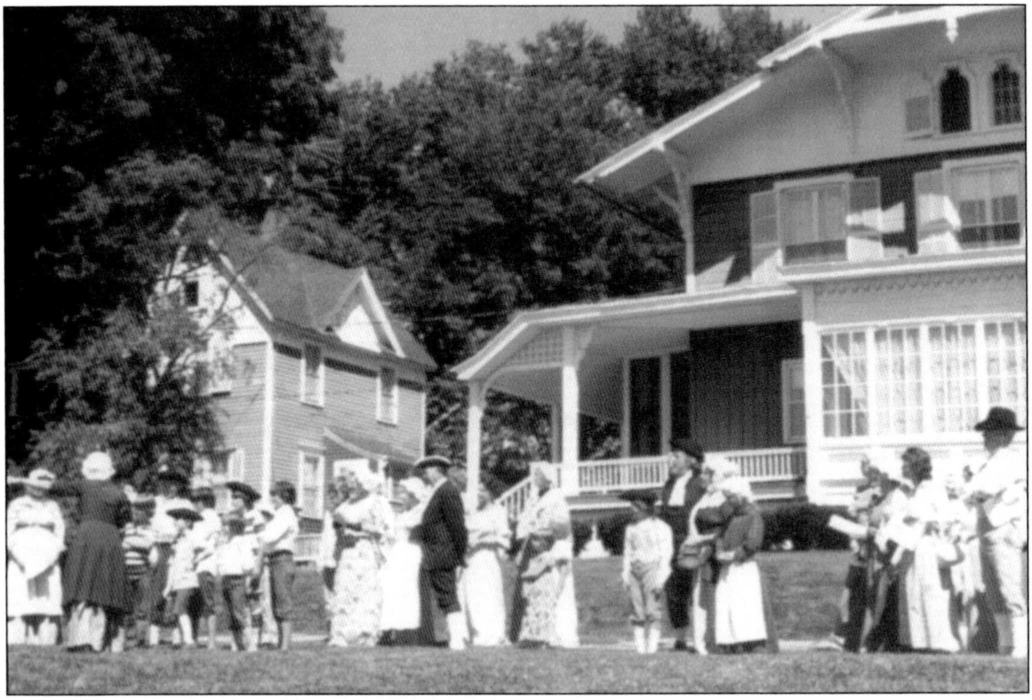

Events were held monthly during the US bicentennial celebration in 1976. A pageant with a cast of nearly 100 people was written and directed by Jano Fairservis. Here, members of the pageant cast rehearse on the lawn of the Bartram Inn. (Courtesy of Barbara Bartram.)

Nine

Moments in Time, Friends, and Family

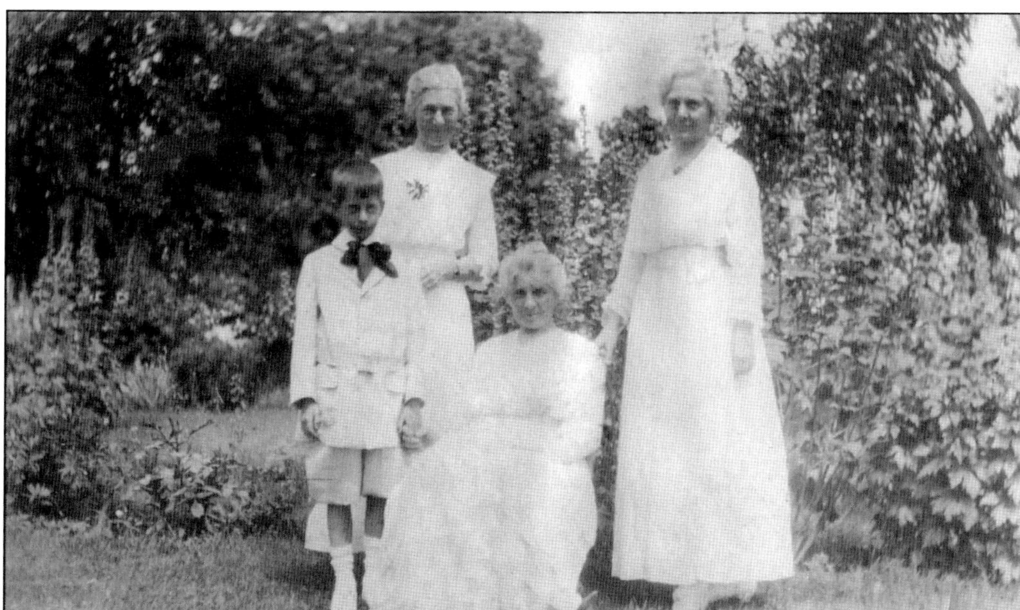

The Wheelers were one of the earliest of the New York families to settle permanently in Sharon, starting a family dynasty. This photograph of members of the Wheeler family was taken in 1923 in Sharon. From left to right are William Herrick, Laura Wheeler, Emily Wheeler, and Caroline Wheeler Schwab. When brother William Ogden Wheeler purchased a second property in 1883, the Wheeler family owned the first four houses on the left traveling south from the intersection with the Sharon & Goshen Turnpike (today's Route 4/Cornwall Bridge Road.) In total, the family's property holdings encompassed over 100 acres of land. (Courtesy of Nancy Trowbridge.)

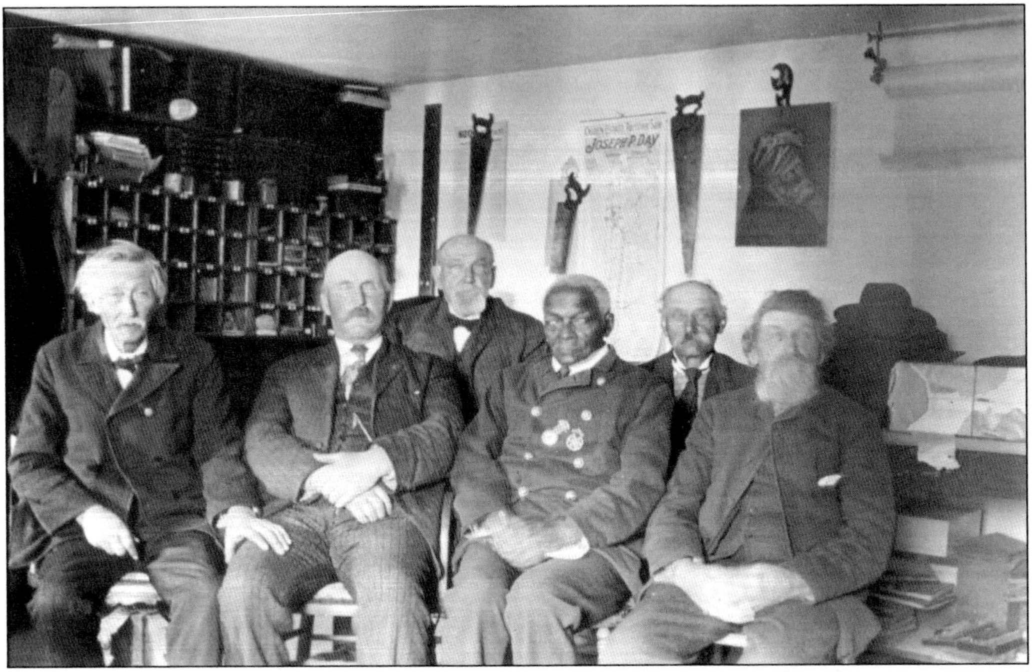

This rare interior photograph of the Gillette Store, at 147 Main Street, dates between 1883 and 1900 and was taken (probably by George M. Marckres) in the portion of the store that served as the post office and general gathering place. Identified in the photograph are George Conklin (second from left) and George World (fourth from left). World was a prominent member of the community, serving as sexton of the Congregational church for many years.

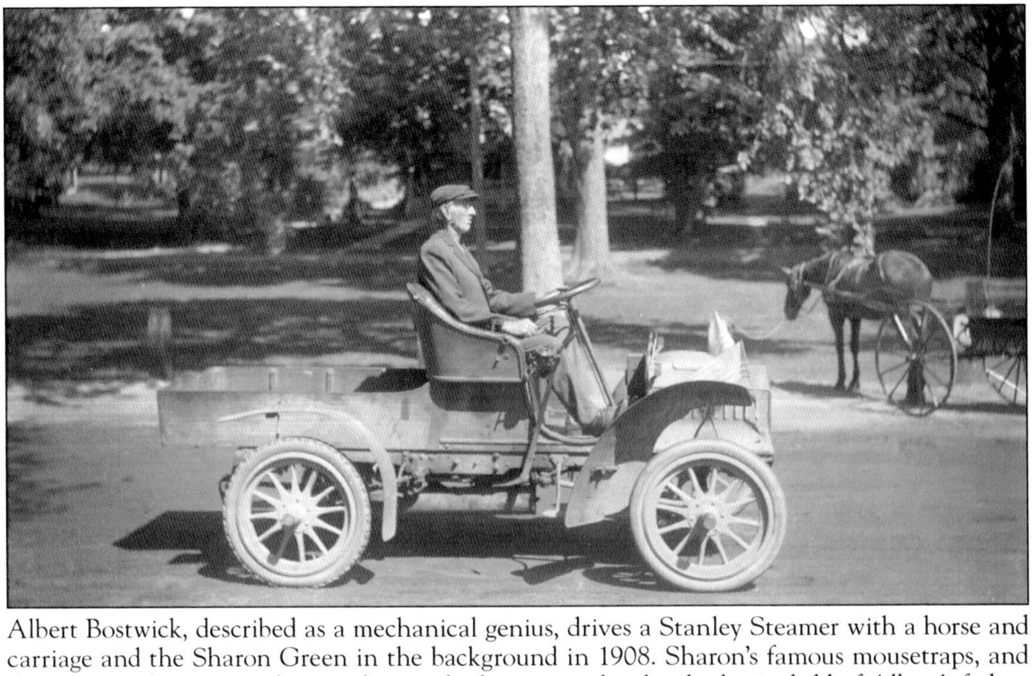

Albert Bostwick, described as a mechanical genius, drives a Stanley Steamer with a horse and carriage and the Sharon Green in the background in 1908. Sharon's famous mousetraps, and the mass-production machinery that made them, is said to be the brainchild of Albert's father, Judson Bostwick.

James B. Wilbur (1856–1937) was the town clerk from 1909 to 1921 and the first selectman in 1904, as well an unofficial town historian. He was the uncle of Charlie, Bill, and Odge Wilbur. (Courtesy of Diane Monroe.)

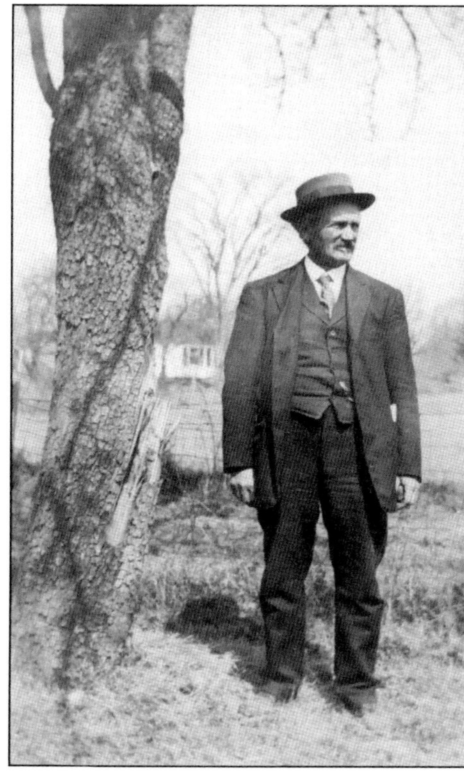

Dr. William Herrick and his son Billy sit in a sandbox around 1916. Known in the community as a very formal man, Dr. Herrick wears his usual garb of suit and tie as he gazes at his young son with obvious love and tenderness. (Courtesy of William Trowbridge.)

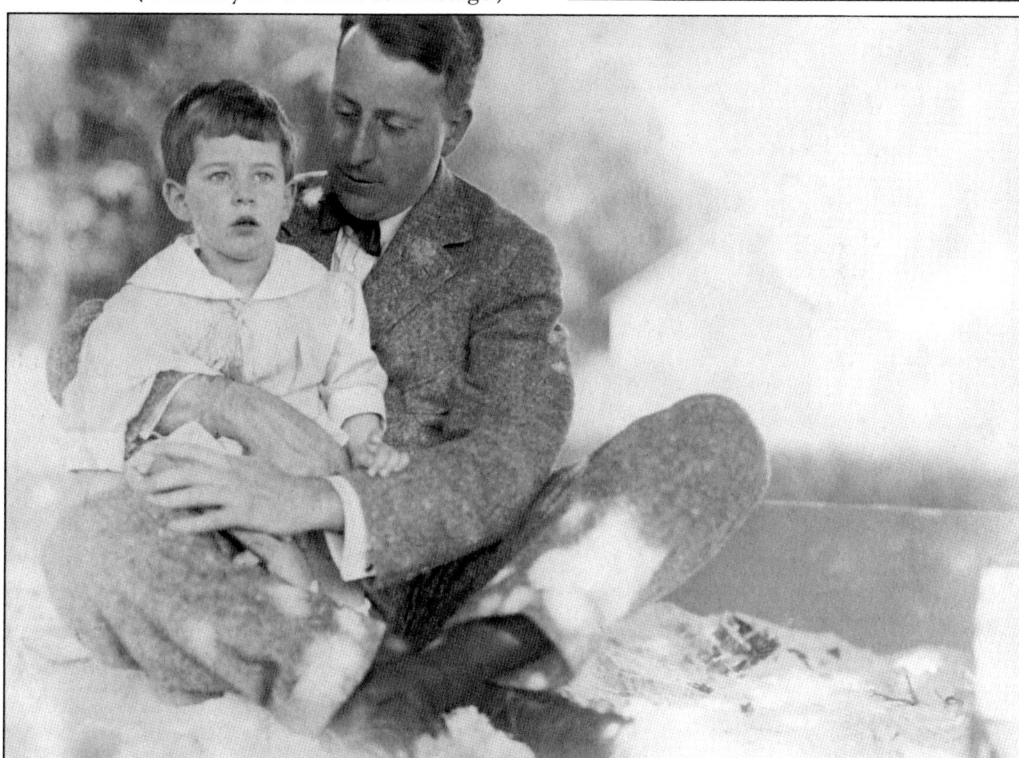

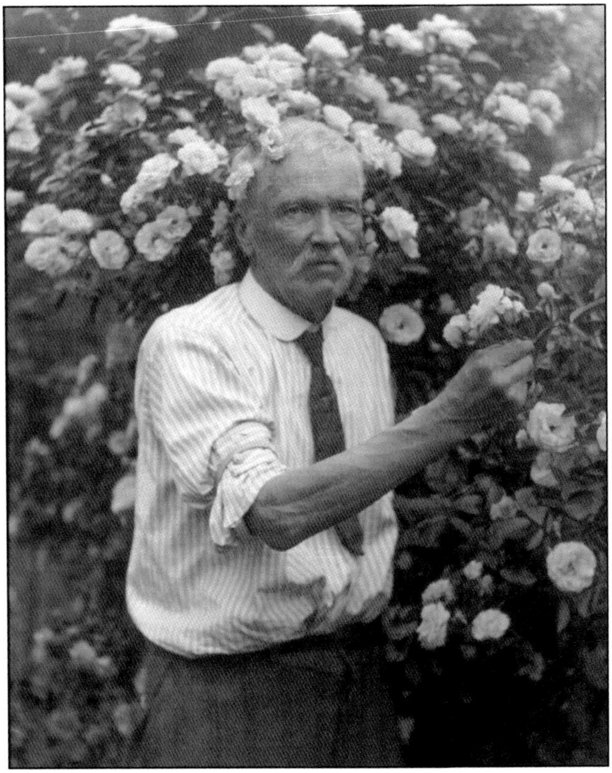

George M. Marckres came to Sharon in 1882 from Albany, Vermont, with his wife, Marie. He ran a small variety store next to the town hall. A jeweler and clock maker by trade, he also organized the Sharon band and was a skilled ornithologist and taxidermist. Above all, he was an artist with his camera. His collection of over 1,000 glass-plate negatives chronicles Sharon history from 1882 until his death in 1937. Noted photographer Fran Kelsey learned her trade at his knee. Together, their images chronicle over 110 years of life in Sharon.

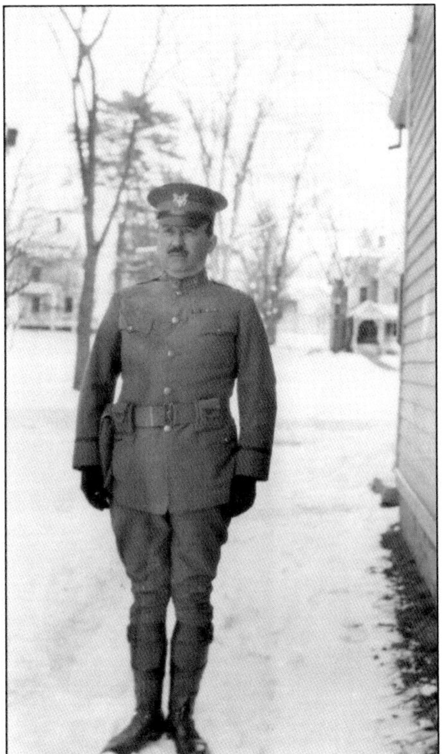

A year before the United States entered World War I, Congress passed the National Defense Act of 1916, which required the use of the term *National Guard* for the state militias and further regulated them. Congress also authorized the states to maintain Home Guards, which were reserve forces outside the National Guards being deployed by the federal government. A series of photographs were taken of the members of the Sharon Home Guard during World War I, probably by George M. Marckres. Shown here is a photograph of Dr. Jerome Chaffee, founder of Sharon Hospital. (Photograph by George M. Marckres.)

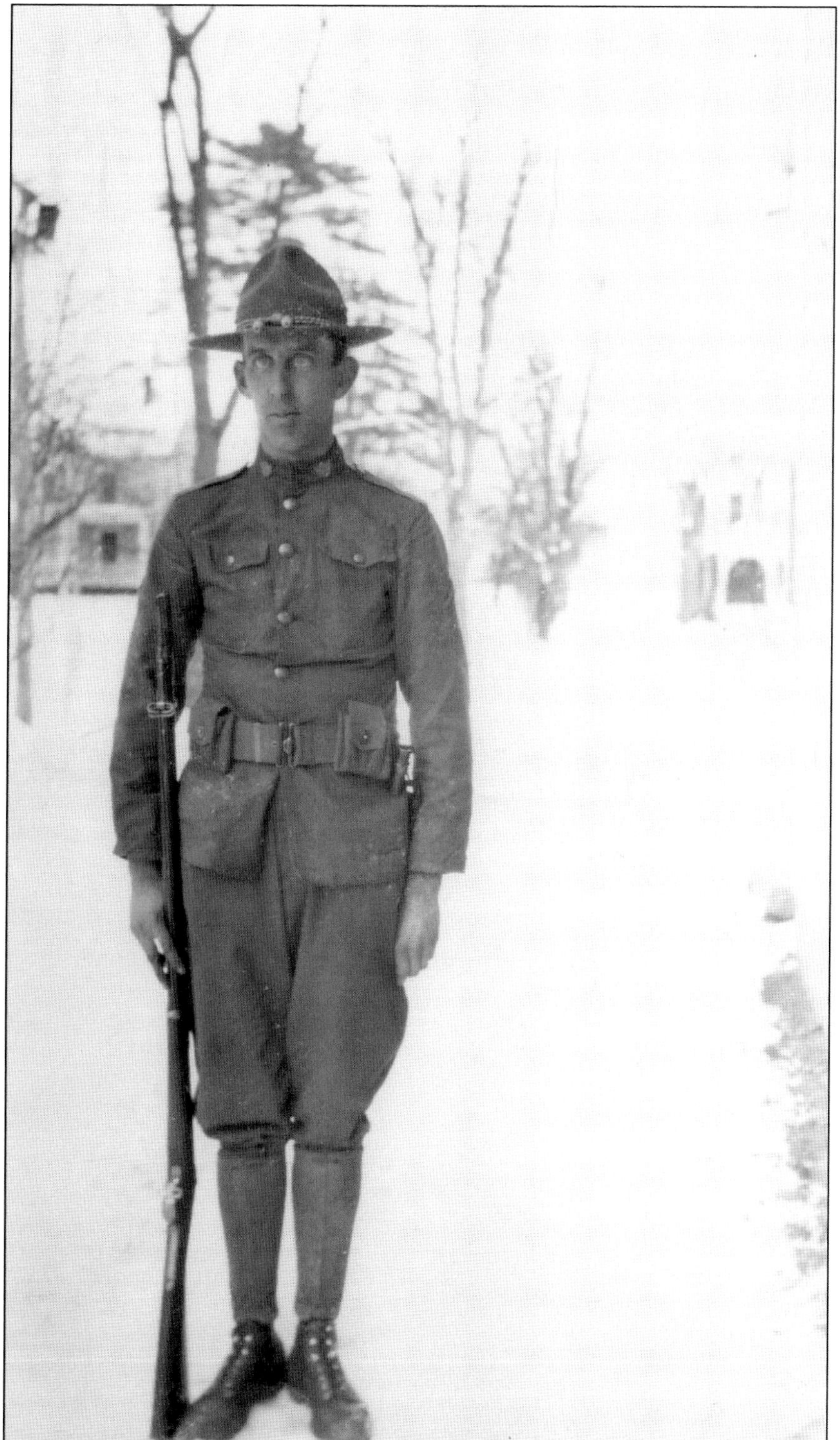

The Sharon Home Guard included Isaac Harry Bartram, the father of Ken Bartram, grandfather of Tom, Mary Ann, and Kathleen Bartram, and great-grandfather of Erin and Emily Bartram.

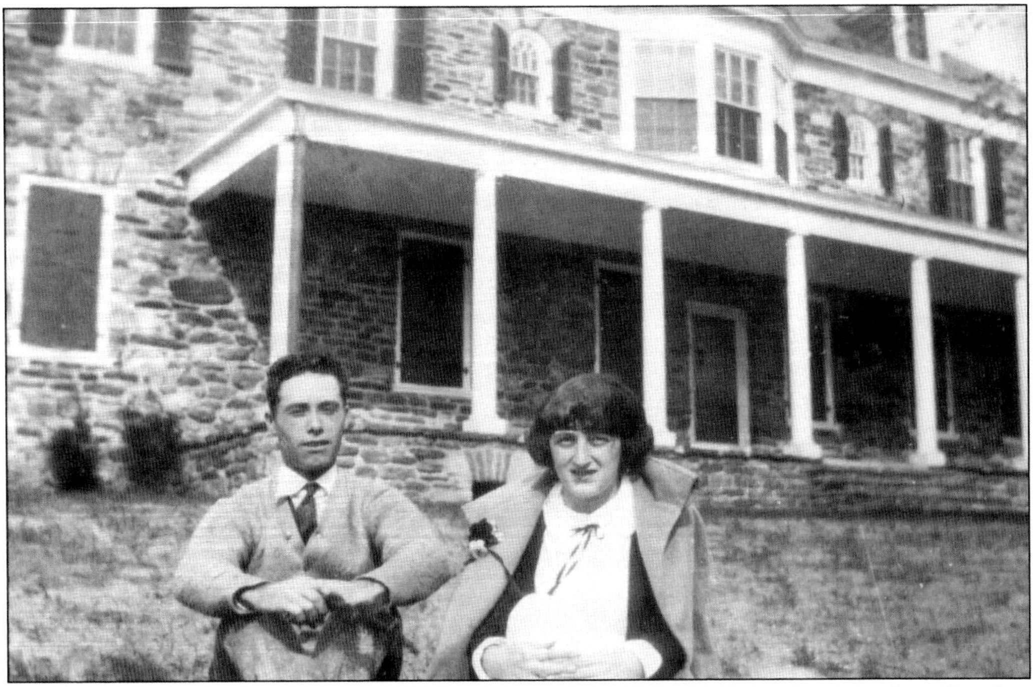

William Riley Jr. and Violet Kinsman Riley are in front of the Jameson estate on Low Road in 1924. Violet's father, Arthur Kinsman, was an outstanding gardener, maintaining the pleasure gardens for the sprawling estate. His son Edward joined the army on December 18, 1942, and served as a private first class in the 33rd Infantry. He was an expert rifleman and was stationed in Trinidad. During the war, he was awarded a World War II Victory Ribbon, a Good Conduct Medal, and an American Theatre Ribbon. He was discharged on January 5, 1946. Edward married Mary Sartori of East Canaan and they built a house on Route 4 in Sharon, among the cluster of houses just beyond Hilltop Road going east out of town. (Courtesy of Tom Riley.)

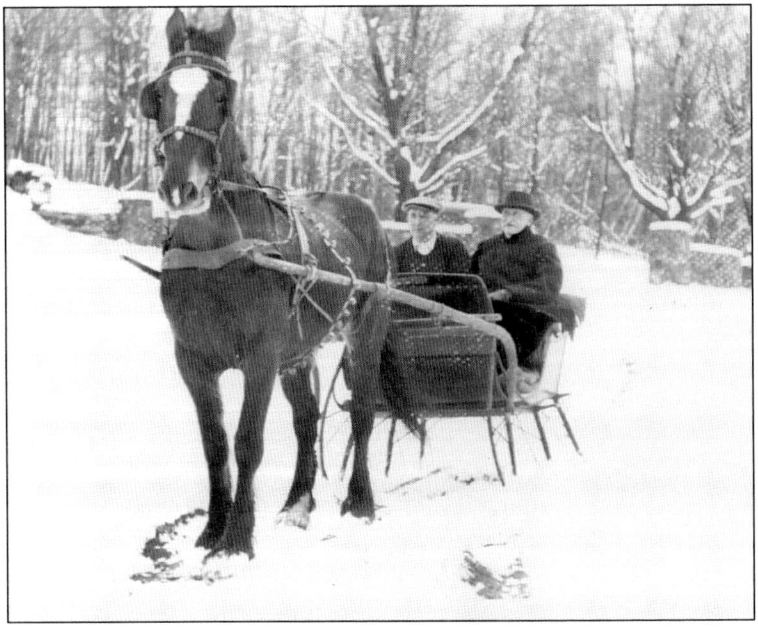

Maynard Bartram drives Augustus Van Cortlandt in a one-horse open sleigh. Bartram was the superintendent of the Van Cortlandt estate, at 40 Jackson Hill Road, and the father of Barbara Bartram. Augustus Van Cortlandt was a well-known philanthropist. (Courtesy of Barbara Bartram.)

Helen Wike Humeston was what was once known as a tomboy. Known for shooting rattlesnakes in her yard as a young woman, she rode horses into her 80s and recently celebrated her 90th birthday in Sharon. Around 1923, Helen resembled a young Annie Oakley. (Courtesy of Lynn Humeston.)

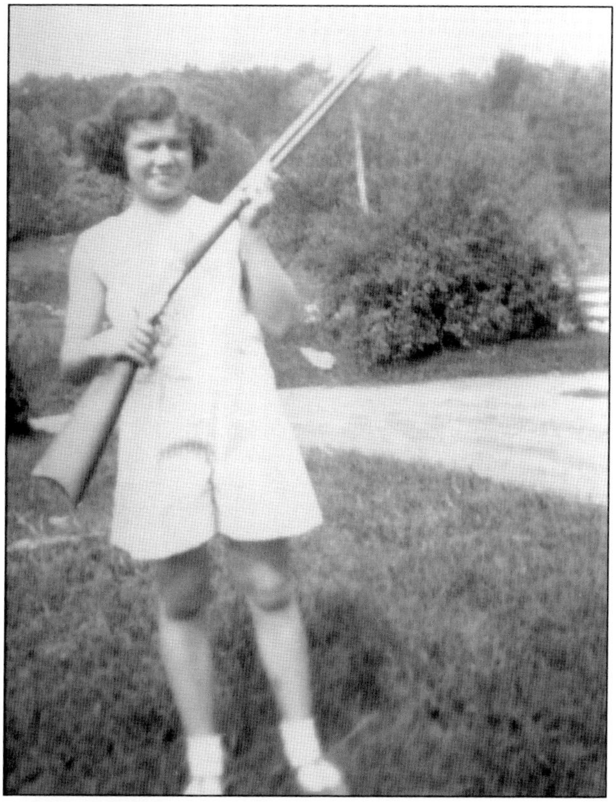

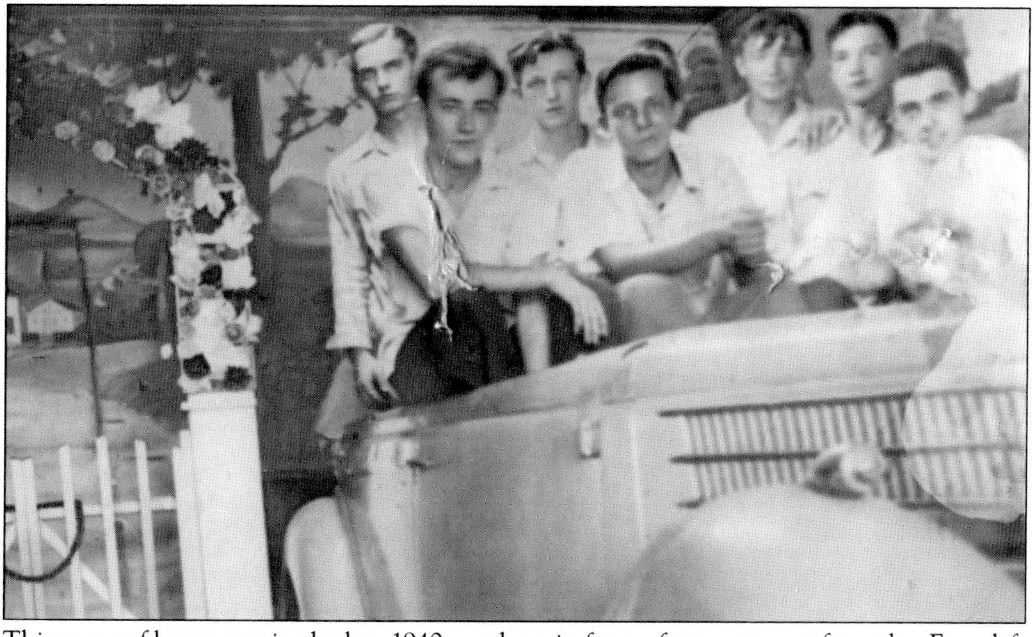

This group of boys poses in the late 1940s, perhaps in front of some scenery for a play. From left to right are William Riley III, Tom Flanagan, Don Carberry, Stub Middlebrook, Francis Carberry, Ray Osolin, and Sid Shoifet. Sid Shoifet and Sully I. Berman Jr. were the two Sharon boys who later died in the Korean War. (Courtesy of Tom Riley.)

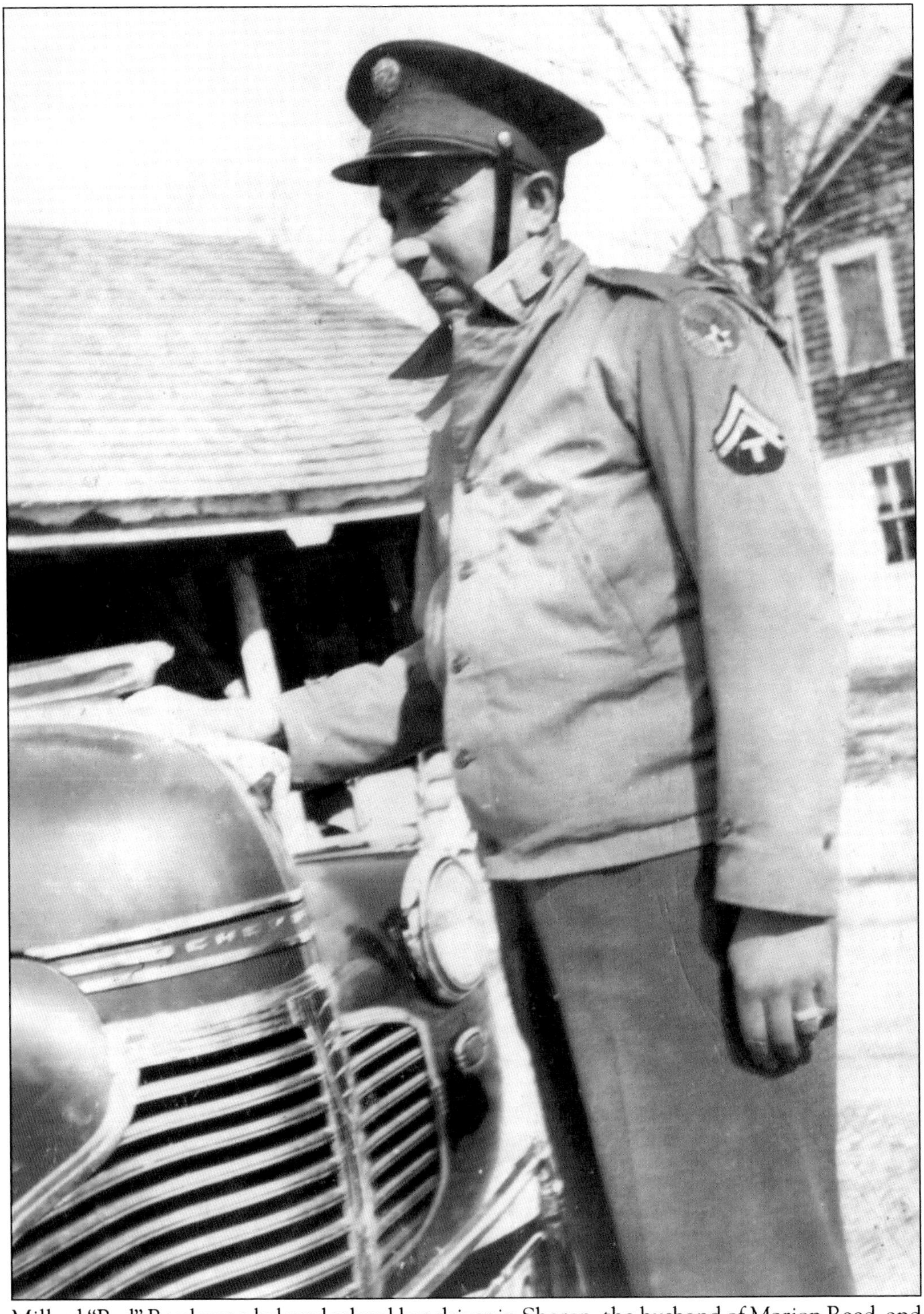

Millard "Bud" Reed was a beloved school bus driver in Sharon, the husband of Marion Reed, and a World War II Army veteran. When Reed had a heart attack, 15 volunteer firemen rushed to his house to help. (Courtesy of American Legion Post 126.)

Nearly everything that was hunted for sport was eaten, even if someone had to spend an hour picking out the shot before cooking it. Here, Norman Wilcox, age 20, and Roy Wilcox, age 15, pose in the field. Both brothers live in Sharon to this day, right across the street from each other. (Courtesy of Catherine Wilcox.)

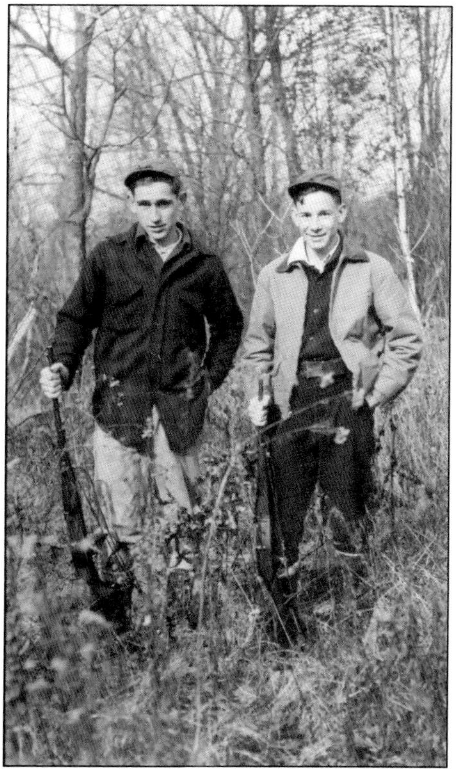

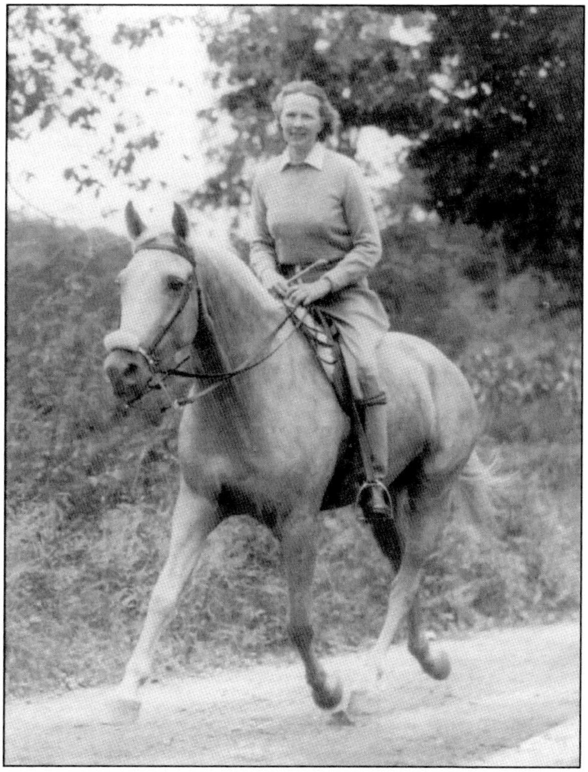

Gertrude Schley lived at the Appollos Smith House in Sharon from 1928 until her death on January 14, 2008. During World War II, Schley put in long hours at Sharon Hospital, where she worked as a nurse's aide in support of the medical staff that had been depleted due to wartime needs for military doctors. She loved horses and dogs. As a passionate equestrian, she took part in riding and driving events locally and throughout the East Coast; in later years, she volunteered at the Little Guild of St. Francis, an animal shelter in Cornwall. It was said that one could set a watch by the regular appearance of Schley on West Woods Road as she rode one of her Morgan horses.

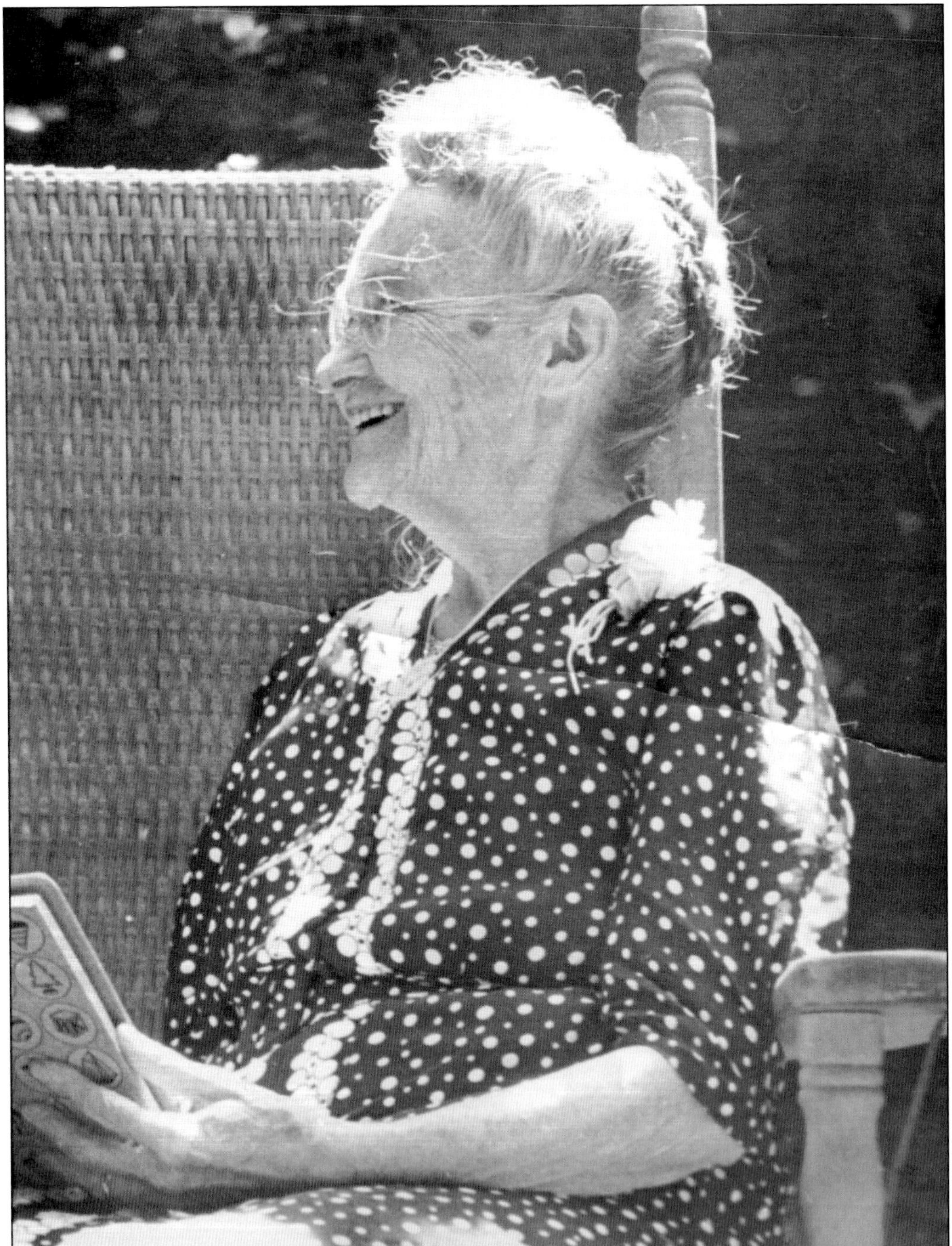

Ann Elizabeth Morehouse Prindle lived her entire 93-year life in Sharon. Upon her death in March 1952, she was memorialized as Sharon's "Aunt Anna." The *Lakeville Journal* remembered her as "the dear little lady of a Victorian generation, loved for her clear reminiscences as well as her wit and gracious charm." Aunt Anna was an accomplished quilter, with her favorite pattern being the Mariner's Compass. Three of her quilts are in the collection of the Sharon Historical Society. (Photograph by Fran Kelsey.)

Julia and Albert Wilcox are shown here in 1954 at the wedding of their son Norman to his wife, Catherine. The Wilcox dairy farm was on Amenia Union Road. Julia and Albert were the parents of Roy, Norman, and Barbara Wilcox, Irene Ruggeria, Dorothy Dean, and Winifred Grindrod. Norman, Roy, Irene, and Winifred lived within a mile and a half of each other all their lives. (Courtesy of Catherine Wilcox.)

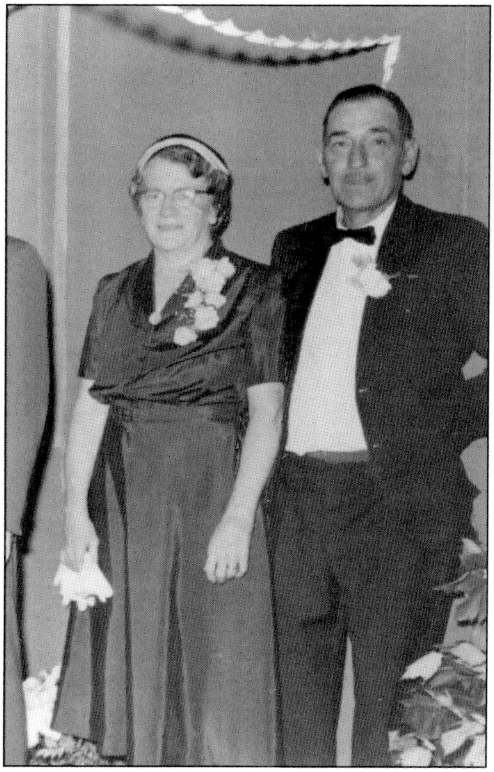

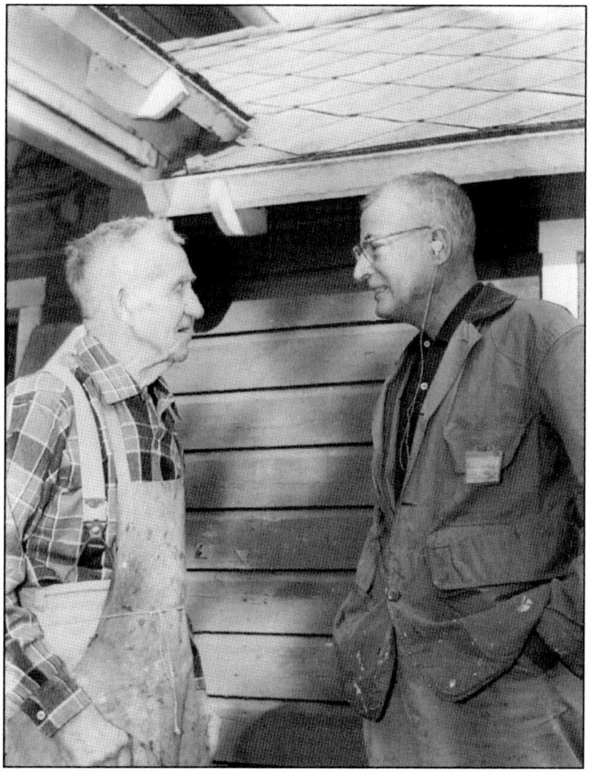

John Carley (left), the father of Richard A. Carley, was a builder and the renovator of many houses on South Main Street. He employed a large complement of skilled craftsmen and taught his son Richard A. Carley, the father of Sharon's Dick Carley, the basics of his trade. He is pictured here with Dr. Bradley Coley, a prominent New York City physician, surgeon, and cancer specialist who was wooed to Sharon in 1918 by Dr. Jerome Chaffee, the chief of medicine at the fledgling Sharon Hospital.

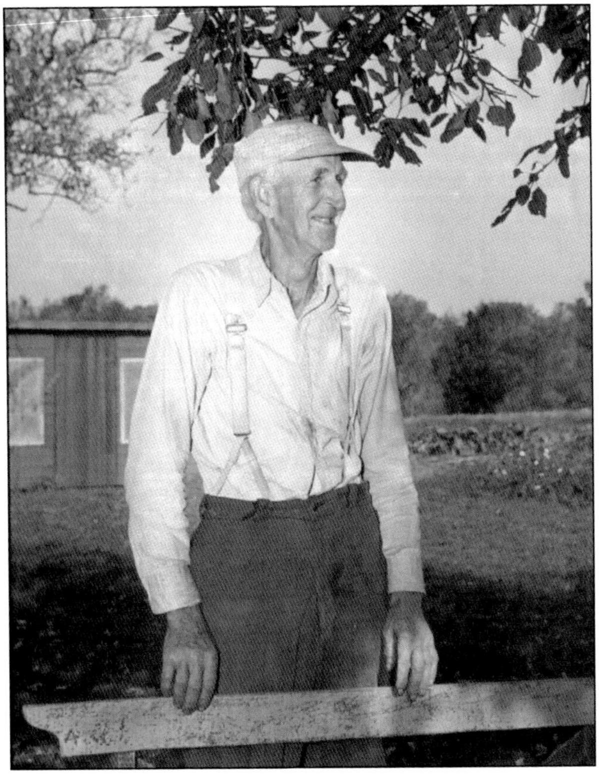

Edwin Prindle was the husband of Susie Brown Prindle, whose family ran Brown's Mill, the last mill to operate in Sharon, which closed in 1916. He is the father of Stuart Prindle.

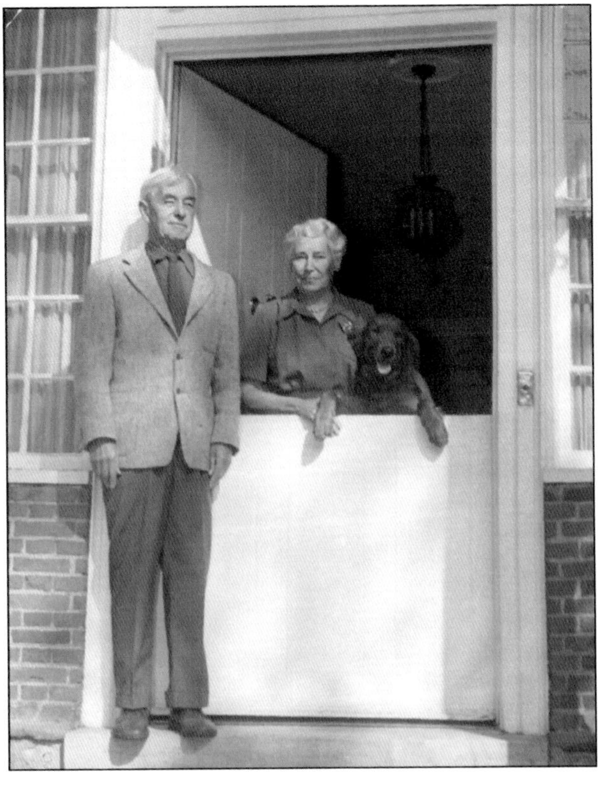

In 1924, Adm. Thomas C. and Caroline Brownson Hart purchased the King House, which had once belonged to Caroline's great-great-grandfather Col. George King. Admiral Hart was the commander of the ABDA naval forces in the Pacific in 1941–1942. Caroline Hart was an active member of the Sharon Historical Society, and Admiral Hart was the first to catalog and curate the society's collection of small arms.

Dr. Harvey and Myrtle Maddox Hayden, the local veterinary team, were always active in town affairs. Myrtle was best known as a talented musician and composer, and many mourned her passing in 2013. Harvey still serves as a volunteer fireman and is on call to help a hurt animal at all hours of the day or night. (Courtesy of Harvey Hayden.)

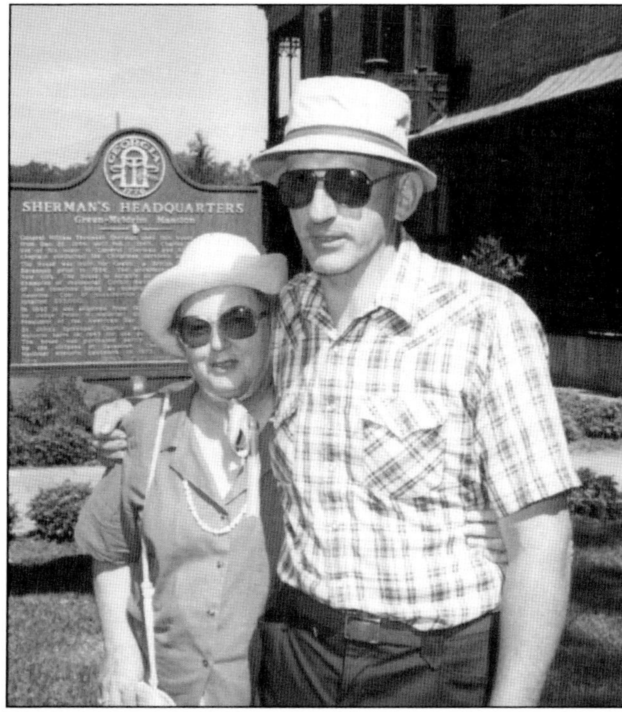

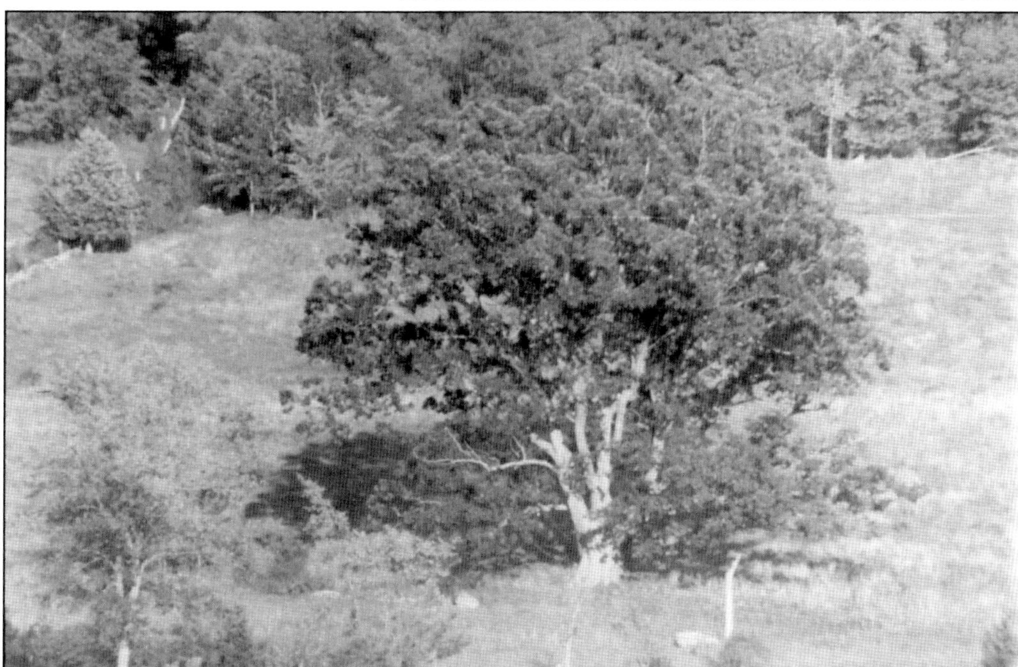

This tree, reputed to be the largest white oak in Connecticut, is situated on Mill Brook (also known as Little River), which runs parallel to Amenia Union Road. In 1988, the tree was 93 feet tall and 21 feet in circumference. It is an old friend and neighbor that has witnessed the passage of so much time and so many people, and it still stands for residents to admire and enjoy. (Courtesy of Catherine Wilcox.)

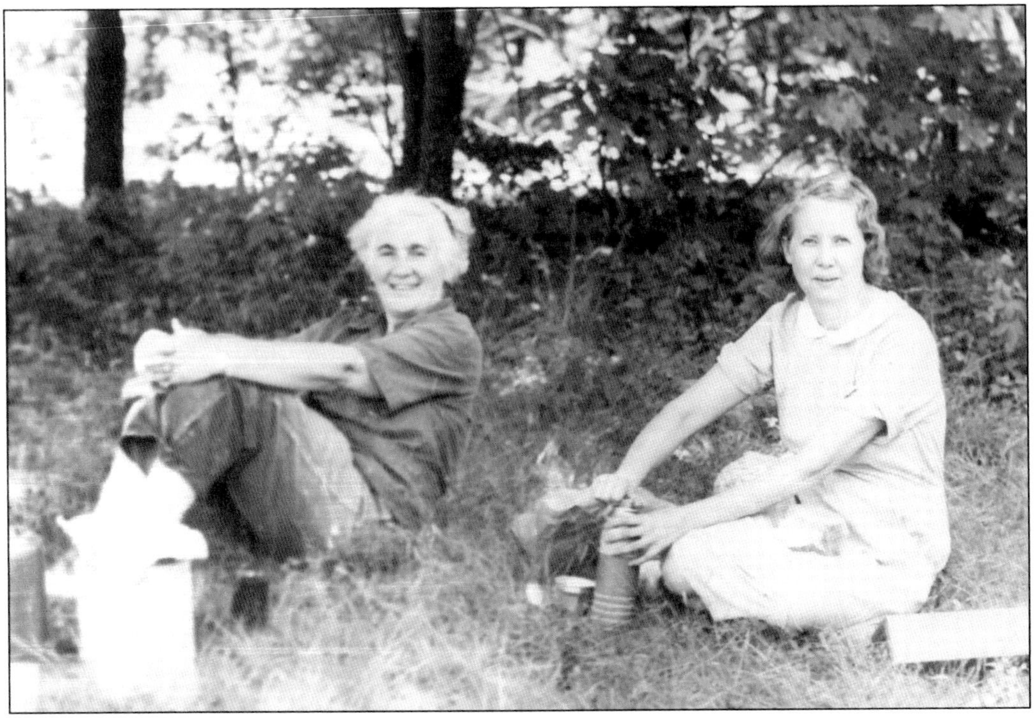

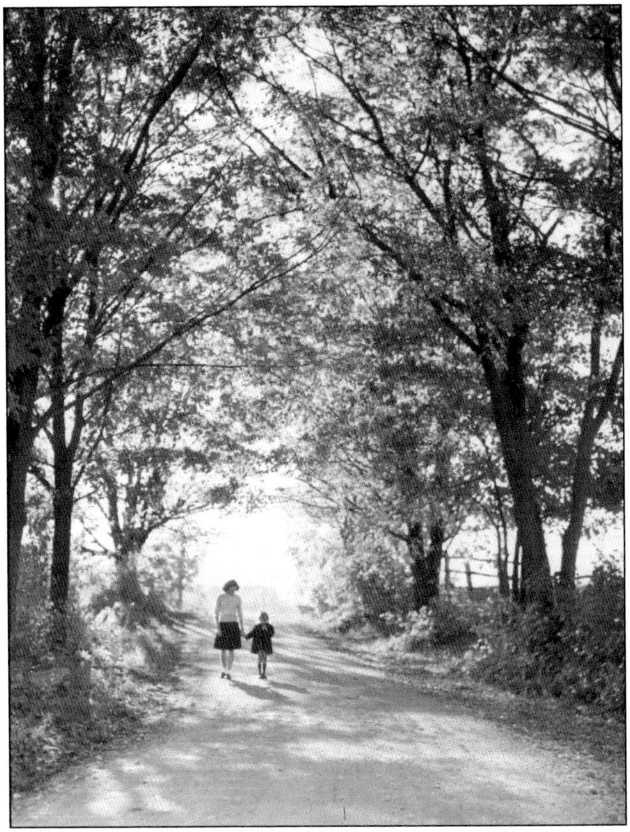

In this image, Mabel Hotaling (left) and Evelyn Pitcher are picking blueberries. A slower pace of life that puts value on simple pleasures is a hallmark of life in Sharon. (Courtesy of Barbara Bartram.)

This photograph, taken by Ward Hutchinson in the late 1930s, illustrates the peace and safety that are associated with life in Sharon. Barbara Riley Farley and her neighbor, young Wanda Hutchinson, stroll on an unpaved Hilltop Road. (Photograph by Ward Hutchinson; courtesy of Tom Riley.)

Bibliography

Carley, Richard L. *Growing Up on the Farm*. Bloomington, IN: AuthorHouse, 2011.
Kelsey, Fran. *Seeing Sharon through a Century of Photography*. Sharon, CT: Sharon Mountain Press, 1993.
Kirby, Ed. *Echoes of Iron in Connecticut's Northwest Corner*. Sharon, CT: Sharon Historical Society, 1998.
———. *Seldom Told Tales of Sharon*. Sharon, CT: Sharon Historical Society, 2004.
———. *Seldom Told Tales of Sharon, Book Two*. Sharon, CT: Sharon Historical Society, 2008.
———. *Seldom Told Tales of Sharon, Book Three*. Sharon, CT: Sharon Historical Society, 2011.
Sedgwick, Charles F.A.M. *General History of the Town of Sharon, Litchfield County, Connecticut*. Sharon, CT: Sharon Historical Society, 2000. Fourth Edition.
"The Original Home Lots of the Town of Sharon." Sharon, CT: Sharon Historical Society, 1963.
Trowbridge, Eunice Herrick. *Family Sketches*. Sharon, CT: self-published, 1989.

Consistent with our mission to preserve history on a local level, this book was printed in South Carolina on American-made paper and manufactured entirely in the United States. Products carrying the accredited Forest Stewardship Council (FSC) label are printed on 100 percent FSC-certified paper.

MADE IN THE USA